BUSINESS LEADERS AND THE PRESS PRAISE

STRATEGIC SELLING

"A practical guide offering new insight into the way salesmen can successfully promote big-ticket items to large organizations."
—*Financial Post*

"Strategic Selling is in a class by itself. . . . We use it to plan all our national account sales."
—**Jack Schang, Chairman and CEO, Ryder/P.I.E. Nationwide, Inc.**

"We use Strategic Selling as a means of substituting analysis for guesswork . . . and for reviewing and following up on major sales."
—**Lowell E. Gutzler, VP and General Manager, Marriott Corporation**

"Thanks to Bob and Steve's conceptual approach to complex sales, we're now a major carrier in the [group life and health] field."
—**William J. Burton, VP, Group Life and Health Sales, Massachusetts Mutual Life Insurance Company**

"A totally professional planning process. If Willy Loman had taken the Miller Heiman program, he'd have been salesman of the year."
—**Walter H. Drew, Senior VP and General Sales Manager, Kimberly-Clark Corporation, Consumer Products Division**

"Miller Heiman's Strategic Selling course provides an effective process for selling our company's products and services which our bankers find invaluable. . . . We have been delighted."
—**William R. Caldwell, EVP, and COO, The Bank of California, N.A.**

"A method that sales professionals can use effectively. The authors clearly and engagingly describe numerous 'workshops,' in which readers can apply what they have just read to their own sales experiences. Professionally yet clearly presented."
—*ALA Booklist*

Robert B. Miller rose from associate to vice-president-general manager for North American operations at Kepner-Tregoe, Inc., which offers consulting services for senior management of Fortune 500 corporations and the federal and state governments. He personally consulted with such companies as Ford, General Motors, Citicorp, and Rolls-Royce. In 1974, he founded Robert B. Miller & Associates, where he began developing the innovative sales systems and other programs that have made Miller Heiman & Associates one of America's top sales consulting firms.

Stephen E. Heiman rose in nineteen years from national account salesman for IBM (where he increased sales in all product areas by more than 35 percent and was in the top 5 percent for total sales and percentage quota) to director of marketing at Kepner-Tregoe, to executive vice-president of North American Van Lines, where he increased sales and profits by 36 percent in four years. In 1978, he joined Robert Miller as co-principal and full partner in what became Miller Heiman & Associates Inc. and has since helped train thousands of sales management executives from top corporations across the country.

STRATEGIC SELLING^{SM}

SELLING^{SM}

The Unique Sales System
Proven Successful by
America's Best Companies

Robert B. Miller
Stephen E. Heiman
with Tad Tuleja

WARNER BOOKS

A Warner Communications Company

STRATEGIC SELLING^{SM} is a Service Mark of Miller Heiman & Associates, Inc., 2150 Shattuck Avenue, Suite #400, Berkeley, California 94704.

Warner Books Edition

This Warner Books edition is published by arrangement with
William Morrow and Company, 105 Madison Avenue, New York, New York
10016.

Warner Books, Inc., 666 Fifth Avenue, New York, NY 10103

A Warner Communications Company

Printed in the United States of America

First Warner Books Printing: March 1986

10 9 8 7 6 5 4

Book design by Patty Lowy

Library of Congress Cataloging-in-Publication Data

Miller, Robert B. (Robert Bruce), 1931–
    Strategic selling.

    Reprint. Originally published: New York: Morrow,
1985.
    Includes index.
    1. Selling. I. Heiman, Stephen E. II. Tuleja, Tad,
1944–   . III. Title.
[HF5438.25.M567   1985b]   658.8′1   85-26566
ISBN 0-446-38922-6 (U.S.A.) (pbk.)
        0-446-37007-X (Canada) (pbk.)

FOREWORD

When Strategic Selling was first introduced to us at Hewlett-Packard some eight years ago, the concept had an immediate appeal. It was an approach to selling that represented the high degree of professionalism and the kind of buyer-seller relationship to which we aspired. Thousands of HP sales engineers worldwide have been trained in Strategic Selling, and its influence can be directly seen in the results they have attained.

Strategic Selling doesn't attempt to teach the sales representative how to make an effective pitch. It doesn't rely on luck or charisma. And most importantly from our perspective, Strategic Selling is not manipulation.

The methodology in this book looks at the buying decision. The focus is outward, on the customers we serve. Their needs—both organizational and personal—are identified. The resultant analysis allows us to better determine how we can add value to that customer's organization and create a long-term business relationship that benefits all parties. Strategic Selling points not only outward to customers, but forward. It aims at creating the kinds of partnerships that will last over the years to come.

Strategic Selling has strengthened Hewlett-Packard's customer focus by providing a common discipline and vocabulary that have helped create a unified customer emphasis throughout the company. Our sales representatives have found it immediately applicable to the accounts they serve. Its usefulness has spanned product disciplines and national boundaries.

Considered a somewhat revolutionary approach when first introduced, Strategic Selling has also spanned the years very well. This is because the objectives it seeks—providing customers with real value and establishing long-term relationships with them—are timeless. Professionals seeking those goals will find this volume a most useful resource.

> —JOHN A. YOUNG, President and
> Chief Executive Officer,
> Hewlett-Packard Company

CONTENTS

OUT OF THE TRENCHES: A NONTRADITIONAL APPROACH TO SELLING

Selling is the largest profession in North America, perhaps the world. Yet it has one of the worst reputations of any profession—second only to that of politics. "Professor" Harold Hill in the classic musical *The Music Man* and Herb Tarlek in the television series *WKRP in Cincinnati* typify the popular image of the salesman: a charming, fast-talking scam artist who wears loud clothes, cons the customer, never delivers on his promises, and is genuinely interested only in filling his pockets with your money.

This stereotype is so pervasive that men and women who sell are rarely called salesmen and saleswomen any more. To disguise their true function, their companies give them high-toned euphemistic titles: marketing consultant, account representative, field engineer, account manager, customer service consultant, marketing specialist—and occasionally sales consultant or sales engineer. They're called anything but what they are.

We were reminded of this not long ago, when we asked a

senior vice-president if "sales" was considered a dirty word by his people. "Oh, no," he assured us. "Everybody is really on board with the importance of selling. But," he went on without batting an eye, "remember that we call it marketing."

Whatever the euphemism used, the implicit point is the same. "Sales" *is* a dirty word to many people, because it has so long been linked to images of manipulation and deceit.

Unfortunately, we sales professionals have only ourselves to blame for this. Many of us have perpetuated the stereotype by the way we've sold our customers. No wonder our methods turn people off—many of them *are* manipulative.

You see this in the sales literature even more blatantly than in the field. Many sales-training systems actually *encourage* manipulation and deceit, by teaching the salesman "tricks" and "techniques" for getting the order in spite of what the customer really wants. Many sales representatives today still adhere to that approach. They believe that their job is to sell their products to as *many* people as possible, whether or not those people really want or need them.

This old-fashioned, "refrigerators to Eskimos" approach is encouraged by corporate attitudes. Companies pay lip service to the idea of customer need but make it clear to the sales force that it's supposed to *make* the customer need what the company has to sell. Therefore, many people in sales go by the old slogan "You can't call yourself a salesman unless you can sell somebody something he doesn't really want or need." And they do or say anything that will get their customers to buy.

The logical outcome of this approach is that the salesperson and the customer come to see each other as adversaries. It's no accident that working out in the field is often spoken of as being "out in the trenches." Many catchphrases of the sales profession testify to a battleground mentality. "Find his weak spot," you'll hear sales representatives say, "so you can sink in the hook." Or, more simply, "Get him before he gets you."

Given the pervasiveness of this attitude, it's not surprising that most large organizations have created professional dragon-slayers to protect their decision makers from sales people. Purchasing agents and buyers often form a defensive perimeter against the supposedly barbarous hordes of sales representatives. Heaven help a manager, the corporate wisdom runs, who is inadvertently cornered by an invading Attila the Rep.

The image is comical, to be sure. But it's also a sad commentary on the way many potential customers view members of our profession.

The amazing thing is that this old "trench warfare" approach to selling works at all. It does work, of course: once, twice, maybe three or four times with a given customer. But eventually it breaks down. If you approach your sales as battles and see your customers as enemies, eventually your customers will lock on to the huckster stereotype and back off.

Why? Because they'll see you as having Won, and themselves as having Lost. Even worse, they'll see themselves as having been *manipulated* into Losing. At which point your credibility—and thus your selling effectiveness—will be gone.

The scenario of "Salesman Wins—Customer Loses" has been entrenched in mythology and in practice for many years. But it's not the only scenario. Through all the years that the Professor Hills and Herb Tarleks have been slogging their way into disrepute, a small, quiet group of salesmen and saleswomen have been rising to the top of the professional ladder—and pulling down enormous incomes—by adopting exactly the *opposite* approach.

These are the sales representatives who have systematically built up customer trust and confidence by *never* treating the customer as an enemy, and by always making sure that the customer Wins on every deal. They're also the people whom everyone else perceives as lucky—although luck has nothing to do with their success.

These "lucky" sales professionals don't concentrate on the traditional tasks of overcoming objections and asking for the order. They know that you only have to overcome objections when you're cramming something down somebody's throat. And they're not interested in "getting" an order that a customer isn't anxious to give them.

They concentrate instead on providing solutions, solving problems, creating opportunities, and in general making their customers feel good about the sale, no matter how much effort that takes. Many of these "lucky" top professionals actually refuse to take an order unless there's a solid match between their product or service and the customer's real needs. They pay much more than lip service to the notion of customer need.

This small cadre of supersuccessful salespeople have adopted what we call an "I Win—You Win" strategy. The essence of that strategy is the recognition of a fundamental truth: The best way for sales professionals to serve their own self-interest is to make sure that the *customer's* self-interest is also served. Success, the Win-Win strategist knows, depends on *mutual* satisfaction.

We emphasize mutual because manipulating the customer into Losing is only one way you can mismanage the sale. Another way is to allow *yourself* to Lose so that the customer Wins. Sales professionals do this all the time, in the usually vain hope that doing their customers "favors" will pay off in the end. Satisfying your customers at your own expense is, in the long term, just as bad as not satisfying them at all. A Win-Win approach to sales involves maintaining a delicate balance: It means keeping your customers happy *without* giving the store away.

Win-Win salesmen and saleswomen don't overstock their customers. They don't pressure, threaten, or cajole. They don't ask for or offer mere "favors." They don't overpromise and underfulfill. They don't misrepresent the match between product and customer need. Instead, they work with their customers to provide satisfaction for *everyone* concerned. They follow up, check up, fix problems, provide liaison to their factories, help the customer move the product, and stick with the customer long after each sale is completed. Far from behaving like their customers' sworn enemies, they act like partners instead.

As a result, they discover an irony. Because of their genuine support and service to the customer, Win-Win sales professionals often are able not only to sell *more* product or service, but to sell it at a higher price than the competition! And they do this not just once, but time and time again, because they help their customers understand that they're getting a "value-added" product.

It takes very little talent to sell somebody something *once*. Even the Herb Tarleks and Professor Hills of the world can do that. But once is never enough. All viable companies today are built on *long-term* relationships, and the main drawback of the old trench-warfare approach to selling is that the Win-Lose scenarios it generates are inherently *short-term*. Adherents of the traditional approach have to start out on each new sale from scratch, because they never create a Win-Win history to build upon. And what good is it, after all, to keep selling new customers at a record pace if you're losing your old ones even faster?

The "lucky" sales professionals understand that long-term success means keeping all of your customers not just sold but *satisfied*. That's what this book is all about. It shows the modern sales professional how to manage every prospective sale into a solid, Win-Win outcome—one that will generate income not just today, but all the way down the line.

If you don't mind seeing your customers as enemies—and if you don't mind their seeing *you* that way—this book is not addressed to you. But if you're fed up with the old slick-talker image, if you don't really enjoy "sticking it" to your customers—most of all, if you want to profit from what the "lucky" sales leaders already know—then welcome to Strategic Selling.

If you're ready to come in out of the trenches, your "luck" is about to improve.

Among the people who have already discovered the value of a Win-Win approach are our clients. Most of these sales leaders handle relatively high priced product or service lines in the face of low-bid competition, so they *have* to "add value" for their customers. Our Strategic Selling programs have helped these already successful professionals to do that in an increasingly effective manner.

But if we've helped them, they've also helped us. Strategic Selling, whose principles form the basis of this book, is a dynamic vehicle. The feedback we've received over the years from our program participants has enabled us constantly to improve and clarify those principles. These behind-the-scenes contributors to this book now number over twenty thousand. To them we express our deepest gratitude.

Rather than list individual names, and risk omitting an important individual contributor, we are dedicating this book to *all* our client companies, and the individuals whose interest and enthusiastic support for Miller Heiman & Associates Inc.'s Strategic Selling programs served as the basis for this book. Our thanks to:

Acme Resin Corporation
Airwick Industries, Inc.
American Bank Stationery Co.
American Can Company
American Cyanamid Co.
American Microsystems, Inc.
Apollo Computer Inc.
ARA Services, Inc.
Arkwright-Boston Manufacturers Mutual Insurance Co.
The Bank of California, N.A.
Bekins Company
Beloit Corp.
Berkey Photo Inc.
Booz • Allen & Hamilton, Inc.
Bourns Inc.
Burroughs Corporation
Bussman Manufacturing Division
Central Paper Co.
Central Rigging and Contracting Corporation
C. F. Mueller Co.
Cincom Systems, Inc.
Coca-Cola U.S.A.
Container Corp. of America
Control Data Corp.
Datachecker/DTS
De Luxe Check Printers, Inc.
Dow Chemical Co.
Emery Worldwide
Exxon Office Systems Company
Fisher Controls International, Inc.
Frito-Lay, Inc.
G. D. Searle & Co.
General Electric Co.
Geometric Data
Frank B. Hall & Co., Inc.
Hallmark Cards, Inc.
Harris Corp.
Hercules Incorporated

The Hertz Corp.
Hewlett-Packard Co.
Honeywell, Inc.
ICI Americas Inc.
Intec, Inc.
International Business
  Machines Corp.
ITT Dialcom, Inc.
James River Graphics, Inc.
Jerrold Electronics Corp.
Johnson & Johnson
Kimberly-Clark Corp.
KLA Instruments Corp.
Lee Way Motor Freight,
  Inc.
Lockheed-California Co.
Lockheed-Georgia Co.
McGraw-Edison Company
Marriott Corporation
Massachusetts Mutual Life
  Insurance Co.
Memorex Corp.
National Semiconductor
  Corp.
NBI, Inc.
NCR Corp.
NL Sperry-Sun
Pallm Inc.
Pepsi-Cola Bottling Group
Pitman Company
Policy Management
  Systems Corp.

Racal-Milgo, Inc.
RCA Solid State Division
Research Cottrell, Inc.
Reynolds Metals Co.
Ricoh of America, Inc.
Rockwell International
  Corp.
R. R. Donnelley & Sons
  Co.
Ryder/P-I-E Nationwide,
  Inc.
Saga Corp.
Shade Information Systems
  Inc.
Shared Medical Systems
  Corp.
Sweda International, Inc.
Synergex Corporation
Sytek
Szabo Food Service Co.
Tandem Computers Inc.
Technicon Instruments
  Corporation
Tektronix, Inc.
Teradyne Inc.
TRW, Electronic
  Components Group
Warner Jenkinson Co.
Wilson Sporting Goods
  Co. (PepsiCo.)
WTC Air Freight

In addition, three unique individuals made such significant contributions that without them this book would not have been written:

The late Tom E. Smith, Ph.D., colleague and friend, worked with us in the early formulation of the Strategic Selling principles. We will be forever grateful for his contributions.

Tad Tuleja, our gifted collaborator, took mountains of written material and, through his expertise and precise skills in wordsmithing, organized and distilled our thoughts and words.

Without Lila Karpf, our literary agent and consultant, we would not have had the guidance and direction needed to start and complete this project. Our deepest appreciation.

R.B.M.
S.E.H.

Berkeley, California
1984

STRATEGIC
SELLING

▲

▶ 1 ◀

SUCCESSFUL SELLING IN A FUTURE-SHOCK WORLD

Not long ago, a major manufacturer of information systems—a company that does hundreds of millions of dollars' worth of business a year—was on the verge of closing a deal involving the sale of a sophisticated computer system to a potentially huge new account. The sales representative who was handling the negotiations, a man whom we'll call Ray, had every reason to be confident. He'd been talking to the client's top management for months, and as the deal moved closer to signing, he knew he was firmly entrenched. The department head who would use the new equipment, the purchasing agent who would sign for it, the data-processing people—all were delighted with his proposal. Ray even belonged to the same club as the company's CEO, and knew that he too was favorable. With a five-figure commission practically in his pocket, Ray was already shopping for a new car.

Ray knew that his wasn't the only company with its eye on this account. A smaller firm had also approached the client, and he was aware of this competition over his shoulder. But judging from the general receptivity to his proposal, he figured he had nothing to worry about. The smaller firm had half the market share of his own, and no matter how good its product might be, he was way ahead on reputation points alone. Rumor had it, he congratulated himself, that the salesman for the other side hadn't even met the CEO.

What Ray didn't know was that the rival firm had one distinct advantage. Many of its best representatives—including his opposite number, an eager young lion named Greg—had recently attended one of our Strategic Selling programs. There he'd acquired a whole new perspective on selling. He'd learned how to identify the critical Buying Influences in a sale, how to minimize his uncertainties about a customer's receptivity, how to prevent internal sabotage of a proposal—and he'd picked up a storehouse of practical information for leveraging from his own strengths and thus maximizing his competitive advantage. When he left the program, he had a detailed, pragmatic system that allowed him to analyze the components of the pending sale far better than Ray could hope to. Armed with his understanding of these components, and of how they all fit together in the sale, he was about to steal a march on the "leader."

It was true that Greg hadn't met the CEO. But thanks to the Strategic Selling program he'd attended, he didn't have to. While Ray was focusing on senior management, Greg was quietly finding out who the real decision makers were for this sale, and what other information he could use in helping him make the deal. Specifically, he wanted to know who would have to give final approval for the sale. He found what he was looking for in Jeff, an outside consultant whom Ray had entirely ignored.

Jeff was able to give Greg two extremely valuable pieces of information. First, he explained that on the specific sale under consideration, it was the division general manager, not the CEO, who was empowered to give final approval. Second, if Greg wanted to sell this critical decision maker, he could do no better than to go through Jeff himself. Prior to becoming a consultant, he had been a valued senior member of the buying company's organization, and the division general manager had relied on him for years to keep him informed about state-of-the-art technology.

What Greg did, therefore, was to demonstrate to Jeff the match between the buying firm's needs and his computer solution—and then let Jeff demonstrate the match to the general manager. Soon all the parties involved in the purchase decision were sold on his product. He was the one who got the new car, while Ray, who supposedly had had the sale tied up, was left wondering what had gone wrong.

When Ray's company realized it had been blindsided, its officers wanted to know how. When they discovered that we had had a part in their misfortune, they sent over their sales management to find out more about our program. Today both Greg's and Ray's firms are our valued clients, and both report regular increases in account penetration and sales performance directly attributable to our principles and planning process.

Anybody who sells for a living can tell you similar stories about how a "sure thing" fell through because the sales representative in charge had failed to cover all his bases, pitched his proposal to the wrong person at the wrong time, or neglected a crucial piece of information that indicated the sale was in trouble. No matter how expert or experienced you are, you've probably felt the pang of disappointment that comes when your competition manages to unseat you from a position you thought was secure.

What you may not realize (and very few salespeople do realize it) is that there's always a specific, clearly identifiable reason that such a sale is lost, even though you may not know what it is. That reason never involves merely "luck" or "timing" or "hard work." When you lose a sale that seemed nailed down, it's nearly always because you failed to bring to that sale what Greg brought to his computer deal: a solidly researched, clearly defined, and reliable program for success that takes into account *all* the elements of the pending transaction, no matter how obscure or "trivial."

This is true in any sales situation, but it's especially relevant in what we call the Complex Sale. That's what our programs and this book are about. The goals of *Strategic Selling* are to help you understand why things have sometimes gone wrong in your Complex Sales, and to give you a tested, reliable system for setting them right from now on.

The Complex Sale: What It Is

Our program is built on reality, not theory, and it would be quite unrealistic to suggest that everyone involved in selling could profit equally from our approach. That's why we have to start by defining the Complex Sale, so that you can determine whether or not, given the type of selling you do, you can benefit from our method. In our programs and in this book we use the following definition:

> *A Complex Sale is one in which several people must give their approval before the sale can take place.*

That sounds simple enough, and it is simple, but the concept has enormous implications nonetheless, both for the business world in general and for your role in it. The variety of people involved in the Complex Sale, and the variety of often conflicting decisions that these people commonly have to make, mean that in Complex Sales the sales representative has to develop a selling method that's quite distinct from, and far more analytical than, that of the old-time Good Joe who made it on a smile and a shoeshine. As the story of Greg and Ray indicates, having this type of method can be the difference between failure and success. It's because we demonstrate it to our clients that our program is in such demand.

If you've ever sold something to a couple as opposed to a husband or wife alone, you know how multiple approval can complicate a sale. If your selling takes place in a corporate or government environment, you know that the complications are even greater when the persons whose approvals are needed are not only individuals, but also committees and boards of review. The bottom line here is that whenever two or more yes votes are needed for a sale to go through, you're dealing with a difficult situation, and you need a very special strategy to handle it.

This is true no matter how simple or complex the product being sold is, and no matter how much or how little it costs. The decisive factor in the Complex Sale is *structure,* not product or price.

Take basketballs—certainly a small-ticket product—as an example. The sales representative who sells a dozen basketballs to old Pop Jones at the local sporting goods store is making a Simple Sale; he doesn't need our help. But the sales representative who's selling a hundred gross of that same product to K mart definitely does need it, since making this sale will require not just one yes but several. A selling method is needed that has been validated in the field with an almost limitless variety of products and services, and found to be equally effective with all of them. That's where we come in.

With this definition of the Complex Sale in mind, you should be able to determine how relevant this book will be to you. If you sell principally over a counter or door to door, you won't find it as helpful, since you rarely need more than one yes to close your transactions. But if you're involved in any aspect of corporate selling, our program can help you hone the skills you already have, develop new ones you may not have thought you needed, and fit them all together into a visible and repeatable strategy for success.

The people who have already gone through our program, and who are now using its principles in their own sales operations, form a Who's Who of American business: We deliver our programs mainly to the Fortune 1,000 Industrials and the Fortune 50 Transportation, Financial, Insurance, and Commercial Banking firms. Many of these firms deal in obviously big-ticket items, such as airplanes (Lockheed) and computer systems (Hewlett-Packard, IBM). Others sell small-ticket products, such as Kleenex (Kimberly-Clark) and basketballs (Wilson Sporting Goods). All of them do business in the arena of the Complex Sale.

In that arena, the people who profit most directly and immediately from our training are field sales representatives and their managers. In addition, we've made significant advances in terms of sales and corporate success for inside salespeople, customer service people, product managers, and numerous senior executives whose work in one way or another involves sales performance.

But you don't have to work for one of these multidivision, *Fortune*-listed giants to profit from our strategic system. Whatever the size of your company, and whatever the product or service you deal in, if you're involved in the Complex Sale as we've defined it here, this book is directed to you. To get the maximum benefit from reading it, however, you should understand its particular relevance to your current sales environment. That environment, you already know, is characterized by virtually constant change. Because this change is often troubling to the sales representative, before we start laying out our program we want to describe very briefly the impact of future shock on the world of the Complex Sale.

Future-Shock Selling: Three Premises

A dozen years ago Alvin Toffler, in his landmark bestseller, coined the term "future shock" to describe the "shattering stress and disorientation that we induce in individuals by subjecting them to too much change in too short a time." As a sales representative, you can probably point to numerous changes that have already induced this future-shock sensation in your environment. You may be experiencing change in your marketplace, your technology, your customer base, your product line, your competitive position, your marketing strategy and tactics—or in a combination of any of these areas. You may be experiencing change as a subtle, gradual erosion (such as Detroit has been seeing since the 1950s), as a sudden event (such as the Arab oil embargo), or as continual growth (such as the computer industry is experiencing now). But whatever the scope or the rate of the changes that are affecting your environment, they can lead to future shock.

This isn't necessarily cause for despair. As Toffler

pointed out, it isn't change per se but the *uncertainty* often created by it that causes the disorientation known as future shock. No matter what changes are going on in your industry, you can still develop effective sales strategies if you learn to sort out the opportunities from the threats in your particular environment, and if you continually develop the specific skills needed to sell in a future-shock world.

This book is designed to give you those skills, whatever your business and whatever your product or service. You'll get maximum benefit from it if you first accept the reality that *change has become a constant.* To close the Complex Sale today, you need to know that yesterday's business as usual is today's outdated system and tomorrow's millstone around the neck. We believe this recognition is so important that we identify the acceptance of change as the first prerequisite for understanding our program, and we even put this in the form of an axiom, or premise, of our system. We phrase it in the following way:

> *Premise 1 of Strategic Selling: Whatever got you where you are today is no longer sufficient to keep you there.*

This premise, we realize, goes against the grain of all those who have been doing things "their way" for twenty years and are comfortable with the established patterns. Yet accepting this premise is essential to continued prosperity in the Complex Sales world of the 1980s and 1990s. The fact is that in today's sales environment instability is about the only thing you can count on. The person who refuses to alter his or her "time-tested" methods of doing things to adjust to this central fact will soon be left behind.

Future shock isn't peculiar to the selling environment, but the specific future-shock changes associated with the Complex Sale are. Our second premise is addressed to this fact. It's meant to identify one of the most important changes you're going to have to make in your approach to selling if you're to carry your current success into the 1980s and beyond, and if you're to make that success the basis for ever increasing sales volume.

> *Premise 2 of Strategic Selling: In the Complex Sale, a good tactical plan is only as good as the strategy that led up to it.*

"Tactics," as we use the term in our programs and in this book, refers to techniques you use when you're actually face to face with a prospect or customer in a sales call. It includes all the time-honored tricks of the trade that you learned in Selling 101, such as questioning techniques, overcoming objections, presentation skills, trial closes, and so on.

By "strategy," on the other hand, we mean a series of far less widely recognized, but equally identifiable and repeatable, processes that you use to position yourself with the customer before the sales call even begins. You use tactics *during* your sales presentation; strategy must come *before* it.

We emphasize to all the sales professionals we work with that in today's corporate selling environment, strategy is a prerequisite to tactical success. We tell them they must understand something that Ray found out to his dismay: that tactics will get you nowhere if you present them to the wrong person, in the wrong fashion, without sufficient information, or at the wrong time. And we explain that good strategy, like good tactics, can be *learned*. In fact the entire focus of the program we'll be presenting in this book is on developing effective sales strategies.

Not that tactics are unimportant. We believe in good presentation skills as deeply as you do, but we emphasize strategy in this book because it's *the single most neglected element* of selling, not only among sales representatives, but even among the very managers and sales trainers who are supposed to be teaching them to cope with the confusions of the Complex Sale. In fact it was our frustration with such training programs that led us to develop our system in the first place. What you have in this book is the first sales program that systematically integrates strategy and tactics into a unified blueprint for selling success in the 1980s and beyond.

Our third and final premise also addresses itself specifically to the sales environment, but is much broader in scope than Premise 2. If Premise 1 identified the reality of general social change and Premise 2 the reality of change in the Complex Sale, then Premise 3 points to the need for personal, internal change as a way of handling what's going on outside.

> *Premise 3 of Strategic Selling: You can only succeed in sales today if you know what you're doing and why.*

This may sound obvious, but it's not—at least judging from how infrequently today's sales representatives apply it in actual sales practice. We can demonstrate that to you by relating an experience that happened time and time again during the years we were sales executives in major corporations. As regional and national sales managers, we interviewed literally hundreds of prospective sales representatives. Most of them were already quite successful when they came to us, and so our task was often to sort out the very good from the excellent in choosing new members of our teams. To do this we devised a simple question to test not their individual performance (we already knew that was good) but their *perception* of that performance. The question we asked was this: "*Why* are you so successful? What sets you apart from the other people in your branch whose sales are consistently below yours?"

The answers were surprising. *Not one in a hundred* of our candidates was able to identify the real reason for his or her success. They talked about luck, connections, or hard work as the essential ingredients. Only a tiny fraction understood that it was the way they went about their work—what we call their *methodology* or *process*—that was the real clue to why they did well.

It was that fraction we sought to hire. Of course we knew that working hard, building up contacts, and luck probably hadn't hurt these people's track records. But we also knew that these were trivial factors compared with sales representatives' awareness of their own working methods, and their willingness to improve those methods to bring about even greater success. What we found for over twenty years as managers was that the person with the best *under-standing* of his or her own effective *way of doing things* was the one who would produce for us. Those were the people we hired, and with few exceptions they did prove to be the excellent material we needed.

This was, and is, only logical. If you rely on luck or territory or connections, your work will always have a high degree of trial and error about it—and trial and error simply isn't a reliable key to success in a world that's as riddled with change, and as competitive, as ours is. Without an understanding of your own method, you're going to be doomed to approach each sale as an entirely new experience. You'll never develop a *testing* procedure to see what works and what doesn't, and you'll therefore see each change in your environment as a signal to go back to square one.

Success today depends on your developing not this kind of catch-as-catch-can approach to your work, but a clearly defined, *professional* approach. Knowing what you're doing and why is fundamental to the strategic professional's profile.

Profile of the Strategic Professional

Surprising as it may seem, many people who sell are reluctant to admit that their profession *is* a profession. The old, unfortunate image of the sales representative as a mere glad-hander, someone whose only skill is "knowing how to talk to folks," still commands a good deal of credence, even among sales representatives themselves. Think of the phrases that come to mind when you think of selling. "A good salesperson is born, not made." "Selling is 90 percent luck." "The real salesman is the guy who can sell refrigerators to Eskimos." Underlying all these adages is the view that it's personality, not understanding; temperament, not training; magic, not skill, that make the top sales representatives what they are. For many, "luck and pluck" is still a watchword of success.

Even if this view was accurate in former days (which is

doubtful), it has no bearing on today's future-shock world. Selling, no less than teaching or medicine or law, is a professional calling, and those who prosper in it are those with a handle on their own professional methods. They're the people who have developed a conscious, planned system of selling steps that are *visible, logical,* and *repeatable.* The person who learns our Strategic Selling system and makes it work never sees success in terms of magic or charisma or luck. No one who makes it big in the Complex Sales of the 1980s will be able to rely on that old mythology. The sales leaders of the next two decades will succeed because they look on themselves as pros.

One of the things these pros will have in common is a special brand of persistence. We're not talking about the simple "Keep knocking on the door until it opens" kind of persistence. That's important, all right, as you can see from a recent survey done by a national association of sales executives: It concluded that 80 percent of the new sales in this country are made by 10 percent of the sales representatives—and that they close those sales only after making five or more calls on the client. But our research shows that another kind of persistence is equally important: the kind the top people show in working on their own selling *methods.*

We've observed one fact countless times in the follow-up surveys we do of our "graduates." If you want to predict the next sales representative of the year, the next star regional manager, the next leading national account executive, find out which salespeople are analyzing their own methodology, which ones are constantly reassessing sales strategy and tactics, which ones are looking for reliable, repeatable methods to improve their competitive edge. An attention to inner process as well as to external change is fundamental to today's (and tomorrow's) sales leaders.

In addition to having a handle on their sales processes and understanding why process is important, all strategic professionals share one other profile characteristic: They're *never satisfied.* This fact helps to explain why the sales representatives and managers who are most excited by our programs, the ones who are most eager to introduce our strategies into their methodologies, are those who are *already* doing well. And it helps to explain why the firms that these commission leaders work for are also already doing well.

As we've already mentioned, our clients are drawn primarily from among the most successful corporations in the country. Why do these firms, which are already leading the pack, have us work with their people? Why do many of them spend fifty thousand to over a million dollars so their sales representatives can learn the principles of Strategic Selling? Why do they spend an average of one thousand dollars per person so their people can attend a two-day program where we present the ideas contained in this book?

For the paradoxical but very good reason that it's the best who always want to do better. In any selling organization, it's that top 10 percent of individuals with persistence and dedication to their own selling skills who ultimately pay the biggest dividends to the company. So enabling that 10 percent to think about their work in the terms we use just makes good economic sense. As you go through this book, you'll see that disciplining yourself to follow these top companies' example makes the same kind of sense for you.

How Strategic Selling Works

What do these people learn in our programs, and how will you learn it from this book?

To begin with, our system isn't derived from a neat, academic theory but from our experiences as lifetime salesmen in the field. Most sales-training programs start with a nice, high-sounding theory that they then impose on the facts. We don't do that. Our program is generalizable all right. As our clients can attest, it's been tested in the hardest arena in the world, the American economy, during good times and bad, during recessions and booms—and it works. But it works because it's *practically,* not just theoretically, sound. The reason that so many national sales managers are insisting their sales forces participate in our program is that it responds to what you're experiencing right now in your everyday sales situation.

The lessons of this book, therefore, aren't designed to expound some abstract "sales philosophy," to impress you with gimmicks, or to give you a briefcase full of five-dollar phrases to throw around at your next meeting. We'll keep the discussion simple and to the point, because the goal of the book is simple and to the point: It's to help you sort through the confusing data associated with the Complex Sale and to give you a method for analyzing the data, positioning yourself better with your accounts, and closing even your most difficult sales. Among the things you'll learn from this book are:

1. How to position yourself with the *real* decision makers and avoid those without approval power

2. How to spot the two key customer attitudes that can make a sale, and the two that usually break it

3. How to get not only the order but a satisfied customer, repeat sales, and enthusiastic referrals

4. How to increase sales penetration in your current accounts

5. How to minimize the uncertainties of a cold call on a new account

6. How to free up the stuck order

7. When to treat an old account like a new prospect

8. How to avoid selling business you don't want

9. How to identify and deal with the four different Buying Influences present in every sale

10. How to prevent sales from being sabotaged by an internal antisponsor

11. How to recognize fail-safe signals that indicate when a sale is in jeopardy

12. How to track account progress and forecast future sales

13. How to avoid dry months by allocating time wisely to three critical selling tasks

14. Why the adage "Look before you leap" is the key to selling in the 1980s and 1990s, and why "He who hesitates is lost" is inappropriate advice

We want you to remember that this is only a sampling of the topics we're going to be covering, and to remember also two major distinctions between our approach and that of sales-training programs you've previously encountered.

First: Our focus is on success, not failure. In trying to avoid failure, many sales-training programs actually guarantee it, by emphasizing long lists of things that can go wrong in a sales call, and by blaming the sales representative when they occur. We don't want you to concentrate on your shortcomings in this way, and for that reason we focus not on *you* but rather on your *account* or prospect: Our goal is to teach you how to understand that account so well that once you get into the sales call, you'll already have dealt with your own uncertainties and will be free to devote your attention to making the presentation count.

Second: The work is on *your* accounts and prospects. Most training programs, in an attempt to link theory and practice, give you a series of canned case studies as illustrative material. By working on these hypothetical cases, you're supposed to develop the skills needed to work on your own accounts. When we were designing our programs, we realized that that was a roundabout and inefficient method of getting you to analyze your own situation, so we eliminated the case study approach and zeroed in on our clients' own problems. This book, like our programs, takes a hands-on approach. Instead of hypothetical situations, you're going to get a series of Personal Workshops that are based on the workshops we use in our programs, and that will help you to use the concepts we'll be presenting to manage your own accounts and prospects better right now.

The people who have been through our programs tell us that this direct, real-case method is one of the most useful and lasting lessons of the experience. An American Can Company regional manager put it well, months after his people had taken the Strategy Selling program, when he said, "I've been to a lot of different courses. This one my people are really using." That pleased us, of course, but it didn't really surprise us, because Strategic Selling is *designed* to be used, and to be used at once. It's meant to help you deal with *your* stuck orders and trouble accounts, *your* inside saboteurs, *your* dry months and difficult renewals. And it's meant to help you do that right now.

By using the workshop method that we developed in our programs, you'll reap the benefits of your own hands-on experience, and turn those benefits to your advantage even before you finish the book. By the time you come to the last page, you'll be able to say, as so many of our sales professionals are now able to say, "It's *the way I go about it* that makes me number one."

▶ 2 ◀

STRATEGY AND TACTICS DEFINED

Suppose you're the coach of the Washington Redskins, and your boys are gearing up for an appointment with Tom Landry's Cowboys. The big game is one week away, and the films of the Dallas team's last couple of games have just come in. Your players are anxious to see them so they can start working out game plans, but you've got a better idea. "No films this year, boys," you tell them. "We're going to spend this week working on the basics. Blocking, tackling, running, kicking, passing. We know the Cowboys are good, but by next week we're going to be better. Just concentrate on how hard you're going to hit them once you get onto the field. The rest will take care of itself."

How long do you think you'd last in the National Football League with an attitude like that? A week? Maybe two weeks at the outside. In a league as competitive as the NFL, it would be suicide to ignore your pregame planning and devote yourself entirely to "basics." In the world of professional football, analyzing your opponents' moves in advance is as crucial as pass pattern drills, and the coach who dared to neglect such pregame planning would soon be looking for a job.

The same principle applies to the world of professional selling and yet, to judge from many sales representatives' reactions when we mention the phrase "sales strategy," it would seem that "hitting the field with the basics" constitutes their entire selling approach. To many people, the only skills that count are those that emerge in the actual sales call: the tricks of the trade that help you deal effectively with the buyer once you're actually in the field.

In other words, it's still *tactics* that are seen as essential. *Strategy*—by which we mean that process you use to lay out your moves in advance of the sales call—is still considered something of a gimmick: a newfangled, computer-age innovation that doesn't have anything to do with how the top person really performs in the field.

This unfortunate view of strategy results partly from the traditional picture of the salesperson as a professional shaker-of-hands, and partly from the insidious influence of sales-training programs that specialize in face-to-face techniques. The old-time salesperson and the trainers who initiate most new sales representatives into their fool's paradise share the view of the representative as an "action" person who would rather be on the road than at a desk any day, and who really only comes alive when the stakes are high and he or she is face to face with a buyer. Many of these gung-ho counselors see strategy as a waste of time. "Get out there and sell!" is their advice. "Get out and get your hands dirty. You're not paid to sit in the office."

We have nothing against dirty hands and, as we've already said, this book promotes a definitely hands-on approach to selling. Nobody can afford to neglect the face-to-face fundamentals. But the tactical techniques you use in the direct encounter will only pay off if you develop a sound strategy beforehand.

Why You Need Strategy First

Both "strategy" and "tactics" are derived from ancient Greek. To the Greeks, *taktikos* meant "fit for arranging or maneuvering," and it referred to the art of moving forces in battle. *Strategos* was the word for "general." Originally, therefore, strategy was the "art of the general," or the art of setting up forces *before* the battle began. In military terms these definitions still apply; with them in mind, you can easily see why strategy must precede tactics in a military setting.

This is equally true in the sales arena. The objective of a good sales strategy is to get yourself in the *right place* with the *right people* at the *right time* so you can tactically make the right presentation. The only way to accomplish that objective is to do your homework first: to log that desk time that so many people in sales resent, so that once you get into the actual selling event, you're certain to have everything you need to make the most effective presentation. It was because he didn't have everything he needed that Ray lost out on his computer sale to Greg. If he'd paid more attention to the uncertainties of the sale—in this case, the "hidden" outside consultant and the competition—he might have closed the deal.

When we ask our program participants what they like best about our program, many of them reply, "It helped me organize my data better." This isn't a surprising answer. Think of the bulk of information you have to deal with in any Complex Sale. Think of the maze of offices, the overlapping managerial decisions, the games of receptionist roulette, the vice-presidential timetables, the sheer weight of paperwork that has to be done before you can close a deal. If you plunge into the selling situation without having a reliable method of sorting, organizing, and analyzing this vast body of data—without being able to assess the entire sales situation as it relates to your selling goal—you're going to be in the same impossible position as the Redskins coach relying on a "wait until the game" approach to give him a victory over the Cowboys.

The mistake that Ray made is a very common one in the Complex Sale arena. In Chapter 5 we'll look at that mistake in more detail, when we talk about how important it is in account selling to distinguish among the various Buying Influences in every Complex Sale, and to understand how the roles played by these Buying Influences can shift from sale to sale. Ray discovered how important that was a little too late to help him. So does every other sales representative who displays tactical wizardry at the wrong time or in the wrong place.

You've probably already run into this situation. You walk into Mr. Wilson's office and give him a classic, textbook presentation. He is suitably awed. "That was terrific!" he says. "I only wish I'd known ahead of time how well your product matches our needs. I would have had Mr. Richards here to approve the sale. I'm sure he would have given the OK, but he's in Nigeria for the month."

Or take an even worse situation. You're in the middle of that brilliant pitch when you suddenly realize by yourself, without being told, that you're talking to the wrong person. And you realize that if you now try to go around him to get to the right person, he's going to cut you off at the knees. There's no way to rescue the sale and you walk out of the office mumbling, tactically flush but strategically destroyed.

Situations like these are always the result of poor planning, of the sales representative's neglecting to get an important piece of information, and of going into the selling event with an overconfident or otherwise distorted view of reality. Only a strategic approach can provide you with a reliable method of *testing* your impressions of the pending sale at every step of the selling cycle, and therefore of being certain of your position before you begin the presentation. Without this strategic testing, you may act on the basis of what you *wish* were true rather than what *is* true, and find yourself in the ridiculous position of the fellow who lost a quarter in the park but decided to look for it downtown because the light there was better.

We're not saying that strategy is "better than" or "more important than" tactics. They're equally important elements of the same overall design. It's too simple to call strategy "planning" and tactics "action," because you can't use tactics effectively outside of a strategic Action Plan, and you can't set out good strategies unless you're attentive to the new planning information that each new tactical encounter gives you. As time goes on and you've been using the principles of Strategic Selling successfully in your work, you'll see that strategy and tactics must work together. We emphasize strategy because, as we've said, it's almost always neglected. And it always has to come first.

Long-Term Strategy: Focus on the Account

The tendency of "tactics only" sales representatives to ignore vital preparation is only one factor in their undoing. Another is a tendency to focus exclusively on the individual *sale* and to ignore the *account*. As we've already emphasized, it's the *selling event* that occupies the bulk of most representatives' attention. There's nothing wrong with attending carefully to the selling event—whether it's a phone call, an introductory letter, or the sales call itself—but it can create real problems if it leads you to forget the larger picture of which the individual sale is only a part.

In a Complex Sale arena, you have short-term and long-term objectives. In the short term, you want to close as many individual deals as you possibly can, as quickly as possible. In the long term, you want to maintain healthy relations with the customers signing for these deals, so that they'll be willing to make further purchases from you in the months and years to come. It would be great if these two objectives always coincided, but you know that they don't. All of us who make a living in sales can point to business that we wish we hadn't sold—to sales that seemed like Wins at the time they were made but that turned out to be disastrous in the long run.

You've probably seen this happen yourself in cases where somebody sells a product to a company that cannot really use it well—where the fit between the product and the company's needs simply isn't as exact as the salesperson would like it to be. What do you do in a situation like this?

If you take only the short-term view, you may be inclined to gloss over the bad product fit and go for the instant pay-off, your commission. But you wouldn't last very long with that account once the company discovered that it had been sold a bill of goods. You could forget about referrals and repeat business. And you would very soon discover that your tactical victory had turned out be a strategic defeat.

One of the hardest decisions you have to make as a sales representative is the decision *not* to close a sale, even though it's possible to do so. One of our major clients was faced with making this decision several years ago, just after completing production on a new computer assembly. The assembly was so sophisticated and difficult to operate that, if it had been put on the market (a market that was very eager to have it), our client would have been deluged in weeks with service calls and angry customers. The company's officers understood this, even though the potential customers did not, and so they made a painful but very wise choice: They allowed a rival company to be first in this hungry but inexperienced field. It was the rival company that had to deal with the disappointed buyers, and our client that eventually profited from its decision to be second in the field.

This story illustrates clearly the importance of taking a long-term, account-centered approach. If you concentrate chiefly on tactics, you'll be prone to forget the account, and to go from selling event to selling event as if they were their own reward. To revert to the military analogy, you'll tend to focus on winning individual battles while forgetting about the war of which these battles are only components. Our strategic approach to selling is designed to offset this self-defeating tendency.

We don't mean to imply, by using the military terms "battle" and "war," that we see successful selling as a victory of the seller over the buyer. On the contrary. We use the military metaphor purely as a shorthand description. In contrast to what you might have learned earlier in sales-training programs, the successful Complex Sale should never be seen as one in which you beat the buyer or trick him into signing. That's another problem with the "tactics first" approach and with the "go get 'em" philosophy of many sales trainers. They set you up to keep score, to gauge your success by how many customers you've beaten.

We all know people who relish "sticking it to the customer," who are continually asking themselves, "How can I *fool this buyer*?" Eventually they do themselves in. The question we stress in Strategic Selling is "How can I *manage this sale*?" Only by asking that question throughout the selling cycle can you avoid the adversarial view that so often turns tactical success into strategic defeat. The successful sales strategist of the coming decades will keep both short-term and long-term objectives in mind when managing the Complex Sale.

Setting the Account Strategy: Four Steps to Success

Now you're just about ready to begin setting strategies for your accounts. Before you can do that effectively, though, there's one further principle we have to introduce. It's the principle of a step-by-step approach. We've found that many potentially excellent sales representatives ignore this principle. They "jump squares," thinking that the sooner they reach the end of their selling cycles, the sooner they'll pocket their commissions. This hurried approach almost always results in lost sales.

In the following chapters, we'll be introducing what we call the Six Key Elements of effective account strategies. To understand and use them well, you have to keep the step-by-step principle in mind. Each time we introduce a new element, we'll ask you to examine its application to your accounts in a logical, step-by-step fashion. We know you may find this overly cautious, but our experience shows us that analyzing strategy effectively can only be done in this way: Good strategic analysis depends on a logical, repeatable sequence. The sequence we use has four steps:

1. Analyze your current position with regard to your account and with regard to your specific sales objective.

2. Think through possible Alternate Positions.
3. Determine which Alternate Position would best secure your objective and devise an Action Plan to achieve it.
4. Implement your Action Plan.

Since from now on you'll be constantly setting, testing, and revising your sales strategies, you should be referring frequently to these steps: We advise you to run through them in your mind every time we introduce a new Key Element of Strategy, and to use them as a benchmark every time you contemplate a change in the way you're approaching an account.

The Four Steps will be relevant to your thinking whenever you're trying to make something happen in an account that isn't happening right now. You could be preparing to sell a new product or promotion to an existing account, to sell a new prospect, to penetrate other divisions of an existing account, or to get back in the door after losing out to a competitor. When we speak about setting account strategies, we're referring to all your selling situations and to all your prospects and accounts—past, present, and future. Strategic thinking is important to them all.

Notice two things about these Four Steps to success. First: Taken together, they illustrate the importance of constant review—or, to use a contemporary expression, feedback—in setting out your plans. Review, feedback, reassessment: Whatever you call it, it's essential to good account planning. What we do in our programs is exactly what you'll be doing in this book: measuring each new element of strategy, before it's translated into action, against this four-step standard.

Second: Notice how frequently the word "position" appears in this four-step design. Understanding your position with regard to a given account is so central to setting good strategies that we often say "having a strategy" and "having a position" are two ways of expressing the same thing. *The whole key to strategy is position.* It tells you where you are now, and where you might have to move to increase your chances of sales success. So we begin with a Personal Workshop to determine your current position.

► 3 ◄

YOUR STARTING POINT: POSITION

To the military strategist, position is an absolutely critical element in an overall campaign plan. The general who doesn't know where he is vis-à-vis the enemy—whether in terms of actual geographical location or in terms of knowledge of forces, lines of supply, weather, or other factors—is simply setting his men up for the kill. On the battlefield, being in the wrong place at the wrong time can be a fatal error, because no matter how brilliantly an army may perform in a face-to-face encounter, it will never get a fair chance to do so if its leaders don't know where they are, or if they're marching in the wrong direction.

The same thing is true in selling. In account strategy, positioning is the name of the game. What "setting a strategy" really means is doing whatever you have to do to put yourself in the best position to accomplish a particular objective or set of objectives. Of course this can entail a great deal. It can involve all aspects of your selling situation—physical, psychological, economic—with regard to a given account or prospect and a given sales objective. Knowing your current position well means knowing who all your Buying Influences are, how they feel about you, how they feel about your proposal, what questions they want to have answered, how your competition is placed—and a host of other factors. It means knowing in effect what all your strong and weak points are before the selling event begins.

But even if you're unclear on some of these points, even if you're uncertain of your position, you nevertheless *have* a strategic position. You *always* have a position, and for that reason you always have a strategy, whether or not you can identify it. If you don't know where you stand with regard to a given account, you are or soon will be lost—and *that* will be your position.

To avoid the unwelcome situation of being positioned in the Great Unknown, the first thing you need to do is to make your current position with each account *visible*. Just as a general would find a fix on a map, you have to fix yourself within the context of your current sales situation, so your starting point will become known. You're going to do that now, with regard to a specific account and a specific sales objective.

First you need to pick the account or prospect. We don't want you to select one in which everything is going fine. That would defeat the purpose of the workshop you're about to begin, and of Strategic Selling itself. We've designed this book, as we've designed our programs, to help you work through the difficulties of your current sales situations, so you want to choose an account where something isn't quite right. It needn't be one in which everything is falling apart—although if that's the one you want to attack, fine. We've discovered in our programs that the best kind of account to work on is one in which, although things may look all right on the surface, you still feel some uneasiness, some element of uncertainty or confusion.

You'll be working with this account or prospect throughout the rest of this book, so be sure the one you choose will repay the effort you put into it. Be sure it's one, in other words, where you're really eager to have answers. As you learn the principles of Strategic Selling, you'll be applying them eventually to setting strategies for *all* your accounts. But for this first run-through, you'll be focusing on a single one. By the time you finish the book, you'll have analyzed all the elements of this one account, and have devised an Action Plan for making your strategic position with it more visible and more effective than it is now.

Once you've decided on an account, you'll need the following tools: a spiral notebook (the side-bound school type rather than the top-bound stenographer's type), some pencils, and some highlighting devices. In our programs we use small Red Flag stickers as highlighters; you can use similar gum-backed stickers or a Magic Marker. Find yourself a place where you can work without constant distractions and give yourself about twenty or thirty minutes to think about your account position. Then work through the following Personal Workshop. It has been designed to identify the causes of your current uncertainty regarding your account, to help you see how those causes affect your current sales objective, and to allow you to make your position visible by measuring how you feel about where you are.

Personal Workshop 1: Position

This workshop is divided into five steps. The first one is designed to help you identify the particular changes in your sales environment that may make handling the account difficult.

Step 1: Identify relevant changes.
Position would be a minor problem if you didn't have to deal with change, and more importantly with the uncertainty that change often makes us feel. In Chapter 1 we mentioned Alvin Toffler's concept of future shock, and observed that it isn't change per se that causes the stress and disorientation of future shock, but the uncertainty of not knowing how to react when confronted with massive and rapid change. You probably can't do very much to stop the changes that you're now experiencing in your selling environment, but identifying those changes clearly is a first

step to being able to deal with them. So take out your pencil and write the heading "Change" at the top of a left-hand page of your notebook. Then make a list, in no particular order, of all the changes that *you* feel are influencing the way you do business. Don't worry about being exhaustive or "correct" in your choices. You're not taking a test; you're trying to get a handle on the external, environmental changes that are inducing future shock in you and your fellow sales representatives. The best standard by which to measure that isn't some economics professor's pet theory, but the way you're feeling about your work.

Since the national economy affects the way all of us do our jobs, some of the changes you list will no doubt be the stuff of nightly news reports. Others will be specific to your industry, your market, your geographical location. Whatever *you* consider a significant change should go on this list. If you spend about five minutes on this step, you shouldn't have any trouble coming up with eight or ten significant changes. Commonly, in our programs, the participants list twenty or more.

Step 2: Rate these changes minus or plus.

Now go down your list of changes and put a plus (+) next to those you perceive mainly as opportunities, and a minus (−) next to those you see mainly as threats. We know that, if you're like most sales representatives, you'll be a little hesitant about this. As our clients tell us all the time, practically any change can be seen as both a threat and an opportunity: It all depends on how you react to it. That's true, but we're not judging your potential reaction here. We're trying to give you an overview of your *current* position with your account. So as you debate between the pluses and minuses, start from where you are *today*. Is the change you're wondering about, right now, primarily good for you or bad?

The decision will be easier to make with regard to some changes than others. If you're experiencing a drastic shift in customer loyalty from one of your lines to a competitor's, it's not hard to identify that as a threat. If your overseas engineers have just discovered a vast new source of a material that will dramatically cut your production costs, this could easily be an opportunity for reduced prices and higher sales. Most changes will be trickier to measure, but you know your situation well enough to make reasonable decisions about rating them. Just be sure to concentrate on how you see these changes today. Take about another five minutes here. You'll end up with a sound personal overview of the current effects of future shock on your situation. Put the list aside; we'll be returning to it in a moment.

Step 3: Define your current sales objective.

Now, on the facing right-hand page of your notebook, write down your current sales objective with regard to the account you've chosen. Remember that you always have a long-term objective with any account, which is to keep the decision makers in that account happy over time. But you also have specific, short-term objectives that change from sales period to sales period, and often more quickly than that. Focus on the short-term objective that you're working to accomplish right now. Define it briefly but precisely, and write down your definition.

In being precise, you should include in your definition exactly *what* you're trying to sell the account, *when* you expect to close the deal, and if possible *what quantity* you expect them to order. Don't say: "Get Newberry chain to buy sofas." Specify which sofas, how many, and when: "Get Newberry chain to order trial package of 100 Slumber Line sofas by June 1." It may strike you as belaboring the obvious to do this, but we have a reason for asking you to be precise. Our work as managers has taught us that many sales representatives are unsure of what they're supposed to be accomplishing. Writing your immediate objective down is one way of forcing you to clarify what it is.

The bottom line is this: *Every sale is unique.* We've found that it's easier to remember that fundamental fact if you remember that every sales objective always has the following characteristics:

- It's *specific* and *measurable*. It gives numerically precise answers to the questions who, what, and when.

- It focuses on a specific *outcome* that you're trying to generate in a specific account. It answers the question "What am I trying to make happen in this account that isn't happening right now?"
- It's *single* rather than multiple. The definition of the sales objective is a simple rather than compound sentence—that is, it's not connected by "and."

This last characteristic is very important. We've found that many Complex Sales go awry because the person responsible for managing them simply hasn't identified a unique objective beforehand. If you think you have two or more objectives in a given sale, look again. The principles of Strategic Selling are designed to help you manage your accounts *sale by sale,* because managing each individual sale on its own ground is ultimately the only way to keep all your accounts healthy over time. In the words of a wry associate of ours, "You can't draw an elephant through a keyhole—unless you do it one hair at a time."

If, like many sales representatives, you're unclear about your current objective, notice this as a possible cause of your general uneasiness about the account. To help you define the immediate objective, write down briefly what you're doing with the account right now, and what you'd like to be doing with it by the end of the next sales period. Think of other objectives you could be pursuing at this time, and which of them would be most gratifying to you not only in terms of immediate commission, but also in terms of maintaining good relations with the account over time. Our program participants have told us that taking a few minutes to think about what they're trying to do with their accounts often reduces their confusion: They find out that they knew things about the account, and about their approach to it, that they weren't aware they knew. And they discover gray areas—areas where they should have information, but don't.

When you've defined your objective, look at that objective and your list of "Changes" side by side. How does each change on your list affect your current sales objective? Are the changes that you've marked as threats creating problems for you in attaining this objective now? Are the ones you've marked as opportunities making it easier for you to attain it? Or can you see some way, now that you're relating these changes to a single objective, in which they could be turned to your advantage? The purpose here is to help you define specifically the connections between general changes and your immediate goal. Doing this won't alter the environment, but it may help to reduce your uneasiness by making you more *conscious* of what's happening.

Step 4: Test your current position.

The next step in clarifying the situation is to test your current position: to find out how you feel overall about your prospects with this account and your chances for making this sale. We do this in our programs by having participants ask themselves a simple question. You should do the same thing now. In your notebook, underneath your objective, write down this question: "How do I feel about_____with regard to_____?" Fill in the first blank with the name of the account you're working on, and the second blank with your defined objective. Then answer the question.

To help our participants define how they feel about this question, we ask them to identify their position along a chart we call the Euphoria-Panic Continuum. We reproduce it on page 49 for you to use. You may feel that none of the "choices" we've listed here is exactly a description of your feeling, and if so you'll have to supply your own. This is not a multiple-choice test, but a guide for you to determine where, along a line from Euphoria to Panic, you feel you belong. Whether you use your own adjectives or ours, the point is for you to define how good (how close to Euphoria) or how bad (how close to Panic) you feel right now.

The use of the Euphoria-Panic Continuum is pretty straightforward, but we do want to make a few comments about it so you'll get maximum benefit from this exercise. First: We caution you to be honest. Unless there's absolutely nothing wrong with your account situation (which happens only in Never-Never-Land), identifying how you feel about the situation is like identifying pain in your body. Your uneasy or worried feelings about the situation signal you that something is wrong, just as pain tells you there's something wrong with your body. Don't ignore the signal and don't kid yourself. Don't simply put on a brave front, adopt a "positive" or "winning" attitude, and forge ahead as if everything were fine. If you don't treat your feelings about your accounts seriously, you'll be like the football player who "plays through pain" with the use of painkillers, and ends up in the hospital because he couldn't feel himself being hurt.

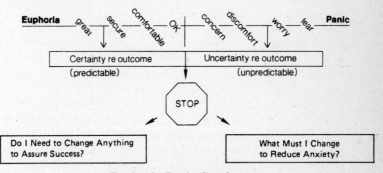

Euphoria-Panic Continuum

Second: It's just as dangerous to be blissfully happy about your account as it is to be in a panic mode. If you find yourself at *either* end of the continuum, be wary: You're probably being unrealistic in your assessment. You cannot function well in either a euphoric or a panic state. In the former you tend to do nothing because you think things are already perfect. In the latter you do everything and anything you can, and most of it has no impact. In either case you're out of touch with reality.

In fact, the person who's euphoric and the one who's in a panic are really much closer than they think, in terms of how they're probably handling their accounts. We illustrate this in our programs by drawing the Euphoric-Panic Continuum not as a straight line, but as a nearly closed circle. When we draw the continuum this way, you can see that the distance from euphoria to panic is very short (see page 50).

EUPHORIA   PANIC

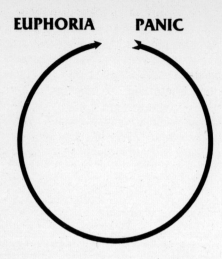

Euphoria, left unchecked, leads to complacency; complacency leads to arrogance; and arrogance inevitably leads to disaster. The cocksure sales representative always overlooks "trivial" pieces of information that indicate the sale is in danger—and soon ends up in a state of panic.

The distance *back* from panic to euphoria, unfortunately, isn't nearly so short. Once you've fallen into panic, you have to work your way back slowly, going through the whole long circle of reality until you're feeling confident again. So be very suspicious of euphoria. As a regional manager in a tough eastern market once told us, "I want my competition to get euphoric. That's when I've got my best shot."

The final point to notice about the continuum is that it isn't a predictive device, merely a descriptive one. Its purpose is to let you test your strategy, or position, *up to this point* by allowing you to gauge your emotional reactions to the situation as it stands. Throughout the rest of this book you'll be making adjustments to your strategy that will move you to the left of the continuum if you're now far off to the right, and ensure that you stay where you are, in spite of changing conditions, if you're already feeling good.

As those conditions change, you'll be reassessing your position many times. The continuum is designed to help you do that efficiently, not only now but in the future.

Step 5: Examine Alternate Positions.

Once you know where you are, you next want to know where to go. In terms of the Four Steps we outlined in the last chapter, you've now finished the first one, analyzing your current position. Now you need to examine alternatives, to discover how you might *reposition* yourself to make the attainment of your objective more likely.

The entire rest of this book will help you to identify and take Alternate Positions. Right now, we want you to focus on what you already know, and to think about areas of possible change—areas in which something *you* do can counteract the environmental changes that are causing you future shock and pain. You'll notice that on the continuum, a predictable, successful outcome is more likely if you find yourself on the left than if you find yourself on the right. But this is only a likelihood, and it too is subject to change. The significant thing to observe at this point is that, no matter how you're feeling about your current account and sales situation, you still must consider change—that is, change that *you* bring about.

The stop sign in the continuum diagram is meant to point you to that necessity. If you're on the right side of the continuum, you need to consider changes in your position so that you can reduce anxiety. If you're on the left, you need to do this also, to ensure continued success. So stop for a few minutes now. Put your pencil down and look at what you have. Look over your list of external "Changes," and at how they relate to your objective. Look at that objective itself: Have you identified it clearly for yourself, or is it an area for possible change? Finally, review how you feel about the account and the objective in question. What changes, in the account or in the environment, would make you feel better than you do? And what can you do right now to bring about that result?

To make your options more visible to you, turn to another page of your notebook and at the top write "Alternate Positions." Then list the things you can do to improve your current position. *Save this list.* You'll be revising it throughout the book. At this point, it's likely to be a short list. That's fine. Learning that you don't have the answers is itself a positive step. And making your current position visible can at least make the field ahead less confusing. Now that you've spent half an hour thinking about the effect of outside changes on your position, you should be more certain about *where* you're uncertain, even if you don't know what to do next. You're in the position of the house carpenter who knows that the south wall needs work, but needs a blueprint before he can begin.

Hold on to your tools and to all the information you've collected in this workshop. Keep your notebook and pencils with you, and keep everything you've written down. You're going to start building a strategy, and we're going to give you the blueprint.

► 4 ◄

A GLANCE AT THE STRATEGY BLUEPRINT: THE SIX KEY ELEMENTS OF STRATEGIC SELLING

You've just done a Personal Workshop to make your current position regarding your present sales goal more visible to you. You've identified areas of uncertainty in that position and drawn up a list of Alternate Positions that you might take to broaden your strategic options. We've acknowledged that, at this point, your Alternate Position list is likely to be short. We're now going to give you the blueprint you need to expand and revise it, so that by the end of the book you'll have turned it into a fundamental working paper for your strategic Action Plan.

That Action Plan will grow out of not one but many Alternate Positions. There's never only one "correct" strategy for a sales objective, but always a choice of options. Indeed, as a sales professional you'll commonly have to adopt several strategies—to change your position several times—between the first sales call and the successful close of any sale. The blueprint we're going to give you will help you do that with a minimum of trial and error, and with the greatest possible understanding of *all* the elements involved in your sales goals.

As we said in Chapter 2, in our years of coaching top salespeople in a vast array of businesses, we've found that every good sales strategy always pays attention to six such elements. These Six Key Elements of Strategic Selling are the fundamental analytic tools you need to move from the position you've just defined to any Alternate Position of greater strength. The Six Key Elements are:

1. Buying Influences
2. Red Flags/Leverage from Strength
3. Response Modes
4. Win-Results
5. The Sales Funnel
6. The Ideal Customer Profile

Future chapters will show you in detail and with examples how to bring these Six Key Elements together into a tested, practical strategy for sales success. In this chapter we're just going to define our basic terms, to give you an overview of the entire blueprint. Treat the chapter in that way—as an overview or glance, nothing more. Don't "study" it or take notes or worry about concepts that are unfamiliar to you. Just give it a quick run-through, to get a basic feel for the tools you'll be using.

Keep one thing in mind as you do. We present the Six Key Elements to you in the same sequence we use in our Strategic Selling workshops, because we've discovered that it makes the material accessible in the most orderly fashion. Don't infer from this numerical presentation that there's any ranking to the individual elements. On the contrary. The element of Buying Influences is discussed first, for example, merely because you can't fully understand the other five elements without it. The Six Key Elements are equally essential to your success. The only proper way to use them is *interactively, as a system.*

Key Element 1: Buying Influences

We've defined a Complex Sale as one in which several people have to give their approval before the sale can go through. Identifying *all* those people accurately, and understanding the role that each of them plays in getting you to your sales goal, are two of the major stumbling blocks for salespeople—even very good salespeople—in the Complex Sale.

Many sales managers address the problem of identifying key players by telling their sales representatives to get in touch with "my old friend Jim Murphy" or to find out the department manager's name. They concentrate on the individuals who have been important in previous sales, who are "friends," or whose position or title in the buying organization suggests they're the people to meet.

We take an entirely different approach. Since corporate structures today are in constant flux, we tell our managers and sales representatives to look first not for people, but for *roles*. Then, we say, look for the people playing those roles for a specific sales objective—irrespective of their titles.

In every Complex Sale, there are *four* critical buying roles. We call the people who play these roles *Buying Influences,* or, more simply, *Buyers.*

To head off a potential misunderstanding right at the outset, we need to emphasize that we *don't* use the capitalized form of the word "Buyer" in the conventional sense, to indicate a department store's "dry goods buyer" or a manufacturing division's "purchasing agent." We know that "buyer" commonly implies someone whose job involves designated purchasing responsibilities, but we use the term quite differently.

When we use the capitalized terms "Buyer" and "Buying Influence" in this book, we are referring to people who play one of the *four buying roles.* There may be four, or fourteen, or forty people in the buying organization who can influence a given sale, but each one of these people always plays at least one of the four roles. We define the four as follows:

- *Economic Buying Influence.* The role of the person who will act as Economic Buyer for your sales objective is to give *final* approval to buy. There is always only one person or set of people playing this role for a given sales goal. The Economic Buyer can say yes when everyone else has said no, and vice versa.

- *User Buying Influences.* The role of User Buyers is to make judgments about the potential impact of your product or service on their job performance. User Buyers will use or supervise the use of your product or service, and so their personal success is directly tied to the success of that product or service. There may be several people playing User Buyer roles in a sale.

- *Technical Buying Influences.* The role of Technical Buyers is to screen out possible suppliers. Their focus is on the product or service itself, and they make recommendations based on how well the product or service meets a variety of objective specifications. Technical Buyers can't give a final yes, but they can (and often do) give a final no. As with User Buyers, there are usually several people playing the role of Technical Buyer for a given sales objective.

- *Coach.* The unique and very special role of a Coach is to guide you to your particular sales goal by leading you to the other Buyers and by giving you information that you need to position yourself effectively with each one. You usually find the other three Buyers in the buying organization. Coaches are different in that they may be found in the buying organization, in your own organization, or outside of them both. Your Coach's focus is on your success; for every sales objective, you have to find and develop at least one Coach.

Understanding these four Buying Influence roles—and then identifying all the people playing them with regard to your sales goal—is the foundation of Strategic Selling.

Key Element 2:
Red Flags/Leverage from Strength

The story of Ray in the first chapter illustrated that even experienced salespeople, like you, can make mistakes in positioning. When sales representatives or managers fail to spot them in time, to understand why they've arisen, or to take them seriously, they can be disastrous to the sale. Our second Key Element of strategy helps you to identify your positioning difficulties with precision *before* they prove your undoing.

We've chosen the symbol of a Red Flag to highlight areas of strategy that need further attention. We use the Red Flag device for the same reason that a road crew does—because it means "warning" or "danger." We want you to think of the uncertainties and problems in your sales in just that way: not as minor annoyances, but as hazards that can jeopardize the sale. In our presentation of the second Key Element, we identify common sales situations that you should consider automatic Red Flag areas. And we stress that Red Flags are *positive,* because they help you identify potential trouble before it finds you.

The Red Flag device, which you'll be using throughout this book, is one of two principal ways in which you will test the effectiveness of Alternate Positions. The other way can be seen as the Red Flag's mirror image. It's the principle we call Leverage from Strength. When you lever from a Strength, you use the information or contacts you already have to eliminate areas of uncertainty. Every sound Alternate Position either leverages from a Strength, eliminates a Red Flag, or does both. You'll be practicing these two halves of the second Key Element interactively in all the remaining Personal Workshops in the book.

Key Element 3: Response Modes

If the foundation of your strategy is knowing who your key Buyers are, the next thing you need to know is how they feel about your proposal. In Strategic Selling, you determine that by identifying their current receptivity to *change,* specifically the change you're proposing.

In the workshop you did in the preceding chapter, you saw that change can be a critical factor in the way you view the sales environment, and that it's always possible to perceive change as positive, negative, or a mixture of the two. But change doesn't influence you alone. It happens to each of your Buying Influences as well. Understanding *their* perceptions of change is what helps you to predict their receptivity.

There are always four possible reactions to change that a Buyer can have in a given selling situation. We call these reactions *Response Modes.* They're determined by:

1. The Buyer's perception of the immediate business situation.
2. The Buyer's perception of how your proposal is likely to change that situation.
3. The Buyer's perception of whether or not that change will close a gap, or discrepancy, between what's seen as the current reality and the results needed. No matter how good a match there is between your proposal and those "objective" needs, no Buyer will be receptive to change unless this discrepancy is apparent first.

In the Response Mode of *Growth,* the Buyer does perceive the essential discrepancy between the way things are right now and the way they should be. It's a feeling that the gap between current reality and the desired results can only be closed if quantity can be increased, quality improved, or both, right away. A Buyer in Growth Mode will thus be receptive to you, provided you can show that your proposal makes it possible to do *more* or do *better.*

The second Response Mode is called *Trouble*. A Buyer in Trouble Mode also sees a reality-results discrepancy, but it's a discrepancy on the down side. Something in the business environment has caused a deviation from the planned course; therefore the Buyer needs help and will welcome any change that looks like a way of taking away the source of the problem. You have another good candidate for a sale—provided you can show that your proposal will quickly eliminate the discrepancy.

The third Response Mode is called *Even Keel*. A Buyer in Even Keel perceives no discrepancy between current reality and the hoped-for results, and is therefore satisfied. With no incentive to change, the probability of selling a Buyer in Even Keel is very low. Buyers in Even Keel consistently demonstrate the truth of the maxim "No discrepancy, no sale."

The same thing is true, only more so, for the Buyer in the fourth Response Mode, *Overconfident*. A Buyer who is in Overconfident Mode perceives reality as being far *better* than the hoped-for results. Such a person is therefore totally unreceptive to change, and the likelihood of making a sale is nil.

In Strategic Selling we stress that the four Response Modes are not descriptions of overall attitude or personality, but rather of the way in which individual Buyers see a given sales situation, and a given sales proposal, at any particular moment. Changing business conditions can move a Buyer from Overconfident to Trouble Mode extremely quickly, so the strategic sales representative develops separate sales approaches for people in each of the four modes.

Key Element 4: Win-Results

You already know from Chapter 2 that in our experience the smart salesperson never thinks of selling as a battle or of customers as enemies to be beaten. It's possible to get an order by tricking or pressuring your customers into signing, but when you do that you're making them "Lose" so that you can "Win." A customer who feels beaten will get out, get even, or do both. In the short run, you may not care. But in terms of the long-range management of that customer's account, you'll be kidding yourself even more than your customer: An order that you get by "beating the buyer" in this way is likely to be your last order.

In Strategic Selling we look beyond the individual order. We concentrate on the account, and we train you to develop ever widening networks of quality sales and new prospects. We make the assumption that, as a sales professional, you're interested not only in the order, but also in:

- Satisfied customers
- Long-term relationships
- Repeat business
- Good referrals

The only way to ensure that you'll get these things—the only way to keep every one of your accounts productive over time—is to approach every one of your Buying Influences as a potential *partner* in your success rather than an *adversary* to be overcome.

There are only four possible outcomes to every buy/sell encounter:

1. In the first, or Win-Win, scenario, both you and the Buyer "Win." That is, you both come out of the sale feeling satisfied, knowing that neither of you has taken advantage of the other and that both of you have profited, personally and professionally, from the transaction. In the simplest terms, you know you have a Win-Win sales encounter when both you and the Buyer come out of it feeling positive.

2. In the second, or Win-Lose, scenario, you Win at the Buyer's expense. You feel good about the sale, but he's already looking for revenge, or how to avoid you in the future.

3. In the third, or Lose-Win, scenario, you allow the Buyer to Win at your expense by "buying the business." You provide a special discount or free time

or other services in hopes of a return favor in the future. Often, it never comes.

4. In the final, or Lose-Lose, scenario, both you and the Buyer Lose. Even though you get the order, neither of you feels good about the sale.

Of these four scenarios, only one can bring you the long-term success that you want. That is the Win-Win, "partnership" scenario. Unless they're actively *managed* into this Win-Win scenario, both Win-Lose and Lose-Win ultimately, and inevitably, degenerate into Lose-Lose.

To be able to manage all your sales into the Win-Win scenario, you have to go beyond the conventional wisdom about why people buy. Many sales-training programs act on the premise that people buy when you demonstrate to them that you can meet their immediate business needs. Such programs are product oriented. The trainers who use them pack sales representatives' heads full of data about "features" and "benefits" of the product, and then send them forth to collect orders from people who "can't help but be impressed" with the product's advantages.

Naturally you need sound product knowledge, but to a sales professional like you, that's not enough, because the reason that people *really* buy is only indirectly related to product or service performance. That's why we don't focus on the product. Instead, we show you how to *use* your product knowledge to give each of your Buyers personal reasons for buying. You can't just meet their business needs. You have to serve their individual, subjective needs as well. You do that by giving them what we call Win-Results.

A *Result,* as we define it, is the impact your product or service can have on the Buyer's business processes. The product-oriented sales representative sells for Results alone.

A *Win* is a less widely recognized, but equally important, factor in buying psychology. It's a personal gain that satisfies an individual Buyer's perceived self-interest.

A *Win-Result,* finally, is a Result that gives one of your individual Buyers a personal Win. Win-Results are the real reason that people buy. We show you how to determine them for each Buying Influence, and explain why delivering them consistently is the only way to keep your accounts healthy—the only way to keep getting Win-Win outcomes all the time.

Key Element 5: The Sales Funnel

Before they come to our programs, even our most successful participants find that their sales figures tend to be way up one quarter and way down the next. They experience what we call the Roller Coaster Effect, in which a January bonanza is followed by a seemingly inevitable April slump. In the words of a West Coast regional manager who has sent us hundreds of his people, "Before I send them to you, putting two great quarters together is the dream of every one of them."

As he's discovered, and as you'll discover, it doesn't have to be a dream. There's a reason for the Roller Coaster Effect, and there's a way to avoid it. In our discussion of the fifth Key Element, we depart for the first time in the book from an emphasis on your specific, chosen sales objective and show you a method for managing *all* your sales objectives, and *all* your accounts, in a way that minimizes the Roller Coaster Effect and fulfills your dream of regular, consistent commissions.

That method involves the use of a conceptual tool that we developed when we were national sales managers, and that we have used with excellent results not only in our own business but in all the businesses that hire us to help their people. We call it the Sales Funnel.

The funnel metaphor may not be entirely new to you. Many salespeople talk about throwing prospects and leads into the top of the "hopper" or "funnel" and then waiting for orders to come out the other end. The difference between our use of the Sales Funnel and theirs is that we don't wait. We actively and methodically *work* the Funnel, so that the prospects that make it through to the order do so on a predictable basis.

Essentially the Sales Funnel is a tool for helping you to use your most precious commodity, your selling time, in the wisest and most efficient manner possible. You know that selling time is a resource of which you never have enough. What you may not know—or may not have articulated consciously—is that every successful sale involves three different kinds of selling work. If you don't divide your time efficiently among these three kinds of work, you can easily end up wasting what little time you have. The Sales Funnel will help you to identify the type of work you need to be doing at any given moment on each sales objective, and bring about a balance among the three. It will also help you determine how much time you should allocate to each type of work, on a regular basis, to ensure predictable commissions.

Key Element 6: The Ideal Customer Profile

Every sales representative you know, no matter how successful, has up to 35 percent poor prospects working at any given moment—prospects that will be impossible to close or, if they're closed, will eventually become liabilities. That may seem like a surprisingly high percentage—but just think of how many times since you began selling you've heard someone say, "I wish I'd never sold that order." Think of how many times you've said it to yourself.

Sales representatives end up regretting these orders for a simple reason. Somewhere during the sales cycle, they allowed themselves to be seduced by the old saw "Any sale is a good sale." They allowed themselves to believe that it's quantity, not quality, that counts. And so they ended up selling a customer with a poor or nonexistent match to their product or service.

When we spoke about maintaining a Win-Win scenario, we said that you *can* sell a customer who perceives the sale as a "Lose," but that this is a very poor long-term account strategy. Our sixth and final Key Element carries that observation to its logical conclusion by introducing a concept we call the Ideal Customer, as both a method of identifying your best prospects and a standard for gauging the probable long-term benefits of working through to the close with each one. Selling to everyone indiscriminately is bound to create bad matches and bad orders. Judging your actual customers against an Ideal Customer Profile will keep those bad orders to a minimum, and ensure that the bulk of your sales have a Win-Win outcome.

We use the Ideal Customer Profile both to anticipate problems in our current customer base and as a sorting device that helps us to cut down on that 35 percent of prospects that shouldn't be in our Sales Funnel in the first place. You'll do the same thing in this book. You'll make up your own Ideal Customer Profile by analyzing the characteristics common to your current and past good customers. Then you'll use it to test your current sales prospects.

This will leave you with a shorter list of prospects than the one you have now. But the shorter list will be *real*. It will allow you to focus on those sales goals that can be achieved with a minimum amount of aggravation in the shortest period of time. Concentrating on those sales goals is what is going to give you Win-Win sales, not only with your present customers, but with every new lead you encounter.

A Final Word of Introduction

You'll probably recognize the use of a customer profile to rate and qualify prospects as an example of a marketing-oriented approach to sales. We're aware of that, and in fact we encourage the people we work with to think in marketing terms rather than in "product first" terms. As we've been stressing, the Strategic Selling system focuses on the *account.* We want you to be successful with your accounts not just for this sales period but for as long as you have them. You do that by really *selling to need,* not just paying it lip service. All the Six Key Elements of the blueprint are designed to help you assess your customers' needs accurately, so that you can give them Win-Results on a predictable, consistent basis. Satisfying their needs in this way, experience proves, is also the best way to satisfy your own.

You've now done all the preliminary work you need to do to understand the principles of Strategic Selling. We've introduced the concept of the Complex Sale and explained why you need to plan both strategy and tactics to manage it effectively. You've made a preliminary assessment of your current position with regard to a particular sales objective and started to consider Alternate Positions to make the attainment of that objective more certain. Finally, we've presented in outline form the Six Key Elements of strategy that you'll use as a sales success blueprint. We know you have questions at this point. We know you want details of the blueprint filled in, and we know you're anxious to begin applying it to your current and future sales goals.

So let's get started.

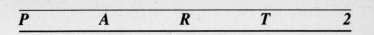

STRATEGIC

SELLING:

THE BASIC

ELEMENTS

▲

▶ 5 ◀

KEY ELEMENT 1: BUYING INFLUENCES

The foundation of every reliable sales strategy is knowing who the key players are. The first Key Element of the strategy you're going to start developing now is to identify *all* the relevant players for your particular sales objective. For now you'll continue to work with the objective that you chose in Chapter 3. But the means and the method of using this Key Element will apply to every sales objective, every time.

Identifying the relevant players may seem like an obvious first step. It is obvious. It's also frequently ignored—and with predictable results. Because most sales-training programs emphasize tactical rather than strategic skills, even very good salespeople sometimes find themselves cut out of a sale at the last minute because they failed to locate or cover all the real decision makers for that specific sale. Unfortunately, most trainers pay little attention to this initial task of identification. They assume that their salespeople already know whose approvals are necessary, and concentrate on telling them how to deal with those people when they meet them.

We don't make that assumption. Experience has taught us that, if left to find the key players on their own without a systematic method of testing their findings, many sales representatives simply end up talking to the people whom they feel comfortable with, who have approved their orders in the past, or who have the "right" titles on their doors. None of these "methods" of identification is reliable. Even if one of them leads you to the right players for a given sale, it cannot help you understand *why* they were the right players, and why they were right *for that sale only*. They're not reliable, repeatable methods of finding out whose approvals count.

You need new, reliable methods because in today's corporate sales arena, the names and faces of the players are in constant flux. You may understand very well who the relevant players were in a ten-thousand-dollar sale you made to the Williamson Tool and Die Company in November. This doesn't mean you necessarily know the right people to contact in making a fifty-thousand-dollar sale—or even another ten-thousand-dollar sale—to the same account the following March. *Every sale is unique.* Therefore, you can never *assume* you know the right people without testing. No matter how well you know the players in a given account, you still need a systematic method for locating the correct ones for your immediate sales objective—and for determining whether or not they're still the correct ones when you return to that account for future sales objectives.

In Strategic Selling we do this by focusing not on what changes from sale to sale, but on what we've found to be universal and constant in every Complex Sale.

Focus on Buying Roles

No matter how many people are involved in a buying decision, and no matter what official functions they play in their organizations, we've discovered that the same *four buying roles* are present in every Complex Sale. The people who play these roles, who may number far more than four, are the key players that we call *Buying Influences,* or *Buyers.*

As we mentioned in Chapter 4, we use the term "Buyer" very differently from the way it's usually used. When you see the word "Buyer" in its capitalized form in this book, we don't want it to decode as "dry goods buyer," "purchasing agent," or anything else that suggests merely a person with specialized purchasing authority. We use "Buyer" as shorthand for the term "Buying Influence." In Strategic Selling, a Buying Influence, or Buyer, is *anyone* who can influence your sale—whatever the title on that person's door.

Some purchasing agents do play a Buying Influence role in many sales. But others do not. Even more to the point, *most* of the people who will act as Buyers in your sales won't have anything to do with "purchasing" or "buying" per se.

The first thing to do in setting an effective Complex Sale strategy is to *position* yourself effectively with *all* the people playing *each* of the four roles. This involves two steps:

1. Understanding the four Buying Influence roles that are common to *every* Complex Sale
2. Identifying all the key players in each of these four roles for *your* specific sales objective

To understand why we focus on roles rather than on past contacts or titles, consider a sports analogy. In football, the lineman who stands in front of the quarterback has a clearly defined position, or "title." He's the center, and his primary role, on most plays, is to snap the ball and then block. On a fourth-down kick, however, his role changes. After the snap, he's still called the center, but the role he's expected to play is that of defensive tackler. If you think the distinction is merely semantic, consider what would happen to a punt receiver who, confronted by a charging 220-pound lineman, said to himself, "I don't have to worry about this guy. He just snaps the ball."

In the Complex Sale no less than in football, a given player in an account can shift roles quickly and unpredictably, even though the player's title and official function on the buying "team" remains the same. A purchasing agent who has routinely approved your three previous sales may suddenly be unable to do so—unable to play her usual role—if your fourth sale is for double the usual order, or for a new product or service. A financial officer who has never been remotely involved in your orders may suddenly become a key Buying Influence because corporate head-quarters has just changed its capital expenditure protocols. Focusing on the four Buying Influence roles that are played in every Complex Sale will help you weave your way through the corporate labyrinths of your accounts and get to the real Buying Influences for *your unique sales goal*.

The four types of Buying Influences that need to be iden-tified and sold in every sale are the Economic Buying Influ-ence, the User Buying Influence(s), the Technical Buying Influence(s), and the Coach. Each has a different business focus—that is, a different point of view regarding your pro-posal and a different reason for considering it. And each one must be sold to close the deal.

The Economic Buying Influence

The Economic Buyer is the person who gives *final* approval to buy your product or service. The role of this Buying In-fluence is *to release the dollars to buy*. For that reason, we sometimes say that the Economic Buyer exercises the "Golden Rule": Whoever has the gold makes the rules. This person can say yes where everybody else has said no, or veto everybody else's yes.

The Economic Buyer's Focus—and Importance
We don't call this Buying Influence the Economic Buyer because his or her major concern is the cost or economics of the sale. The focus is never price per se, but *price perfor-mance*. With direct access to the needed money and a dis-cretionary use of funds, this Buyer can adjust the budget to "find" or release unbudgeted funds, if your product or ser-

vice seems to match the firm's priority needs and is good value for the money. The ultimate focus—the ultimate business reason this person will buy—is the bottom-line impact you can make on the organization.

Although the identity of the person filling the role of Economic Buying Influence often changes from sale to sale within the same account, there's always only one Economic Buyer *per sale*. Only one person gives final approval, even though many others may give recommendations and advice. Thus it's critical to find out who gives the final yes for *your* sale.

The role of Economic Buyer may be played by a board, a selection committee, or another decision-making body acting as a single entity. But even when such a group is involved, there's usually one person within the group who is first among equals and whose final approval is necessary. You always have to determine, when you're selling to such a group, who really has direct access to the funds. It may not be the best strategy for you to contact this individual personally, but it's always your responsibility as "director of strategy" for the sale to identify accurately the single person filling the Economic Buyer role.

Failing to do so can be fatal, as an American airplane manufacturer found out recently when it tried to sell a consignment of jets to a Middle Eastern country. Everybody in that country loved them—the king, the air force generals, even the pilots who would eventually fly the planes. But when the manufacturer drew up the contract and presented it to the king for his signature, he looked both pleased and bemused. "Ah, yes," he said. "This is very nice. Now all we have to do is to ask our friends the Saudis to lend us the money for the planes." And a multimillion-dollar "sure thing" was suddenly on hold, pending approval of a hitherto unidentified Economic Buying Influence.

This is an extreme example, we know. Few of us are ever going to be involved in a sale of this magnitude. But the same principle applies in Complex Sales of any size. If you don't identify the source of funds—and do it *early in the selling cycle*—you run the risk of handing the ball to the competition.

The Profile Box below summarizes the focus and importance of this first critical Buying Influence.

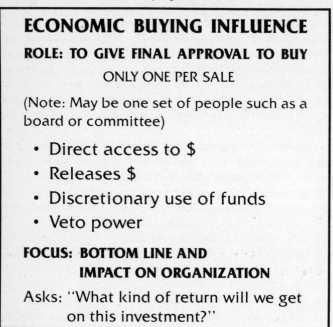

ECONOMIC BUYING INFLUENCE

ROLE: TO GIVE FINAL APPROVAL TO BUY

ONLY ONE PER SALE

(Note: May be one set of people such as a board or committee)

- Direct access to $
- Releases $
- Discretionary use of funds
- Veto power

FOCUS: BOTTOM LINE AND IMPACT ON ORGANIZATION

Asks: "What kind of return will we get on this investment?"

Finding the Economic Buyer

In identifying Economic Buyers in your sales, you have to know where to look. Almost by definition you don't find people who give final approval far down on the corporate ladder. People playing the Economic Buyer role are usually highly placed in their organizations. In smaller firms the CEO or president himself may play the Economic Buyer role for many sales. But you don't always have to go that far up. The Economic Buyer role, like all buying roles, can shift from sale to sale, and the organizational position of the person playing that role depends on a number of variables. Five critical variables are the dollar amount of the sale, business conditions, the buying firm's experience with you and your company, the buying firm's experience with your product, and the expected organizational impact.

1. Dollar Amount. The greater the dollar amount of your sale, the higher up in the buying organization you need to look for the Economic Buyer. Every company, as you've undoubtedly observed in your business, has its own cutoff points at which final approval for purchases passes up or down the company ladder. These points relate to the dollar amount of the sale *relative to the size of the buying company*. The president of the Apex Food Company, which does a hundred million dollars' worth of business a year, may feel he has to personally approve every sale over ten thousand dollars. In Multiplex Toys, where annual sales amount to half a billion dollars, the president may only get involved—may only be called in to play the Economic Buyer role—in purchases over fifty thousand dollars. Sales that in a small company have to be approved at the top may, in a large concern, be handled by middle management.

There are no hard-and-fast rules here. You always have to search for the person acting as the Economic Buying Influence from square one, in each individual company and for each unique sales objective.

2. Business Conditions. In hard times management starts counting paper clips. Therefore, the less stable the overall business environment, the more likely it is that your Economic Buyer will be found higher up in the organization. We have seen this numerous times in our client companies. One of them is a major computer firm that does several billion dollars' worth of business a year. In "normal" times, the company CEO has to approve every expenditure over fifty thousand dollars. During the 1980–81 recession, however, he became the Economic Buyer on expenditures as low as five thousand dollars. This is not an uncommon practice even in Fortune 500 firms.

3. Experience with You and Your Firm. It always takes time, even for the most reliable of salespeople, to build trust in the selling firm's capabilities. Lack of trust means greater perceived risk for the buying firm, and greater perceived risk means that the final decision to buy will move up the corporate ladder. Conversely, the more experience a buying organization has had with you and your firm—that is, the better you've established your *credibility* and that of your company—the more likely it is that top management will entrust the Economic Buying Influence role to middle management.

4. Experience with Your Product or Service.

Even if a buying organization has had a good history of interaction with your company, its Buyers may still be unfamiliar with the specific product or service involved in your current sales proposal. If that's the case, the Economic Buyer role is going to move up. The same thing is true if they've bought your type of product before, but not from you. A buying organization's initial decision to introduce robotics into its manufacturing division is obviously going to require a top-level Economic Buyer. So is a subsequent decision to shift suppliers—to start buying the same type of automation from a different supplier. Once they have experience with your particular robotics line, though, they'll be willing to entrust future decisions about servicing and replacement to a lower-level executive.

5. Potential Organizational Impact.

Since the Economic Buyer's business focus is on long-term stability and growth, buying decisions that more radically affect those areas will involve a higher-placed person playing that role. The decision to computerize billing procedures for an entire company will be made at the top; subsequent decisions about personnel retraining, service, or supplies may not have to go that high.

A critical point to remember is that there's never a single Economic Buyer for a company or account. There's no such thing as "the Apex Company's Economic Buyer." There are only people filling that role for *individual buying decisions*. Within any account, the identity of the person playing the final approval role usually varies from sale to sale, depending on the above factors.

In looking for the Economic Buyer, many of our best program participants have found it useful to ask the question *"At what level in my own organization would such a decision have to be made?"* The answer may not be the Economic Buyer's title for your sale, but it will start you looking at the right corporate level. That's one way of focusing in on the person who actually controls the funds. Another way is to utilize your Coach. More about that critical and unique Buying Influence in a moment.

User Buying Influences

The role of the User Buyer is filled by someone who will actually use (or supervise the use of) your product or service. The role of the User Buyer is *to make judgments about the impact of that product or service on the job to be done.*

Focus of the User Buyer

The key phrase here is "on the job." User Buyers are concerned primarily with how a sale is going to affect everyday operations in their own areas or departments; their focus is therefore much narrower than that of an Economic Buyer. People acting as User Buying Influences will ask you about areas of immediate, day-to-day concern, such as the product's reliability, service record, retraining needed, downtime record, ease of operation, maintenance, safety, and potential impact on morale.

Because the focus of User Buyers is how a sale will affect *their* jobs, their reactions to sales proposals, and their predictions about performance, tend to be subjective. This doesn't mean that they're unsound, or that you can ignore them as "irrelevant." It does mean that you have to take subjectivity into account when selling to them, because their personal success hinges on the success of your product or service. User Buyers want good performance not only because it makes their people productive, but also because better productivity looks good on their own records. You get one on your side, therefore, by answering one simple question. "How will your product or service work *for me?*"

Most Complex Sales involve more than one person playing a User Buying Influence role. But there's always *at least* one person whose central focus is the job to be done. If you're selling group insurance to a large company, User Buyers might be the employee benefit manager, a personnel manager, and the parties being insured. If you're selling laboratory equipment, they might include a technical administrator, an R&D manager, and lab technicians. If you're putting thirty new word processors into a branch office, they might include the branch manager, a head of data processing, and individual operators. In the case of the airplane sale we just mentioned, the User Buyers were the military personnel—the pilots and their commanders—who would actually operate the planes. The primary focus of all these people is the job to be done.

The role and focus of the various User Buyers in your sale are summarized in the Profile Box below.

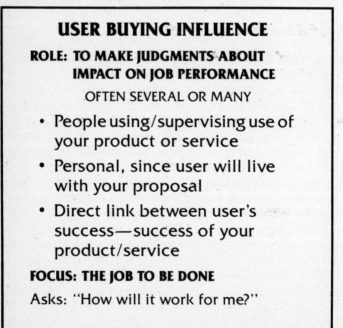

USER BUYING INFLUENCE

ROLE: TO MAKE JUDGMENTS ABOUT IMPACT ON JOB PERFORMANCE

OFTEN SEVERAL OR MANY

- People using/supervising use of your product or service
- Personal, since user will live with your proposal
- Direct link between user's success—success of your product/service

FOCUS: THE JOB TO BE DONE

Asks: "How will it work for me?"

User Buyers Can't Be Ignored
If the key User Buyer isn't sold, you'll have a very difficult time closing the sale. Management can, and sometimes

does, approve orders for products that the User Buyers just as soon wouldn't buy; but the eventual outcome of these sales is generally bad for everyone concerned. You have to please User Buyers because the way they use your product directly affects how that product is viewed by everyone else in the buying organization. Even if you manage to get around a User Buyer's no, the chances are good that future orders to that department will be hampered by resentment, lack of cooperation, or outright sabotage.

A friend of ours encountered just this type of sabotage several years ago, when he sold a half-million-dollar training program to a major textile firm. The program was designed to help mechanics and other skilled laborers trouble-shoot more efficiently. The president of the textile company was so impressed with its possibilities that he agreed to give it a trial run in every one of his twelve mills. Unfortunately, our friend neglected to contact the managers of those mills before he made the sale. When he showed up after the papers had been signed to help implement the program, they saw him as an outside agitator who had gone over their heads to The Boss. Miraculously, a month after the program went on line, trouble-shooting in every one of the twelve mills was far *less* efficient than it had been before the sale. There was nothing wrong with the program itself. The User Buyer managers, annoyed at having been ignored, had just seen to it that it wouldn't work. As a result, the end of the trial period was also the end of the program.

Our friend learned a valuable lesson from the experience. Realizing that he'd been done in by his own ignorance of the players, he vowed never again to overlook a User Buyer. "The next time somebody's going to use my stuff," he told us, "he's going to *want* it first!"

Technical Buying Influences

User Buyers *can* be difficult, but Technical Buyers *have* to be. A disgruntled sales representative we know once described these Buying Influences as "people who can't say yes, only no—and usually do." Like User Buyers, they're often found in multiples rather than singly—Complex Sales usually involve several people playing different Technical Buying Influence roles—and because their input is so often negative, their combined presence poses a real problem for the salesperson.

The Technical Buyer as Gatekeeper

Technical Buyers say no because it's their job to do so. The Technical Buyer's role is *to screen out*. They're gate-keepers. You might call them the professional Saint Peters of the Complex Sale. A Technical Buyer at a wedding might be the one to stand up and say, "Hold it! I know a reason why these two should not be married!" On a hockey team this kind of person would be unanimous choice for goalie. It's the Technical Buyer's task to limit the field of sellers; they don't decide who wins, but they do decide who can play.

The objections of people serving as Technical Buying Influences may seem petty at times, but these people serve a necessary function. The screening that Technical Buyers do on candidate vendors makes it much less likely that, as a close approaches, an unforeseen technicality will get in the way. We call them Technical Buyers, in fact, because they screen out based on technicalities.

That's not the same thing as technologies. Some Technical Buyers are concerned with technology, but many of them are not, and even one whose area of expertise is electronics or flow mechanics will still know less about specific products in those fields than the salesperson does. Technical Buyers make judgments about the measurable and quantifiable aspects of your product or service based on how well it meets a variety of product specifications—specifications that may or may not be technological. Your customer's legal counsel, for example, may know nothing at all about your product from a technological point of view. But the lawyer can still screen you out based on the terms and conditions—the legal technicalities—of a contract.

Purchasing agents often serve as Technical Buyers. They

screen out vendors based on price, delivery time, failure to meet quality control specs, logistics, even references. These people can stop negotiations even when there's an otherwise perfect match between your product or service and the company's needs. Financial officers can screen out suppliers based on credit terms or conditions of the sale. A personnel manager can hamper a sale because of a potentially harmful impact on morale. A government agency can block one because of regulations. In each of these examples, a Technical Buyer, judging on technicalities, can block a sale everyone else wants.

In identifying these gatekeeping Technical Buyers before they shoot you down, you have to know that their principal focus—the reason they'll recommend you or show you to the door—is *the product itself.* All they really want to know is how well it meets their screening tests. Therefore, the better you know your product and understand all the tests it might have to meet in a given sales situation, the better your chances of getting all the Technical Buyer's recommendations.

The Profile Box below summarizes the critical facts you need to remember about gatekeeping Technical Buyers.

TECHNICAL BUYING INFLUENCE

ROLE: TO SCREEN OUT

OFTEN SEVERAL OR MANY

- Judges measurable, quantifiable aspects of your proposal
- Gatekeeper
- Makes recommendations
- Can't say yes (i.e., final approval)
- Can say no—often does

FOCUS: PRODUCT PER SE

Asks: "Does it meet specifications?"

The Hidden or Camouflaged Technical Buyer

Technical Buyers are often more difficult to spot than either User Buyers or Economic Buyers, and for this reason they pose special problems for the sales representative. It can be fatal to underestimate the power of a Technical Buyer, or to assume that because someone playing a screening role isn't immediately evident in the buying organization, that person is irrelevant to the sale. A financially troubled airline found this out recently, when it tried to use some of its grounded planes to reorganize as a limited entrant in the commercial carrier market. The troubled company's creditors, the court that handled its default, and the unions were all in agreement on the deal, but at the last minute the Federal Aviation Agency stepped in to inform everybody that the critical airway slots—the old firm's defunct takeoff and landing rights—could not be made available; they had already been assigned to other airlines.

If the parties had thought through all the ramifications of the deal strategically before negotiations were under way, they would have realized that there were hidden Technical Buyers in the FAA who would have to be contacted and sold on the idea before anything final could be signed. Because that key Buying Influence was taken for granted, the entire deal fell through.

While some Technical Buyers are thus seemingly invisible, others are all too visible. Technical Buyers can be difficult not only because of their screening role but because, in playing that role, they often run interference for the Economic Buyer, making it hard for you to see, or even identify, that person. In fact, the favorite game of Technical Buyers is to try to convince you that they *are* Economic Buyers—that they give final approval. Believing in this camouflage can get you into trouble even before you begin.

Some of the Technical Buyers who play this game deliberately lie about their role in the sale, but this isn't always the case. Some Technical Buyers actually believe that they *do* have the final say. Although the Technical Buyer's role is to say no rather than yes, that may not be clear to the person playing that role if he or she has gotten mixed signals from the real Economic Buyer. An Economic Buyer, trying to save time, may ask a Technical Buyer for a "recommendation" in confusing terms. "We'll take whoever you say, Margaret," he may declare. "Just run it by me first." If Margaret is a totally rational person with no ego to defend, she'll read this as it is meant: "You give me your input, and I'll make the decision." But if she's a normal human being, it will be easy to read it as "I trust you, Margaret. You decide." So you can easily find yourself confronted by an earnest, well-meaning Technical Buyer who misunderstands her role in the sale. If you simply take her at her word, you can misunderstand it too.

It's to help you avoid problems of misidentification like this one that you need the fourth Buying Influence, your Coach.

Your Coach

The role of a Coach is *to guide you in the sale* by giving you information you need to manage it to a close that guarantees you not only the order, but satisfied customers and repeat business as well. Your Coach can help you identify and meet the people who are filling the other Buying Influence roles for your sales objective, and can help you assess the buying situation so that you're most effectively positioned with each one. To close any Complex Sale, you should develop *at least* one Coach.

Looking for a Coach is different from looking for your other three Buying Influences. The first three Buying Influences already exist. They're waiting to be identified, and you just have to find out where. Your Coach, on the other hand, has to be not only *found* but *developed*. The first three Buying Influences will already be playing their roles when you find them. The Coach's role is one that you, in effect, create.

In doing that, you must remember that the Coach's focus

is your success in the specific sales objective for which you want the Coaching.

The Profile Box below outlines the salient facts about this fourth, unique Buying Influence.

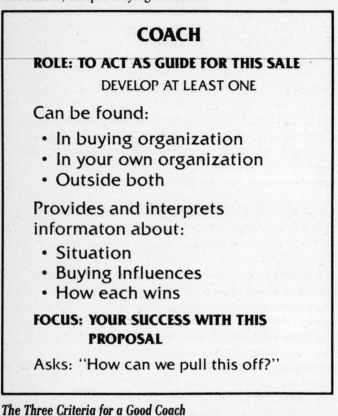

COACH

ROLE: TO ACT AS GUIDE FOR THIS SALE

DEVELOP AT LEAST ONE

Can be found:

- In buying organization
- In your own organization
- Outside both

Provides and interprets informaton about:

- Situation
- Buying Influences
- How each wins

FOCUS: YOUR SUCCESS WITH THIS PROPOSAL

Asks: "How can we pull this off?"

The Three Criteria for a Good Coach

In searching for someone to develop into a Coach, you judge by three criteria:

1. You have credibility with that person. Usually this is because the Coach has won in a sale with you in the past. By definition, then, a good place to find potential Coaches is among your own satisfied customers. If you sold someone a product last year and he has been thanking you for it ever since, you've got an ideal candidate for a Coach in terms of this first criterion. This person's past experience with you is that you can be *trusted*. That's what credibility means.

2. The Coach has credibility with the buying organization.   Once you find somebody who trusts you, you then have to be sure that your candidate is in turn trusted by the buying organization. A potential Coach who doesn't have credibility with the buying organization is going to be a poor liaison to its people, and the information you get about the sale may not be reliable.

Because credibility with the buying organization is so important, you'll often find good Coaches within that organization itself. We've already noted that people can play more than one Buying Influence role in a sale. A Technical or User Buyer who's on your side can serve as an excellent Coach. The best of all possible scenarios is to turn the Economic Buyer into a Coach in the buying organization.

3. The Coach wants you to succeed.   This doesn't necessarily mean that this person wants you to succeed in life or in your sales career in general. A good Coach may be, but is not necessarily, a mentor or a friend. But by definition the Coach wants you to succeed in this particular sale. For some reason—it doesn't matter what the reason is—this person sees that it's in his or her own *self-interest* for the buying organization to accept your solution.

Because the Coach's focus is your success, you can find good ones within your own organization as well. One of the most innovative uses of a Coach that we've seen recently was demonstrated by a Midwest sales representative who dramatically increased penetration in an account by turning his own boss into a Coach. The boss had come up from the ranks and had sold in that account himself; since his sales had been solid ones in which both buyer and seller had Won, the boss had credibility with the Buying Influences. The sales representative was a sales leader himself, so he had credibility with the boss. And because the new business would obviously benefit the selling organization, the boss wanted him to succeed. So on all three counts, the sales representative had developed an excellent Coach.

Asking for Coaching

You may not always be lucky enough to find potential Coaches who perfectly fulfill all three criteria. But when those criteria suggest that someone *might* be developed into a Coach, test that person's potential usefulness by asking him or her for Coaching. Seldom will a real Coach refuse to give you the assistance you require. In fact our data indicate that most people welcome the opportunity to do Coaching. Being a Coach, in our culture, has a very positive connotation, and few professionals will turn down the chance to demonstrate whom, and how much, they know. Even a potential Coach who doesn't really have the information you need about the sale can often guide you to someone who does. As you nurture and develop Coaches for different sales over time, you'll eventually build up a network of reliable sources that can guide you to the key players in any account, no matter what your specific sales objective.

Asking for Coaching, however, isn't the same thing as asking for a referral, or for assistance in making the sale. You don't want your Coach to do your selling for you, and you can't give that impression. Not only are you the best person to sell your product or service, but your Coach already has enough work to do without taking on your responsibilities. When you say, "Can you help me talk to Jackson?" Or "Will you recommend me?" it can easily decode as "I'm incompetent to manage this sale. Please do my work for me." You can't sustain credibility with a Coach who hears that message.

Instead of asking for a referral, we recommend that you seek information and direction. You want the Coach to help you *think through your position with the other Buying Influences.* By asking for Coaching rather than a referral, you make it clear that *you* will be running the plays, and that you just need some advice to help you do it. What you want the Coach to hear is "I'll take accountability for the sale, but I could use your expertise. I'll do the selling if you'll explain how a couple of things work." The irony of this approach is that, while a salesperson who asks for a referral almost never gets Coaching, the one who asks for Coaching usually gets it—and the referral besides.

A Clarification for Consumer-Product Sales Professionals

Many of the people who attend our Strategic Selling programs work in the mass-merchandising area, selling packaged goods and other consumer products to large retail outlets such as supermarket, department store, and drugstore chains. Our clients from Coca-Cola, Wilson Sporting Goods, and Kimberly-Clark, for example, do not sell directly to industrial or other business end users, but to retailers like Sears, K mart, Walgreen, and Grand Union.

If you work in complex consumer-product sales, you know that they differ in some respects from Complex Sales to other businesses. For one thing, the end users of your product aren't the people you sell to; your customers act as middlemen between you and the final consumer. For another, turnover is very important, and is related to a constant battle among vendors for the best shelf and display spaces—what retailers call facings. Typically in mass merchandising you sell not just products but *product promotions* designed to convince the retail organization that giving you the best facings will result in the quickest and most lucrative turnover.

In addition, there's a *terminology* that's unique to the consumer product field—and it's because of this terminology that we offer a clarification.

You know that we use the term "Buyer" in a special sense, to describe people playing one or more of four Buying Influence roles. We've explained the distinction between titles (such as "parts buyer") and roles (such as the User Buyer role). And we've cautioned you not to assume that everybody with purchasing responsibilities can automatically be identified as a Buyer for your particular sale.

In our experience, however, in spite of caveats like

these, the term "buyer" still remains a trigger word to many people in the consumer product field: it means somebody who buys product lines in a large retail store or chain. Because this is not the kind of Buyer we're talking about, we offer an alternate terminology. In the programs we present to consumer-product and mass-merchandising people, we don't refer to the Economic Buyer, User Buyers, or Technical Buyers. Instead, we use the terms *Veto Power* Buying Influence, *Logistical* Buying Influence, and *Merchandising* Buying Influence to describe roles that are different in some respects from the roles in end-user industrial sales.

The Veto Power Buying Influence

The equivalent of the Economic Buyer role in the consumer product field is called the Veto Power Buying Influence—so named because the person playing that role, like the Economic Buyer, can always *veto* your sale or promotion. The characteristics of this Buying Influence are presented below.

VETO POWER BUYING INFLUENCE

ROLE: TO GIVE FINAL APPROVAL TO BUY

ONLY ONE PER SALE

(Note: May be one set of people such as a buying committee)

- Has authority to allocate $
- Has discretionary use of funds
- Buys your product or promotion

FOCUS: BOTTOM LINE AND
IMPACT ON MERCHANDISING
AND RETAILING POLICY

Asks: "What kind of return will we get
on this investment?"

You can see these characteristics are virtually identical to those of the Economic Buyer. Notice, though, that in addition to the Economic Buyer's interest in the bottom line and organizational impact, the person playing a Veto Power role also has a special interest in something peculiar to consumer product sales: *merchandising and retailing policy.*

That policy is constantly, and immediately, affected by the turnover of individual items, and this gives rise to a distinction between Economic Buying Influences as a class and people playing the Veto Power role as a "species" of that class. Most Economic Buyers decide whether or not to release the required funds for a specific sales objective. People playing the Veto Power role usually decide not *whether* to release the money, but *where* to allocate it to ensure the best turnover of merchandise.

There's seldom a shortage of budgeted funds for consumer product purchases—only a question of how much money each product or promotion should get, and when. Selling a Veto Power Buying Influence, therefore, involves convincing him or her that, out of the already available budget, your promotion deserves the lion's share.

Logistical Buying Influences

The approximate equivalent of the User Buying Influence in the consumer product field we call the Logistical Buying Influence. We say approximate because, while User Buyers and people acting as Logistical Buying Influences are similar, there's one difference. Unlike User Buyers, Logistical Buying Influences don't personally *use* the products you sell them—the only real user in consumer product sales is the consumer. Instead, Logistical Buying Influences are concerned with logistics, which the dictionary defines as "the handling of the details of an operation."

Logistical Buying Influences *handle,* or *manage the handling* of, the consumer product through all the stages of the retailing process, from original marketing to the checkout counter.

The role of any Logistical Buying Influence is to make

operational judgments about how the product is to be most effectively guided through that process. People playing this role are interested in anything that affects the retailing flow: for example, space requirements, stocking, display needs, warehousing. Their interests are summarized in the box below.

LOGISTICAL BUYING INFLUENCE

ROLE: TO MAKE OPERATIONAL JUDGMENTS

OFTEN SEVERAL OR MANY

Manages handling of your product.

FOCUS:
Retail Space Requirements
Stocking
Retail Pricing
Service Reliability
Positioning Consumer Demand
Point-of-Sale Display Materials
Retail Merchandising Support

Asks: "How will it work for me?"

As with User Buyers, there are often a number of people playing Logistical roles for a given sale or promotion. This type of role, for example, may be taken by district managers, warehousing managers, retail store managers, and the department heads of local outlets. All of these people have a common interest: They want to know how the product is going to move efficiently through *their* departments. You'll recognize this as an analogy of the User Buyer's wanting to know how a product will *perform*. Like User Buyers, people playing Logistical roles want the product to work for them personally, on the job.   -

Merchandising Buying Influences

People playing Merchandising Buying Influence roles are approximately equivalent to Technical Buyers. They too are *gatekeepers,* serving to *screen out* vendors and make *recommendations.* Their characteristics appear in the box below.

MERCHANDISING BUYING INFLUENCE

ROLE: TO SCREEN OUT AND MAKE RECOMMENDATIONS

OFTEN SEVERAL OR MANY

- Evaluates your products and promotions
- Removed from **direct** involvement
- Gatekeeper

FOCUS: Costs
Product Quality
Packagings
Advertising And Promotion
Merchandising Follow-through
Merchandising Allowances

Asks: "Does it meet specifications?"

Just as Technical Buyers in general are often removed from the on-the-job use of the product or service, so too Merchandising Buying Influences are usually one or more steps removed from direct involvement with your product or promotion. While Logistical Buying Influences generally affect the retailing process, people playing Merchandising roles are often found further back in the product delivery flow. Many of them make judgments about the product or promotion *before* it gets into the stores.

These judgments, like those made by Technical Buyers, will often be less subjective and more quantifiable than those of people playing Logistical roles. People in Merchandising roles bring various types of external expertise to their evaluations of the product. Major concerns of these gatekeepers are such areas as price, quality, packaging, advertising, promotion, profitability, service, and merchandising follow-through.

One proviso, however. The evaluations of Merchandising Buying Influences aren't always objective—and this points to a significant difference between this role and that of Technical Buyers. If a person playing a Merchandising role buys a product or promotion that fails badly, he has to answer for the failure: It's his job and reputation on the line. Therefore, people playing Merchandising roles share with User Buyers a concern with how the sale will affect their jobs, personally. In every Merchandising Buying Influence, there's a mixture of User Buyer and Technical Buyer.

The same thing can be said about Logistical Buying Influences. Although their focus is product "performance," they're also interested in the product's size, weight, shape, and other "logistical" features—and these features are objective, not personal. So in every Logistical Buying Influence too, there are elements of both User Buyer and Technical Buyer.

No Other Differences
We offer this alternate terminology as a way of heading off any uneasiness you might feel about the use of language a bit more appropriate for an industrial sale. And we hasten

to assure you that, beyond this minor terminological quibble, there's absolutely no difference between the way Strategic Selling works in consumer product sales and the way it works in industrial and other Complex Sales. Thousands of our mass-merchandising program participants can testify to that.

If you feel uncomfortable with the term "Buyer," we suggest that, throughout the rest of the book, you mentally substitute this alternate vocabulary. Whenever you see "Economic Buyer," think "Veto Power Buying Influence." Whenever you see "User Buyer," think "Logistical Buying Influence." And whenever you see "Technical Buyer," think "Merchandising Buying Influence."

But remember the proviso we just mentioned about Logistical and Merchandising Buying Influences having elements of both User and Technical Buyer in them. You can't simply plug in one terminology for the other. Instead, as we emphasized at the beginning of the chapter, you have to search for all the individual people playing each of the buying *roles* for your particular sales objective. Keep in mind that, while there will always be only be *one* person playing the Veto Power role, there may be *several* people playing Logistical and Merchandising roles; in addition, a single individual can always play *more than one* role in your sale.

The term "Coach," it's evident, is used in the same way in all types of sales. And *all the other elements* of the Strategic Selling system are used in the same way as well.

Selling All Your Buying Influences

Soon after we founded our company, officers of one of the largest food-products manufacturers in the country began looking over our programs. The package they were considering involved training hundreds of their sales representatives, and the prospects looked very good. We'd received extremely favorable reactions to our presentations from the president of the company himself, and were already beginning to talk about possible sites for the programs.

The only hitch was a nervous sales-training manager who thought our program was a threat to his own. He was used to running things his way, and although he couched his objections in phrases like "incompatibility of design" and "basic structural impasses," his real reason for opposing us was obviously fear. In his estimation, if we got in, he was out.

We handled his resistance in a rather perfunctory manner, not only because we knew his fears were unfounded—in fact the whole design of our program was intended to let him take over once we'd given the program—but also because we already had the top dog in our pocket.

This cavalier attitude proved to be a big mistake. When the president heard about the training manager's misgivings, he withdrew his support of our proposal. He still liked it, but not enough to jeopardize his good relations with a subordinate he'd relied on for many years. As a result he backed off, and a "surefire" order went down the drain.

This story illustrates the important principle that, in every Complex Sale, you have to sell your proposal not just to one or two but to *all four* of the Buying Influences. Selling the Economic Buyer alone, as we tried to do here, can be just as disastrous as forgetting about him and only selling someone who doesn't give the final yes—as the airplane manufacturer tried to do in the Middle East. What we should have done in this case was to turn our Economic Buyer, the president, into a Coach, and get him to help us convince the training manager (who was filling both a User Buyer and a Technical Buyer role) that his fears about his job were misplaced. Instead we made the all-too-common error of assuming that as long as Mr. Big is sold, everything else will fall into place. We paid a heavy price for that assumption.

Many sales representatives are still paying this price, whether they focus on the top (as we did) or on the middle-range decision makers (as the airplane manufacturer did). It's very hard to break with tradition, and traditionally sales representatives try to build their account sales around the people with whom they're most comfortable. Sales representatives with electronics firms, for example, are often engineers, and in fact are often referred to not as salespeople but as "field engineers." Since they're comfortable with other engineers, they become adept at selling their products to User and Technical Buyers who are also engineers. But because they're much less comfortable with top management, they often ignore their Economic Buyers, and find themselves losing out to sales representatives who cover all four Buying Influences.

When we emphasize this point in our programs, someone usually objects, "But what about the sales where one guy does it all? Aren't there situations where one person plays all four roles?"

The answer is almost always no. We realize that there are still a few small firms around where The Founder seems to run everything, and we know that when you're selling to such a firm it may look as if every buying decision is made by that single individual. But before you conclude that all four Buying Influence roles are played by that one CEO and nobody else, look further. Does he really read all the firm's legal documents himself? Is he really going to be personally involved in using every product or service you want to sell him? Does he really dispense entirely with advice and consent? Or, when you look at how buying decisions are made for his firm, don't you find that his people play roles that are more complicated, and more fundamental, than the ones they appear to be playing?

The true one-man company is virtually a thing of the past, and the sale that can be decided by one vote is not now, and never again will be, a reality. In corporate sales today, complexity of decision making is the rule almost without exception. So if you find a situation in which only one Buyer seems to be involved, be careful. We've acknowledged that key players can play double or multiple roles, but if you can find only one key player in a major account sale, it's almost a certainty that you're misreading the situation.

Personal Workshop 2: Buying Influences

To give you some practice in reading your own Complex Sales, you'll now do a Personal Workshop in which you apply the Key Element of Buying Influences to an analysis of your chosen sales goal. To do this workshop, you'll need your large notebook and the small, adhesive-backed stickers that you're using as Red Flags.

Step 1: Draw up your Buying Influences Chart.

We've defined the role of each of the four Buying Influences that appear in the Complex Sale. As a way of reviewing them and of making them constantly visible, we suggest that you write them down in a format that you can use throughout this book whenever you redefine your position with regard to your sales goal. It's called a Buying Influences Chart.

Turn your notebook so that the longer side of the page is horizontal, and at the top of the page write "Buying Influences Chart." Divide the page into four equal boxes. At the top of each one write the name of one of the four Buying Influences and, below that, the role that each one plays in the Complex Sale.

You'll want to write small enough so that you can add material to this chart in future Personal Workshops. When you have the Buying Influences Chart set up, it should look something like the example on page 97.

Step 2: Identify all your Buyers.

Now, with your *specific sales objective* in mind, write down in the boxes the names of the people who are currently filling the four roles for your sale. Remember, there's going to be only one Economic Buyer, but in the other three boxes you may have one or a number of names. Remember also that a single individual may appear in more than one of the boxes, if that person is playing multiple roles.

There are two ways of identifying your Buyers, the right way and the wrong way. The wrong way is simply to list the people you're currently calling on and fit them into the four slots you've just drawn. This *labeling,* or pigeonholing, approach is a tempting but ultimately disastrous shortcut. If you start from your own current prospects, or from an organization chart of the buying firm, and paste an Economic Buyer label on Black because he's chairman of the board, a User Buyer label on Snyder because she's head of production, you'll be certain to confuse titles with roles. You'll be force-fitting your data into preconceived (and probably misconceived) categories.

```
┌──────────────────────────────────────────────────┐
│         BUYING INFLUENCES CHART                    │
│                                                    │
│  ECONOMIC : releases $$  │  USER : judges impact   │
│                          │              on job     │
│                          │                         │
│                          │                         │
│──────────────────────────│─────────────────────────│
│  TECHNICAL : screens out │  COACH (ES) : guides me on│
│                          │              this sale   │
│                          │                         │
│                          │                         │
└──────────────────────────────────────────────────┘
```

The right way to identify your Buyers—the way that will clarify for you how the buying decisions are going to be made for your specific proposal—is to *search* for the people who are playing the four roles for your current objective right now. You can zero in on those roles—and thus find the people playing them—by asking yourself the following questions:

- To locate your single Economic Buyer, ask, "Who has final authority to release the money for *this sale*?"
- To find your User Buyers, ask, "Who will personally use or supervise the use of my product or service on the job?"
- To find your Technical Buyers, ask, "Who will

make judgments about the technicalities of my product or service as a way of screening out vendors?"

- To find the people you can most effectively develop into Coaches, ask, "Who can guide me in *this* sale?"

Write in the names of your Buyers in the relevant boxes of the chart, in a single column at the left-hand side of the box. When you're done, the chart should look like the example below.

BUYING INFLUENCES CHART

ECONOMIC : releases $ $

DAN FARLEY

USER : judges impact on job

DORIS GREEN

HARRY BARNES

TECHNICAL : screens out

GARY STEINBERG

WILL JOHNSON

HARRY BARNES

COACH (ES) : guides me on *this* sale

DORIS GREEN

ANDY KELLY

Step 3: Test your current position.

Now look at each name in turn and ask yourself where you stand with that person right now. Remember, you always have a position even if you don't know what it is. In this step of the workshop, you're objectively assessing your current position with each key player with regard to the role each one is playing in your sale. You're making your position visible.

In testing your position with your Buyers, you should ask yourself two questions, designed to locate areas of uncertainty that we've found to be extremely common:

1. Have I identified *all* the key people who are currently playing each of the four Buying Influence roles for my sales objective?

2. Have I covered the bases with every one of these key players?

The first question is self-explanatory: Since we've stressed that there may be many players filling the four buying roles, you should look at the entire account situation and dig for the key players rather than say, "OK, I've got four; I'm in good shape."

The second question relates to a concept that we'll explain more fully in a moment. For now, just think of "covering the bases" as a synonym for "contacting" or "qualifying."

In looking over your Buying Influences Chart, ask yourself whether you've personally contacted each Buyer identified, or whether you've arranged for someone else to do so. A Buyer whose role you understand, but who hasn't yet been called on, is an *uncovered base.*

Next to the names of those players whose roles you're not absolutely sure of, next to each uncovered base, and in any Buyer box for which you don't have at least one name, stick one of your Red Flags—or mark the name with red pencil. This will call your attention to uncertainties in your current position. Don't worry if your Buying Influences Chart has one or more of these Red Flags. If it didn't, you'd already have the order. We're going to show you now how to use them to improve your position.

► 6 ◄

KEY ELEMENT 2: RED FLAG FOR DANGER—OR OPPORTUNITY

In a recent Strategic Selling program, our participants were in the midst of identifying their various Buying Influences, as you've just done for your sales goal, when one of them, an energetic young man who had twice been the top sales representative in his division for the year, threw his pencil on the table and looked up with an expression of bemused elation. We could see from looking at his worksheet that it was covered with tiny Red Flags. "You know," he said with a kind of sardonic pride, "I just discovered something. I thought this was one of my best accounts. Now I realize I don't even have a prospect. I guess I'm going to have to do some rethinking."

We were delighted with his discovery, and even more delighted at the conclusion he'd drawn from it. It wasn't hard to see why he'd been consistently successful. He was using the Red Flag element of strategy in exactly the way it was meant to be used: as a way of calling his attention to problems with the sale while he still had time to fix them. It's a consistent pattern in our programs that the sales commission leaders, the people who regularly pull down 200 or 300 percent of their quotas, are those who find the *most* Red Flags in their accounts when they begin their strategic analysis. It's those people who most fully appreciate the value of the Red Flag highlighting system—and who most consistently react to the discovery of Red Flags as this top salesman did, by committing themselves to rethinking the sale.

As we mentioned earlier, we chose the term "Red Flag" because in everyday language it's a signal for "warning" or "danger." That's exactly the way you should view those areas in your sales strategy that are incomplete or uncertain. You should consider them not merely "fuzzy" areas, but areas of immediate danger, threatening the completion of your sale. We use the Red Flag symbol for the same reason that a road crew or the Coast Guard uses an actual red flag: to call your attention to a hazard before it can do you in.

"Automatic" Red Flags

The things that can threaten the Complex Sale are virtually numberless. We'll be discussing many of them in this book. We want to begin, however, by discussing five things that are so prevalent and so dangerous to sales that we consider them "automatic" Red Flag areas.

1. Missing Information
In the Personal Workshop you just did to identify your Buying Influences, we asked you to place a red sticker next to the name of any Buyer whose role you didn't understand, and also in any of the four Buyer boxes for which you couldn't find a key player. In both cases, we were asking you to highlight areas of *missing information* that you need to fully understand the sale. You should always consider such missing information a signal that *your sale is in danger*—whether the lack of data relates to your Buying Influences or to any of the other Key Elements that we'll introduce later in this book. Whenever you have a question

about the sale but no answer, then it's time to reassess your position.

2. Uncertainty About Information

It's just as important to reassess that position when the answer you have is hazy or provisional. In our Strategic Selling programs, we see a clear distinction between situations where sales representatives simply lack the relevant data and know it, and those where they have some data, but aren't certain what it means to the sale. Often the latter situation is more hazardous than the former. At least when you know you're missing a piece of the puzzle, you can take steps to track it down. When you have a piece that "looks right" but doesn't quite fit, you run the risk of force-fitting what you already "know" into your analysis—and ignoring what you really *need* to know.

Because uncertainty about "known" information is such a common impediment to successful sales, we'll give you the same advice here that we give our program participants. Whenever you're "pretty sure" or "almost certain" or "90 percent convinced" that you understand a piece of information you need to close a sale, *look again*. And reach for those red stickers.

3. Any Uncontacted Buying Influence

We also mentioned this Red Flag area in the last Personal Workshop, when we asked you to place a sticker next to the name of any person playing any of the Buying Influence roles in your sale who had not yet been contacted either by you personally or by someone better suited to do so. *Any Buyer ignored is a threat.* We sometimes call such a Buyer an uncovered base. The baseball metaphor accurately suggests the trouble you'll get yourself into by failing to contact, or cover, every key player. You *can* field a team without a second baseman or a shortstop, and you *can* close a Complex Sale without contacting all of the relevant players. But you'll do so under conditions of extreme uncertainty—so why try?

You don't have to contact and convince each of the key players yourself. That's not always the most effective strategy. But setting up an arrangement so that all the people in each of the four Buying Influence roles are contacted by *someone* is a principal element of your responsibility as the manager of your Complex Sale. Like the manager of a ball team, you have to see to it that each base is adequately covered by *the person best qualified to do so*.

In some cases that person will be you. In others it will be another member of your organization, or one of the Buying Influences who is favorable to your proposal, or your Coach. Many of our clients—Saga, Coca-Cola, Hewlett-Packard, and Ryder/P.I.E., to name a few—employ the strategy of *like-rank selling* to cover the various bases in their sales. Since they understand that organization people are usually most comfortable talking to others at their own level, they arrange a system of sales calls in which vice-presidents talk to vice-presidents, middle-management people talk to other middle managers, lawyers are used to sell lawyers, and so on. No two such arrangements are identical, since no two sales are identical. The successful arrangements, however, all share a common element: They cover *all* the Buyers.

4. Any Buying Influence New to the Job

The appearance of new faces in the picture is a third reason for an automatic Red Flag, especially if you haven't yet contacted them. Even if you've contacted new potential Buying Influences, however, you should still consider them possible threats to the sale until you've determined positively what Buying Influence roles they're playing and how they feel about your proposal. This may sound overly cautious, but since Buyer roles—and therefore Buyer perceptions—change quickly and subtly in the Complex Sale, the point is really only common sense.

A friend who sells hospital supplies discovered, after he'd actually *closed* a deal with an East Coast medical center, how hazardous it can be minimize the threat of a new player. The Economic Buyer was a vice-president of finance named Jeffries. He'd already placed an order when the vice-presidency was taken over by a new man named Cole. Our friend, wrongly assuming that the deal was solid because the ink was dry, told himself Cole was irrelevant and took a brief vacation. When he returned, the order was still sitting on the loading dock and he was out a fat commission. Cole, the new Economic Buyer, had overturned Jeffries's decision and canceled the order in favor of a less costly bid.

Ignoring a new Buying Influence in this way is the wrong way to manage a sale. The right way was demonstrated by a program participant of ours from a New England insurance firm. He was in the middle of negotiating a contract for group insurance with a company that employed three thousand people when the company suddenly brought in a consultant—an expert in group insurance. Our participant knew that his chief competitor for the account, one of the country's largest insurers, wasn't as well positioned with the buying company as he was. If he'd rested on his laurels and forgotten that new players are hazardous, he might have ignored the consultant, and lived to regret it. Fortunately, he was familiar with the Red Flag concept and immediately spotted the consultant as a threat. Instead of ignoring her, he approached the consultant and was able to convince her that it was in the best interests of everyone concerned—including the consultant herself—for his company to get the order. The larger carrier, which *had* ignored the consultant, found itself strategically outclassed, and our participant carried the day. It was a classic example of a strategy-wise sales representative converting a potentially dangerous Technical Buyer into a valuable ally.

So new Buyers don't have to *remain* threats. Indeed, one of your roles as a sales representative is to transform as many of those new faces as you can into sponsors of your proposal. You can only do that if you consider every new player relevant—and if you refuse to take any of them for granted.

5. Reorganization

The introduction of a new Buying Influence is a relatively easy danger signal to spot. A much more difficult one is presented when the faces in a given account remain the same, their titles and supposed functions remain the same, and yet their *roles* for your particular sale are very different from the ones they've played in the past. We've stressed that the identities of the people playing the four Buying Influence roles are always in a state of flux, even in the most stable corporate environments—and that you therefore have to reidentify your Buyers every time you propose a new sales objective. This admonition is twice as important when the buying company is undergoing, or has just undergone, any kind of internal reorganization. Hirings, firings, promotions, consolidations, expansions, trimming operations—anything that alters the organizational structure of the decision makers—should be read as an automatic Red Flag.

When reorganization takes place on a wide, corporate level, it's generally pretty easy to spot. If two billion-dollar firms merge, or if the presidency of a Fortune 500 company changes hands, you don't have to be a wizard to sense that it might affect your sale. It's much harder to spot this fourth automatic Red Flag when the reorganization is subtle and internal. An especially difficult reorganization to spot is one in which the players retain their titles and their ostensible responsibilities in the buying organization, but no longer have the same authority.

We knew a vice-president for a large consumer-products group, for example, who had been in the same office and exercised essentially the same responsibilities for ten years. Those responsibilities included approving any sale to his division that exceeded ten thousand dollars: He was the Economic Buyer for those sales. Two years ago, he was "promoted" to the position of senior vice-president. He stayed in the same office with a modest increase in salary, and as far as the casual outsider was concerned, he seemed to enjoy the same privileges and exercise the same buying role. But that wasn't the case. As is true in many instances of an executive being kicked upstairs, he'd lost his Economic Buyer role when he took the "senior" title. After his promotion, sales of ten thousand dollars and above had to be approved by a "junior" vice-president down the hall. The sales representative who casually assumed that nothing had changed might easily have wasted time—and imperiled sales—by presenting proposals to an Economic Buyer who no longer existed.

In these days of mergeritis and administrative razzle-dazzle, corporate reorganization is anything but a rare occurrence. As one of our program participants told us in complaining about a notoriously unstable banking client, "Their 'constant' is ninety days. Reorganization is the most important Red Flag there is." A word to the wise should suffice. Whenever the buying organization shifts gears, you'd better take a new look at the account and reidentify the players who are filling the four Buying Influence roles.

The five automatic Red Flag areas discussed here, and highlighted in the box below, are the most obviously and consistently dangerous ones you'll encounter in your sales. But they're only the tip of the iceberg. Every sales goal can be blocked in countless ways. Therefore, sales success is always a direct result of constant vigilance against hazards. The Red Flag technique for locating those hazards only works with optimum effectiveness when it's so fully incorporated into your strategy that you use it again and again without hesitation—when it has become second nature.

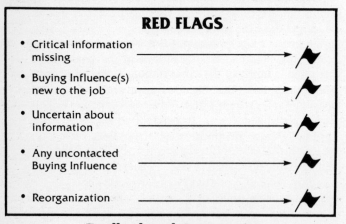

RED FLAGS

- Critical information missing
- Buying Influence(s) new to the job
- Uncertain about information
- Any uncontacted Buying Influence
- Reorganization

Feedback and Opportunity

Used in this way, the Red Flag technique is a "continuous assessment" device, a feedback mechanism that enables the strategy-conscious sales professional to maintain an effective sales position in the face of every contingency, because it shows, every time it's used, where your current position is shaky and where an Alternate Position may be needed.

Because they enable you to test and reposition yourself in the face of change, you should always consider Red Flags *positive,* not negative. Ideally they serve not only as "road hazard" signals, but as signposts to *opportunities* that you might have overlooked without them. The best people in sales understand that a strategic analysis without Red Flags is one without opportunities. Like our program participant who discovered "I don't even have a prospect," top people *welcome* Red Flags. They know that without the constant checking of position that these devices offer, it's very easy to fall into a fool's paradise.

Sales hazards, like road hazards, are most dangerous when they're unflagged and hidden. That's why people who are afraid or embarrassed to identify what's wrong with their positions always get run off the road. They allow themselves to feel blindly confident right up to the moment when the sale falls through, and they're thrown into blind panic. If you think back to the Euphoria-Panic Continuum that we introduced in Chapter 3, you'll recall that being euphoric, just like being in a panic state, means you're out of touch with reality. The Red Flag "early warning system," by forcing you to uncover what's hidden, keeps reality always at hand.

Leverage from Strength

When you know a Red Flag is there, you then can work to eliminate it. You do that by using a principle we call Leverage from Strength. Leverage from Strength can be considered the "better half" of the Red Flag technique. It's what enables you to turn the weaknesses uncovered by your Red Flags into opportunities for improvement.

As effective as it is in improving position, it's surprising how infrequently Leverage from Strength is employed, even by very good salespeople. Many sales representatives, faced with an obvious roadblock, choose either to hammer

away until it moves or to run around it as if it weren't
there. Both these reactions are ways of avoiding the unknown, and they both have a boomerang effect: They send
the sales representative careening *into* the unknown, and
give the order to the competition.

To see how these reactions fail, and how Leverage from
Strength works, consider a typical sales picture. Suppose
you're working with an account in which two of the principal players are a production manager acting as a User
Buyer and a financial vice-president serving as the Economic Buyer. The User Buyer is clearly on your side; he's
ready to put in your order. But the Economic Buyer won't
sign. Moreover, you can't even get close; like many Economic Buyers, this one is insulated from salespeople and
won't even return your calls. Consider three approaches
you could take.

Scenario 1: Hammering Away
In this common scenario, you assume that the reason
you've been unable to see the vice-president is that you
haven't tried hard enough. It's *your* fault that the Economic Buyer is inaccessible. If you only adopt a more
positive attitude and keep leaving phone messages, your
persistence will be rewarded. We've already told you how
worthless we've found this kind of "better mental attitude"
approach to be. Even if the fates (or a secretary) smile on
you and you get five minutes with the vice-president, it's
extremely unlikely that you'll be able to turn it to your advantage: You'll still be the same unknown that you were
before getting in. Thus you'll probably only end up advertising your weakness.

Scenario 2: Ignoring the Roadblock
In this scenario you forget about the Economic Buyer entirely. You accept the fact that you can't get in and focus
your presentation on the User Buyer, who's already favorable to your proposal. Of course there's nothing wrong
with talking to a User Buyer who wants you in (in fact, by
not doing so you could easily create a new roadblock). But
since no sale can go through without a release of funds,

you're still going to be weakly positioned to close the sale if you talk only to the User Buyer. An Economic Buyer who's an uncovered base is a major Red Flag in any sale. Relying on your good relationship with the User Buyer to offset that serious weakness is like playing stud poker with a deuce in the hole.

Scenario 3: Leverage from Strength

A strategy that would most likely succeed in this sales situation would use Leverage from Strength. Using this principle, you would go to the User Buyer for assistance in getting the Economic Buyer covered. By turning the User Buyer into a Coach for the sale, you would be relying on an established Strength (his desire for you to make the sale) to eliminate a Red Flag (the vice-president's reluctance to see you). "This sale is obviously good for the two of us, Joe," you could say. "But the money is tied up in Finance. How can we show them up there that buying will increase productivity?"

Joe will have some ideas about that. He may simply offer to introduce you to the vice-president. He may offer to make a presentation for you or suggest that the two of you go in together. In any event, as a production manager in the vice-president's own company, Joe already has better credibility with Finance than you do; since you also have credibility with Joe, and since he wants you to make the sale, he's an ideal candidate for a Coach.

The User Buyer may or may not become your Coach for this sale. But involving him in your approach to the Economic Buyer at the very least consolidates your position with him. Ideally, you can capitalize on that Strength to improve your overall position in the sale. The point is that the Economic Buyer, as a Red Flag, has to be covered by *somebody;* a friendly User Buyer can help you find out who's best qualified to do that.

Referring to the mechanical advantage of a simple lever and fulcrum, the Greek mathematician Archimedes is reputed to have said that with a lever long enough and a place to put the fulcrum, he could lift the world. His seemingly extravagant conjecture illustrates an important principle and an important reality: Leverage enables us to move by indirect force objects that we could never budge with an equal, or even greater, amount of direct force.

That principle is as applicable to sales as it is to mechanics. You gain a distinct strategic advantage when you apply indirect rather than direct pressure on recalcitrant or inaccessible Buying Influences. Much of your repositioning in Strategic Selling involves looking, as Archimedes might have, for a place to put your "fulcrum." Invariably you'll find that that place is one where you're already solidly positioned.

In summary of our second Key Element of strategy, we can say that the dual principle of Red Flags/Leverage from Strength involves three sequential techniques:

1. Locating areas of weakness (Red Flags)
2. Locating areas of Strength
3. Using those Strengths to remove the Red Flags

You'll use this combined principle now in a Personal Workshop to assess your position with the Buyers for your stated sales objective.

Personal Workshop 3: Red Flags/Buyers

In the Personal Workshop on position that you did in Chapter 3, you assessed your feelings about your current position with regard to future shock and change. Now that you've been introduced to the first two of our Six Key Elements, you can reassess that position using objective criteria. So get out the Buying Influences Chart that you drew up in the last chapter, and your Red Flags.

Step 1: Identify Red Flags and Strengths.
Now take out your Red Flags and use them to identify uncertainties. Place one in any box of the Buying Influences Chart for which you have not identified at least one player. Then, remembering the automatic Red Flag situations we discussed earlier in this chapter, put a Red Flag next to the name of any of the following players:

- Anyone about whom you have insufficient data—about whom you have a question you can't answer
- Any uncovered base
- Any player involved in a recent or current corporate reorganization
- Any new player

Once you've identified your roadblocks, start looking for areas of Strength from which you can use Leverage to remove them. Which of your Buyers are most enthusiastic about your proposal? Which of them could best be utilized as a Coach? Have you spoken to these people yet about helping you move to a stronger position?

As you look for places to put your "fulcrum," *be alert to your positioning patterns.* That is, notice whether you're consistently well positioned with one category of Buying Influence and out of touch with those in another category. We've mentioned the danger in adopting the traditional approach to Complex Sales, which is to build the sale around the people whom you've known the longest, whom you can contact most easily, or with whom you feel most comfortable—and to ignore other critical Buying Influences. Identifying the *patterns* in how you cover your Buyers will help you determine whether or not you're unconsciously falling into this trap.

The bottom line here is this: To close a quality sale, you have to cover *all* the key players filling *all four* of the Buying Influence roles.

Take about five or ten minutes to analyze your Buying Influences Chart as a whole. Think about each Red Flag in turn, considering what specific opportunity it offers you to improve your position. And for each one, locate a possible Strength from which you can work toward the improvement.

Step 2: Revise your Alternate Positions list.

You now have a lot more information about your account situation than you did when you first drew up your Alternate Positions list in Chapter 3. Right now you're going to begin a process that you'll be carrying through all the remaining Personal Workshops in the book. You're going to use the information you've just acquired to revise and expand on that list; by Part 5 of the book, where you draft an Action Plan for your chosen sales objective, you will have worked over the Alternate Positions list several times, and will have transformed it into the basic working paper for that Action Plan.

Since you'll be performing this revision process continually throughout the book, we want to lay out a few basic guidelines here that will enable you to do it most effectively. As you go down the list point by point, we want you to be *inclusive,* to be *specific,* and to *test* your Alternate Positions.

By being *inclusive* we mean you shouldn't worry too much at this point whether or not every one of your Alternate Positions is ideal for the situation. The Key Elements of strategy that we have yet to introduce will help you to thin out the list so that only the best options remain. But right now don't throw out too much. It's still too early to put all your eggs in one basket.

Be *specific* because you're not making out a list of theoretical sales principles; you're developing the basic working paper for *your* chosen sales objective. In listing alternatives, you can't just give yourself a cheery pep talk and resolve to "do better" with Dan Farley. If Farley is the Economic Buyer for your sale but he won't let you in the door, then "getting to Farley" is not an effective Alternate Position. You need to write down something like the following: "Get Doris Green (my enthusiastic User Buyer) to show Farley how we can increase their productivity by 15 percent."

Of course, using friendly Doris to get to the boss won't make the sale for you. It will just get rid of one Red Flag. Once you see Farley, you may find new Red Flags (maybe he's had bad experiences with your company in the past, or maybe productivity isn't a high priority at the moment), and you'll have to reposition again. Take it one step at a time. And use the leverage principle again and again as you work your way toward your objective.

Finally, *test* each Alternate Position. Don't make the unwarranted assumption that *any* change at all in a bad position is necessarily going to be a change for the better. Every Alternate Position you list should do one of two things:

1. Capitalize on an area of Strength
2. Eliminate a Red Flag—or at least reduce its impact

Of course, the best Alternate Positions do *both* these things. In the example given above, for instance, getting Doris Green to see Dan Farley both capitalizes on a Strength (a friendly User Buyer) and eliminates a Red Flag (the Economic Buyer's reluctance to be seen). Don't bother listing Alternate Positions that don't accomplish *at least* one of these two objectives.

We introduce the Red Flags/Leverage from Strength Principle early in our programs because we want our participants to use it in analyzing all subsequently introduced Key Elements. The checking mechanism you've applied to your sales goal here will be useful to you throughout your selling cycle. We'll return to it periodically throughout this book.

So put your Buying Influences Chart and your Alternate Positions list aside, but keep them handy. You'll be adding to them soon.

► 7 ◄

BUYER LEVEL OF RECEPTIVITY

Up to now you've been focusing largely on your own perceptions of the sales situation, as a way of making your position regarding your current sales objective more visible and of highlighting areas of uncertainty in your strategy. Now you're going to shift your focus to the perceptions of the various Buyers for your sales goal. We've said that after you determine who all those Buyers are, the next thing you have to do is to find out how each of them feels about what you're trying to accomplish in his or her account. The third Key Element of strategy—Response Modes—will clarify your Buyers' receptivity to your proposal, and help you to position yourself more effectively with each one.

You need to be able to gauge your Buyers' receptivity to your proposal because, without an understanding of this receptivity, you can easily end up trying to sell a Buyer who isn't really there—one whose perception of reality is so different from your own that the Buyer is utterly incapable of understanding why you'd want the sale in the first place.

Sales representatives who are inattentive to Buyer receptivity frequently fall into one of three fatal traps:

1. They take their *own* perceptions of reality as the key to the sale.
2. They assume their perceptions of reality are the *same* as those of their Buyers.
3. They recognize that the Buyers' perceptions of reality are different from their own, but conclude that they're *wrong* or *irrelevant*.

Our third Key Element of strategy is designed to help you avoid these common errors of judgment by focusing on what really counts in the sale: how the Buyer is likely to react to the *change* that your proposal is offering.

Change: The Hidden Factor

In the Personal Workshop that you did in Chapter 3, you listed the future-shock changes that are influencing your current sales environment, and analyzed your feelings about them with regard to your chosen account. You'll recall that some changes seemed to be primarily positive, while others appeared mostly as threats. You'll also remember that, no matter what the external "facts" of your sales environment, most changes could be seen as either threats or opportunities, depending on your response.

The same thing goes for the people playing Buying Influence roles in your sale. The elements of future shock that you listed are influencing their business environments too, and like you they can have a variety of responses to those elements. In addition, however, they have to respond to *one* significant change that you by definition see as an opportunity, but that they can easily as a threat. That's *your sales proposal itself.*

You probably don't like to think of your sales proposals as threats, but Buyers can, and often do, see them in just this way. The strategic sales representative understands that *anytime you ask someone to buy something, you're asking that person to make a change.* Neither the seller nor the

Buyer may consciously identify the sales proposal as an offer to make a change, but change is nonetheless a *critical hidden factor in every sale.* Since people react to change in different ways, and since virtually every change can be viewed as either threat or opportunity, there's always the chance that a Buyer will perceive your sales proposal as threatening, even when it's "obvious" to you that it's not.

The nonstrategic sales representative often ignores the hidden factor of change. Dazzled by the elegance of your own presentation or impressed by the "perfect fit" between your product and the Buyer's objective needs, you may overlook the Buyer's potential perception of the proposal as an unwanted or threatening change, and assume that the Buyer will respond in the "obviously" sensible manner— that is, affirmatively.

Experience has proven to us and to our clients again and again that this is a dangerously myopic approach. No matter how good the "facts" of a given sales situation, they may still look terrible to your Buyer. If that's the case, it's the facts, not the Buyer's perception of them, that become irrelevant to your sales objective. Understanding the Buyer's perception of reality is what will help you predict his or her response to your proposal.

The Buyer's Perception of Reality

By "perception of reality" we don't mean the Buyer's general outlook on life, philosophy, or overall approach to business. We mean the Buyer's perception of the *immediate* business situation and view of what will happen to that situation if the change you're offering is accepted.

A Buyer can bring four different reactions, or Response Modes, to a sales situation. Each of these four modes derives from a different perception of the immediate business reality. And each one leads to a different level of Buyer receptivity to incoming sales proposals.

Because each of the four perceptions of reality leads to a different Response Mode, and because each mode leads to a different level of receptivity, the strategic sales representative has to develop *a different sales approach for each of the four perceptions*. We're going to show you how to do that now, as we introduce the four Response Modes.

We need to stress, however, that these Response Modes are *not* descriptions of attitude or personality. They aren't categories of people, but descriptions of ways in which Buyers perceive immediate, specific situations. They show you where the Buyer is coming from in relation to the specific change you're offering. That's all. You can speak of a given Buyer being in a certain mode with regard to a given business situation. It makes no sense to say that someone is *always* in that mode.

This is a critical point, because in many account situations you'll find yourself selling to a positive, growth-oriented person who, at the moment of your approach, sees your sales objective as nothing but trouble. If you focus on personality, you may erroneously conclude that this person is just a grumpy type who will never let you in the door. If you use the Key Element of Response Modes to assess his or her reaction, however, you may find that it's only your approach that's off. You may find that, if you change your strategy, the Buyer could become your strongest supporter. As we'll see now, your Buyer's perceptions of reality, like most things in the Complex Sale, are often notoriously unstable. Understanding our third Key Element of strategy will help you turn this fact to your advantage.

KEY ELEMENT 3: THE FOUR RESPONSE MODES

The level of receptivity of each of your individual Buyers to your proposal is a function of that person's perception of three things: the *immediate* business situation, your proposal as a way of bringing *change* to that situation, and a possible *discrepancy* between current reality and the results that the Buyer wants to achieve.

The last chapter illustrated how the first two of these three perceptions influence receptivity. To understand the critical importance of *discrepancy* as a factor in that receptivity, you need to be introduced to the third Key Element of sales strategy, Response Modes. As we've said, there are always four such possible modes for any Buyer in a given selling situation.

The First Response Mode: Growth

The perception of the Buyer in Growth Mode is represented by the chart on page 119.

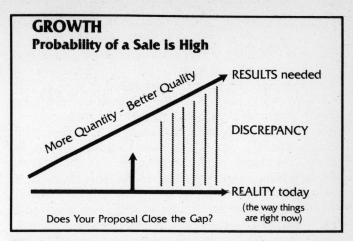

GROWTH
Probability of a Sale is High

More Quantity - Better Quality

RESULTS needed

DISCREPANCY

REALITY today
(the way things are right now)

Does Your Proposal Close the Gap?

The bottom line here illustrates the way the Buyer perceives the *reality* of the current business situation. The top line shows where the Buyer would like that situation to be—the desired *results*. The space between the two lines is a reality-results gap, or *discrepancy*. Because that discrepancy exists, the probability of making the sale is high.

We say this because experience has shown us that a Buyer's *perceived* discrepancy between the current situation and the goal or target is invariably a crucial factor in readiness to buy. You already know that predicting this readiness—that is, predicting the right *time* to call on your Buyers—is one of the great unknowns in most selling situations; knowing *when* to approach a customer is often just as important, but usually not as predictable, a factor in your presentations as knowing *what* the customer needs. You can have a product that's tailor-made to those business needs, but if you approach at the wrong time of the month, or week, or selling cycle, you can easily find yourself— through no fault of your own—going up against a blank wall.

We take some of the uncertainty out of knowing when to approach a Buyer by giving you a simple rule of thumb:

> *Someone buys when there's a discrepancy between that person's perception of reality and his or her desired results.*

In spite of the many nuances that can affect a buying decision, we've found this rule to hold true in all buying situations. Understanding it can be of more value to you than reading any number of texts on buyer psychology and on "assessing your customers' business cycle."

A Buyer in Growth Mode is by definition ready to say yes to *somebody's* proposal—though not necessarily to yours. This person perceives the essential discrepancy and, being in this Response Mode, believes that it can only be eliminated by more or better results, and faster ones. There may be a rising production quota to fill, more orders to fill than products, or a recent memo to step up quality control. Whatever the Buyer's reason for wanting to do *more* and/or *better,* you have a good probability of getting a commitment—*provided that your proposal is seen as the change that will eliminate the discrepancy.*

Buyers in Growth Mode typically use trigger words like "more," "better," "faster," and "improved" that signal they're receptive to change. This mode is often the easiest of the four to sell to. For that reason sales representatives are often attuned to Growth themselves—and are instantly ready to comply when a Buyer is in this mode.

But there's a danger here. It's in confusing corporate growth with the very *personal* Growth Mode of an individual Buyer within the corporation. When we speak of Response Modes, we mean the personal, individual reactions of the people acting as Buying Influences to your sales proposal, not the "growth profiles" of their firms. Since you always have to adopt an individual selling approach for each of these people, you can run into serious difficulty if you assume that all the Buyers in an obviously expanding company are in an expansive Growth Mode themselves. That won't necessarily be the case.

You remember the salesman we described in Chapter 5 who lost an important renewal because he sold a textile company's president a trouble-shooting program without also contacting the mill managers who would be the program's User Buyers. Ignoring these key Buying Influences wasn't his only error. He also assumed incorrectly that, since the company as a whole was now growth oriented, all the Buyers wanted to do more and/or better too. In fact the User Buyers in this situation wanted nothing to do with the growth he was offering them; they wanted things to remain as they were. The salesman's failure to address this fact was a major reason that the renewal was blocked.

No matter what the current economic status of a buying organization, selling to it will always involve addressing the individual perceptions of Buying Influences for your sale— *not* the "perception" of the company at large. In Strategic Selling there's no such thing as a company-wide perception of reality. Only individuals can have perceptions. And all of them must be taken into account if a quality sale is to be made.

The Second Response Mode: Trouble

The probability of a sale is also high in Trouble Mode. Don't be put off by the name. When you confront a Buyer in Trouble Mode, it's not you who is in Trouble. The chart below shows why.

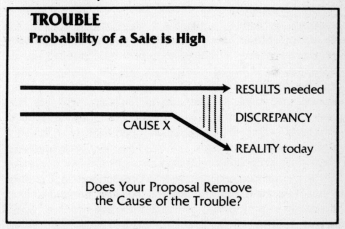

TROUBLE
Probability of a Sale is High

RESULTS needed

DISCREPANCY

CAUSE X

REALITY today

Does Your Proposal Remove
the Cause of the Trouble?

Again, the bottom line shows the Buyer's perception of current reality and the top line his perception of the results he needs to "win." And again there's the necessary discrepancy between reality and results that indicates the Buyer will be receptive to change.

The discrepancy here, however, is a reversal of the discrepancy perceived by the Buyer in Growth. The Buyer in Growth Mode welcomes change as a way of improving an already good situation; the Buyer in Trouble Mode is begging for immediate change as a way of reversing a defeat. Things had been going along well, but then a crisis hit. That crisis has created the discrepancy between the desired reality and actual performance. All the Buyer wants is to fix whatever it is that's wrong—to get things back to normal.

This means that the Buyer in Trouble Mode is ready, indeed eager, to buy—*but not necessarily from you*. The proposal that will be approved is not going to be the most beautifully presented one, or the cheapest bid, or the most technically advanced. It's going to be the one that will *most quickly* remove the cause of the problem.

The Urgency of Trouble

Many people forget this. We constantly run across good sales representatives who are so attuned to Growth and "improvements" themselves that they have difficulty understanding, and selling to, the real needs of a Buying Influence in Trouble Mode. This is especially common in high-tech industries, where the latest, state-of-the-art product developments are a major component of the selling arsenal. You'll probably recognize this exaggerated devotion to technical improvements as part of the "bells and whistles" approach to sales. It's also part of the product-oriented approach, which, as we've already pointed out, is of only limited value in Strategic Selling. The sales representative with this approach is continually stressing the latest features of the product or service, the most recent technical refinements—the bells and whistles that make the company's line always three days ahead of the competition's.

This works fine with Buyers in Growth Mode, but selling technical improvements to Buyers in Trouble is almost always an error. Buyers in this mode are hurting. They're on the panic end of the Euphoria-Panic Continuum. And when people are up to their ears in alligators, they don't want to hear about the sophisticated pumping system that you're going to use to drain the swamp. They want out of the swamp, fast. When Buyers are in Trouble Mode, you don't talk about how your product will improve their lifestyle. You sell survival. Period. The moral here may be stated as an axiom:

> *Trouble always takes precedence over Growth.*

This doesn't mean that Growth is unimportant, only that, to a Buyer who's feeling pain (remember, it's the *perception* that counts), doing more and/or better can *wait* until you've fixed the cause of the pain. Selling Growth to a Buyer who feels in Trouble is like selling a new roof to a farmer whose barn has just caught fire. Even if the barn needs a new roof, it certainly doesn't need one *now*.

When Growth Feels Like Trouble

The truth of the axiom "Trouble always takes precedence over Growth" becomes immediately apparent when you confront a Buyer who's frantically asking for "more" with an urgency that suggests Trouble rather than Growth. Although Buyers always display one Response Mode more dominantly than the others at any given moment, their feelings about their business situations are also constantly in flux. Therefore you frequently have to sell to Buyers who are in the process of moving from one Response Mode to another. A common example of this situation is the case of the person who has just received a directive to increase production or quality, but without an immediate increase in the means to do so.

A production manager we know in a West Coast appliance plant was faced with this situation last year. Sales management had just made a sale to a catalog house that would require him, within a matter of months, to increase his output by 30 percent. The company was obviously growing—but our friend definitely wasn't in a Growth

Mode. "I need everything yesterday," he told us. "We're moving so fast, if I don't get the parts I need by next week, we're all sunk."

There were, and are, two ways to interpret a statement like that. Either you can see it as a pure Growth statement—"I need to do *more* right now"—or you can see it as a desperate Trouble Mode plea: "I need to do more *right now!*" The difference in emphasis is crucial. If you try to sell simple Growth to a person in this situation—if you emphasize the state-of-the-art aspects of your product or service without addressing the customer's problem—you're likely to lose out to a competitor who understands that the first order of business is to get the guy away from the alligators.

We've said that Trouble Mode perceptions arise because something has happened to the Buyer to change his or her reality from what it was (normal) to something worse. The cause of the Trouble doesn't necessarily have to be something bad. There's nothing bad about a 30 percent increase in orders. But that development becomes a source of Trouble when it's perceived by one of your Buyers as a personal difficulty. In this case, such an increase *was* perceived by our manager friend as a problem—and he was therefore, by definition, in Trouble Mode.

Because nobody will say outright to you, "I'm in Trouble Mode here," or "I feel terrific; all I need is better results," you have to be attentive to nuance whenever you're uncertain whether an individual Buying Influence feels himself to be in Trouble or Growth. If your product or service answers the needs of both Trouble *and* Growth, of course, you're home free. But you still have to design your approach to each Buyer based on which of the four Response Modes that person is in at the particular moment you lay out your proposal. As always, the bottom line is that you stress those aspects of your product or service that speak to that individual Buyer's *perception of immediate reality*.

The Third Response Mode: Even Keel

The first two Response Modes provide relatively easy selling situations. The next two do not. In Even Keel, your chances of making the sale are low because the Buyer doesn't perceive the essential discrepancy between current reality and desired results. The perception of a Buyer in Even Keel can be represented by the chart below.

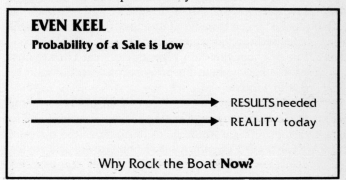

EVEN KEEL
Probability of a Sale is Low

RESULTS needed
REALITY today

Why Rock the Boat **Now?**

Here the top line, representing results, and the bottom line, representing reality as the Buyer perceives it, coincide. (For visual clarity, we've drawn two separate lines. You should think of them as the Buyer does—as superimposed, or identical.) Thus there's no gap for your proposal to close and therefore no receptivity to change. Buyers in Even Keel consistently demonstrate the truth of the maxim "No discrepancy, no sale."

To a Buyer in Even Keel Mode, moreover, your proposal will very likely be seen as a threat. Since results and reality already coincide, this person can only perceive the change you're offering as a potential undoing of that coincidence. The Buyer in Even Keel is by definition wary of *any* change. What this person is usually thinking—and will often say to you—is "Go away. Don't rock the boat."

Raising the Probability of a Sale
When a Buyer is firmly entrenched in Even Keel, only three things can raise the probability of your making the

sale. The Buyer can see Growth or Trouble coming, he can be pressured by another Buyer already in Growth or Trouble, or you can demonstrate a discrepancy the Buyer didn't see.

1. The Buyer sees Growth or Trouble coming. The User Buyers in the textile plant sale we mentioned earlier were clearly in Even Keel Mode. They saw the trouble-shooting program that our friend had sold without their approval as an unnecessary and potentially unsettling change—one that would undo a comfortable status quo. Our friend might have increased the probability of their approval if he'd convinced them either that his proposal had great Growth possibilities, or that, without his program, they would soon be moving into Trouble.

Generally speaking, there's less risk involved in selling Growth possibilities than in selling "Trouble avoidance," so the general rule here would be to try to move the Buyer in Even Keel toward Growth. But selling Growth and selling Trouble avoidance to such a Buyer aren't mutually exclusive strategies: Trouble avoidance can be seen as a kind of Growth. By selling a Buyer in Even Keel something that will prevent *future* Trouble, you're saying, "I know things are going great with you right now. And I have a way for you to keep them that way."

You'll be best prepared to do that if you can see the Trouble coming. That's why keeping on top of your prospects' objective needs is just as important when there's no possibility of a sale as when the signing is just around the corner. If you know how your product can help a Buyer, you also know how being without it will eventually create problems. Knowing that, you can plan your "I can get you out of this mess" presentation while the Buyer is still in Even Keel. He's going to beg you to deliver it when reality finally breaks in.

2. You use pressure from another Buying Influence. Often, an effective indirect way of getting a Buyer in Even Keel to reassess a position is to get another Buyer—preferably a superior of the one in Even Keel—to put pressure on the resistant Buyer to reconsider the situation. Buyers in Even Keel listen much more attentively to the views of Growth or Trouble superiors than they ever will to a salesperson's "warnings."

People playing the Economic Buyer role are generally the best candidates to put this kind of pressure on the other Buyers—precisely because the Economic Buyers are usually quicker to spot Trouble coming than Buyers in other roles. Because of their relatively narrow focus, for example, Technical Buyers and User Buyers are often notoriously slow to recognize storm signals. Often they just don't want to know that, six weeks from now, their boat will be underwater. Economic Buyers, on the other hand (since they're paid to forecast the future), are well attuned to coming storms, and they're much quicker to make changes.

Therefore, one useful strategy is to sell Growth or Trouble avoidance to the Economic Buyer and then get that person to convert the Buyer in Even Keel Mode. This is a way of circumventing resistance by employing the principle of Leverage from Strength. Buyers in Even Keel often cycle out of their sit-tight condition as a result of such pressure even when a sales representative isn't involved. Anything you can do to intensify that pressure—without alienating the Buyer in Even Keel—is going to work to your advantage.

If the Economic Buyer is in Even Keel, however, the probability of making the sale in the short term is remote. Don't count on getting an order soon in this situation.

3. You demonstrate a discrepancy.   Since people will buy only when they perceive a discrepancy between reality and desired results, a third way to increase the probability of sales to Buyers in Even Keel is to show them discrepancies that they hadn't already perceived. You can do this in one of two ways: You can show them that reality actually isn't as satisfactory as they currently believe, or you can show them that the results they've settled for are far short of those they can achieve. In either case, if you can demonstrate that current reality and possible results do *not* in fact coincide, you'll have created the discrepancy that's a pre-requisite to any sale.

A production line manager, for example, who's ac-customed to turning out 500 units a day and who's now turning out 510 won't perceive Trouble; most likely, such a person will be in Even Keel. But if you demonstrate that a rival company, with equipment that you've sold it, is turn-ing out 700 units a day of an equivalent product, the man-ager will probably understand that the competitive results needed are in excess of current production. And receptivity to change will rise.

These three strategies for selling a Buyer in Even Keel frequently prove effective. But they also have their risks—risks that derive from the fact that Buyers in Even Keel Mode find their sit-tight posture *comfortable* and don't like to be disillusioned. Because it's difficult to break down the comfort zone of Buyers in Even Keel, the wisest strategy to adopt with them is often to play an alert waiting game. Re-member that while there may be no match between your product or service and the Buyer's perceived needs today, there could well be one tomorrow.

The Fourth Response Mode: Overconfident

The same principle applies to Buyers in Overconfident Mode. This is the most difficult of the four Response Modes to sell to. In fact, the probability of making a sale to a Buyer who's in Overconfident Mode is, for all practical purposes, zero. The chart opposite indicates why.

When a Buyer is in this fourth mode, there's clearly a kind of discrepancy between reality and perceived results, but in this case the discrepancy works against rather than for the sales representative. An Overconfident Buyer per-ceives reality as outstripping the desired results. Because this person is already doing much *better* than anticipated, there's no incentive to change. Like the Buyer in Even Keel Mode, this one doesn't want you to rock the boat—and that boat, in the Overconfident Buyer's view, is not only watertight, but is winning the America's Cup. When you suggest a change, therefore, you'll be treated as if you were crazy. "I never had it so good," the Buyer will boast. "Things are too good to be true. You want to sell me something that could change that? Get lost!"

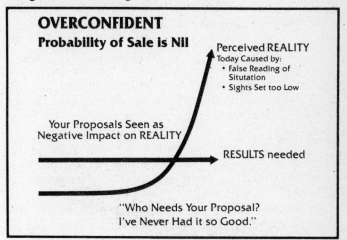

OVERCONFIDENT
Probability of Sale is Nil

Perceived REALITY
Today Caused by:
• False Reading of Situtation
• Sights Set too Low

Your Proposals Seen as Negative Impact on REALITY

RESULTS needed

"Who Needs Your Proposal? I've Never Had it so Good."

What Buyers in Overconfident Mode don't realize is that things *are* too good to be true. Their perception of reality is distorted, usually for one of two reasons:

- They are misunderstanding the situation, out of ignorance or wishful thinking.
- Their goals are set so low that the poor performance isn't obvious.

These two reasons are the primary causes of Overconfident Mode. Buyers in this mode typically tend to be complacent and out of touch; to sales representatives they can be dismissive, even arrogant.

We've all seen the dangers of Overconfidence, in and out of the business world. Many examples of the self-deluding mentality that characterizes people in this mode are provided by recent history. Look at Vietnam, the Watergate fiasco, the demise of the shah of Iran, and the failure of the air traffic controllers to achieve their stated demands. All illustrate what we call the impotence of positive thinking.

All remind us how close euphoria is to panic on the Euphoria-Panic Continuum. And all show that, given enough time, *Overconfidence always cycles into Trouble.*

Killing the Messenger

Being in Overconfident Mode, in spite of the fact that it feels great to a Buyer in that mode, is really a kind of perceptual disability. It's an illness for which the only cure, experience has proved to us again and again, is massive doses of reality. But as we constantly caution our people, to a Buyer in this mode, as to one in Even Keel, you may be the worst person in the world to offer that cure. Buyers in Overconfident Mode are even more difficult to budge than those in Even Keel. Firmly entrenched in their delusions, they don't welcome the news that they're reading the situation wrong. Therefore, you always run the risk, when trying to "convert" a Buyer in this mode, of being seen not as helpful but as intrusive.

In ancient Greece, you may recall, a messenger who brought a king bad news was sometimes taken out and put to death for incurring the ruler's displeasure. As a bringer of unwelcome reality to a Buyer in Overconfident Mode, you risk a similar displeasure, if not a similar fate. We're sure you can think of many sales situations in which an overeager, honesty-smitten sales representative ruined all chances for repeat business by badgering an uncooperative Buyer to "face facts before it's too late."

Waiting for Reality

Because it's so difficult to dislodge Buyers in Overconfident Mode from their misperceptions, our general advice is not to try. Our most successful clients tell us that, faced with a Buyer in this intransigent mode, a wise strategy is for the sales representative simply to maintain a low profile and wait for reality to intrude. The salesperson should keep the lines of communication open, keep the pressure off, and, when the Buyer inevitably cycles into Trouble, be in position to fix the problem.

A client from a West Coast computer company recently used this strategy to good effect in managing a major software sale. The buying organization, which produced a line of multiplex boards for telephone construction, was experiencing an upsurge in orders. It was producing only fifty boards a day, and because of increased demand wanted to up that figure to five hundred. There was concern about quality control at this new pace, however, and that was how our client got involved: She was a specialist in QC systems.

The program that was already in use, she knew, wasn't doing the job well enough. It was barely capable of detecting errors efficiently when the line ran at fifty boards a day; at the new rate of five hundred a day, it would become virtually useless. She said as much to the quality control supervisor—a combination Technical and User Buyer—and was met with disbelief. "You're exaggerating the problem, Diane," the Buyer told her testily. "The system's doing just fine. We could run it to a thousand a day."

The supervisor's cocky attitude was a classic example of Overconfidence, and so our client managed the sale with the waiting strategy we'd recommended. For three months she bided her time, quietly keeping in touch with the supervisor and letting him know that, if he ever needed her help, it was available. Then the weak system started to crack, defective boards started to get through, and service orders began to pour in. Suddenly the supervisor was in Trouble. "I've got a 27 percent return rate on these damn boards," he complained. "How soon can you get me a better system?" "Right away," our client replied. And she proceeded to put in the system she knew had been needed all along.

The moral of the story is simple: Don't waste your precious selling time working on an Overconfident Buyer. This mode is highly unstable. It always, eventually, cycles into Trouble. Just plan to be there when it does.

Matches and Mismatches of Modes

The sales representative's ideal situation with regard to Buyer receptivity is to have all of the Buying Influences in either Growth or Trouble Mode. When all your Buying Influences are saying, "I want to do more now," or "I need better results," they're obviously ripe to be sold. Similarly, when all your Buyers are hurting, you also have a golden opportunity—if you can convince them that your proposal will eliminate their problems. Whenever there's a match of perceptions among your Buyers in Growth or Trouble, there's a higher probability of a sale than when the modes are mixed.

Given the volatility of sales situations, though, and given the personal idiosyncrasies that can influence Buyer perceptions, you aren't likely to come upon these perfectly matched fields of Buying Influences very often. More commonly, you'll be confronted with a mixed or mismatched field, in which, for example, four different Buyers have four distinct perceptions of the same business "reality."

The salesperson unskilled in strategy often mishandles a mixed field. As we've mentioned, a natural tendency among those sales representatives who like to play things by ear is to focus on the Buyers they like, or who like them, rather than see to it that all the relevant bases are covered. You see this all the time with regard to Response Modes. A sales representative who sees Growth possibilities approaches the ABCO company with a proposal designed to boost production. He finds that only a lone User Buyer perceives the situation as he does; all the other Buyers are in Trouble, focusing on a "trivial" problem. But because he and the User Buyer agree, the sales representative concentrates on him—and quickly loses the order to a competitor who addresses the Trouble seen by the other Buying Influences.

The same sales representative might approach ABCO six months later with a surefire cure for absenteeism—a problem revealed by a Technical Buyer in personnel. It turns out that all the other Buyers are now in Even Keel. They're willing to live with the time loss because productivity has never been higher, and they don't want to jeopardize what they have. Crying Trouble in this kind of situation might bring the sales representative closer to the personnel manager, but it would alienate everyone else.

The strategic rep doesn't simply play ball with the Buyer

whose perception he shares. He adopts a selling strategy that covers all of the bases, and that takes equally seriously the perceptions of all the Buying Influences involved in the sales goal.

Covering All the Bases—Again

One of the most serious errors you can make in a Complex Sale is to ignore or abandon a key Buying Influence because that person's perception of current reality doesn't match yours. You don't have to see eye to eye with your Buyers in order to sell them. You do have to respect each one's perception, since it's to that perception you're selling.

We've emphasized the importance of covering all the Buying Influence bases for your sales goal, and of your managing the contacts with the key players in such a way that each one is covered by the person best qualified to do so. It's also important that the people you arrange to have covering those bases understand that it's the individual Buyers' perceptions of reality, not their own, that determine how best to approach each one. The starting point is always the same: It's how the individual Buyer *feels* about the current situation.

These feelings will almost always be at variance with each other, even when the "facts" are obvious to you. Frequently, a situation that spells Trouble to one Buying Influence will simply reinforce the Overconfident attitude of another Buying Influence in the same company. Therefore, you have to manage each sale on the admittedly unconventional assumption that there's no such thing as reality— only individual perceptions of reality. And you have to see that each base is covered by a person who's willing to take the individual Buyer's feelings about the situation as a valid starting point for discussion.

You, as the manager of the sale, need to survey the entire field of players, and work toward a match of modes whenever that's possible. Generally the best way to do that—the way that most effectively employs the principle of Leverage from Strength—is to approach your Buyers in Trouble and Growth first, and then get them to work with you on the Even Keel and Overconfident Buyers.

In summary, it's possible to sell a proposal to a mixed field of Buyers, but only if you employ the basic principles of Response Modes:

1. The starting point for approaching each individual Buyer is to learn that Buyer's current perception of the business situation and his or her perceived discrepancy between reality and results.

·2. Each Buyer base must be covered by a person who accepts this as the starting point, and who's best qualified to approach that individual Buyer.

3. Always use Leverage from Strength to bring about a match of modes from a mixed field of responses.

You'll practice these principles now, in a Personal Workshop on Buyer Response Modes.

Personal Workshop 4: Response Modes

Step 1: Identify each player's Response Mode.

Take out the Buying Influences Chart you started in Chapter 5 and focus in on how each Buyer in turn feels about the *immediate* situation, with regard to the specific change *you* are offering to introduce to that person's business environment—that is, your sales proposal. Ask yourself how that proposal affects the environment, and whether or not it can close a perceived gap (discrepancy) between reality and results. Then, on your chart, write in the letters *G* for Growth, *T* for Trouble, *EK* for Even Keel, and *OC* for Overconfident, depending on how each Buyer perceives the situation. Your Buying Influences Chart should now look something like the example on page 135.

You may find—in fact you almost certainly will find—that identifying your Buyers' modes isn't an entirely straightforward process. Inevitably you'll come across a Buyer whom you can't figure out, or one who seems to be straddling the fence between Growth and Even Keel. That's all right. Since Buyers can be erratic in their perception, and thus in their responses, it would be unreasonable to expect them to fall into slots like pegs into prearranged holes. It would also be unrealistic to expect them to stay there throughout the selling cycle. In reality the Response Modes often appear as permutations and combinations, off the "norm." And they're *dynamic,* not static. That's why we emphasize the need for constant reassessment of position.

```
BUYING INFLUENCES CHART

ECONOMIC : releases $ $        USER : judges impact
                                            on job
  DAN FARLEY    G              DORIS GREEN    G

                               HARRY BARNES   EK


TECHNICAL : screens out        COACH (ES) : guides me
                                            on this sale
  GARY STEINBERG    T          DORIS GREEN    G
  WILL JOHNSON    OC           ANDY KELLY     T
  HARRY BARNES    EK
```

But you can still identify where your Buyers are right now, with regard to your current proposal. The emphasis is on *this moment.* Remember that the four Response Modes aren't categories or types of people; they're *situation perceptions.* All we want you to do is to identify each of your Buyers' responses *today* to the change you're offering. Ask yourself how each one is talking at this point in the developing sale:

- If Dan Farley is asking for faster delivery or bigger orders, he's by definition in Growth Mode.
- If Gary Steinberg has an inventory problem, he's by definition in Trouble Mode—even if he's often oriented toward Growth.
- If Harry Barnes is saying, "I like things just the

way they are," he's in Even Keel; if he's smugly self-assured about how great things are, he's probably Overconfident.

If after about five minutes on this step you still can't determine a Buyer's current Response Mode, place a Red Flag by that name. Then move on to the next step.

Step 2: Rate your Buyers.

Now that you've identified and listed on the Buying Influences Chart all of the relevant players for each of the four Buying Influence roles for your sale, and each person's Response Mode, assess where you stand with each of them by asking yourself one key question:

> *How does each person feel right now with regard to my current sales proposal?*

Notice that you're not trying to find out how the Buyers feel about *you* as a person, or about *your company,* but how they feel about *your current sales objective.*

In our programs we ask our participants to rate their Buyers on a scale of −5 to +5. You should do the same thing now. Each of your Buyers will be somewhere on that scale: wildly enthusiastic about your proposal, vehemently opposed to it, or somewhere in between. Next to the names of those who are enthusiastic sponsors, place a +5 on your Buying Influences Chart. Next to those who are strongly opposed or who won't even see you, place a −5. For the Buyers who are somewhere in between, place appropriate numerical ratings (+1, −2, +4) next to their names.

Rating your Buyers in this fashion isn't an exact science. It's not meant to be. What you're trying to do is to determine *how well each base is covered,* based on how you perceive each Buyer to feel about what you're trying to do. Trusting your gut reactions here is just as important as it was in the workshop on position, when you concentrated on your own feelings about the sale. Those feelings, we know, are not infallible, but they remain a necessary guide in assessing which Buyers are already in your camp and which ones are likely to cause trouble.

Step 3: Test these Ratings.

In our programs we use the informal scale below to test our participants' assessments of their Buyers' feelings.

RATINGS

+ 5 Enthusiastic Advocate

+ 4 Strongly Supportive

+ 3 Supportive

+ 2 Interested

+ 1 Will Go Along

− 1 Probably Won't Resist

− 2 Uninterested

− 3 Mildly Negative

− 4 Strong for Competition

− 5 Antagonistic Anti-Sponsor

Measure your Buyer ratings now against this scale. Look at the numbers you've placed next to their names and then ask yourself the following questions:

- If I've rated this Buyer as +5, is the person really an enthusiastic advocate of my proposal?
- If I've rated someone as +1, will the person definitely at least go along with the proposal?
- If I've rated someone as −1, will that Buyer at least stay out of the way? Will any resistance be slight?
- If I've rated a Buyer as −5, is this a major imped-

iment to the proposal? Will the person work actively to block the sale.

Ask yourself similar questions about the Buyers who fall elsewhere on the informal scale. And note two important points:

One: It's only theoretically possible for a Buyer to be neutral to your proposal. You see that we have no zero on our rating scale; that's because, in our experience, Buyers are always at least slightly positive or slightly negative about sales proposals. If you have a Buyer who seems firmly on the fence, you're probably misreading that person's feelings.

Two: The same thing is true of those Buying Influences whom you haven't yet contacted at all. Remember, this is an exercise in testing how well you've covered the bases; an uncontacted Buyer is by definition an uncovered base. Don't guess about how such people feel. Until you know for sure how each one feels, you should consider every one a Red Flag. They may not turn out to be strong antisponsors; but *in terms of your current position* with them, you have to consider them so.

After you've rated your Buyers and tested those ratings against the scale, your Buying Influences Chart should look something like the example below.

BUYING INFLUENCES CHART	
ECONOMIC : releases $ $	USER : judges impact on job
DAN FARLEY G +2	DORIS GREEN G +3
	HARRY BARNES EK −2
TECHNICAL : screens out	COACH (ES) : guides me on *this* sale
GARY STEINBERG T −4	DORIS GREEN G +3
WILL JOHNSON OC −4	ANDY KELLY T +4
HARRY BARNES EK −2	

Step 4: Analyze your information.

You now have each Buyer assessed twice: once in terms of modes and again in terms of overall feelings about your proposal. Now compare these two assessments. Looking at the mode and numerical ratings you gave your Buyers, determine your current strengths and weaknesses (Red Flag areas) based on the composite picture. Look especially for inconsistencies. If you have a Buyer in Overconfident Mode, for example, whom you've rated as +3, there's something logically inconsistent in your analysis. That Buyer is either Overconfident or +3, not both. Label that kind of inconsistency with a Red Flag: You need to learn more about this Buyer to develop an effective strategy.

Similarly, if you have a Coach who isn't *strongly* in favor of your proposal, look at your data again. The best Coaches are generally in Growth Mode, but to be really effective—to fulfill their role of helping you to make the sale—they *have* to be in either Growth or Trouble. If you've labeled your Coach EK or OC, or given that person a rating of less than about +3, then you don't really have a Coach. "Fire" this Coach and find someone else.

In comparing the two assessments, finally, remember that Buyers you've rated with a plus must always be in either Growth or Trouble, although Buyers in Growth and Trouble Mode can also rate minuses—they might, for example, still like your competitor's proposal better than yours. Buyers in Even Keel and Overconfident Mode are by definition negative: There is no such thing as a +3 Buyer in Even Keel.

Look also for matches of mode—both those that already exist and those you might be able to create. Think about not only how the various Buyers relate individually to you, but how they're integral parts of a composite response to your proposal. Which Buyers share Growth or Trouble Mode? These Buyers constitute your areas of Strength. How can you use these Buyers to overcome the poor receptivity to change that's evident in Buyers in Even Keel or Overconfident Mode?

Step 5: Revise your Alternate Positions list.

You should now have a pretty good idea of the level of receptivity of each of your key players to your current sales proposal. Now take out your Alternate Positions list again and use the data you've uncovered in the last two chapters to revise it. Go over each option on the list and ask yourself this question:

> *How does the level of receptivity of each of my Buying Influences affect the viability of this option?*

Then drop those options that no longer seem workable. Modify those that should be modified. Add any new options suggested by the lessons of these two chapters.

We'll make the same provisos here that we did in the previous workshop:

- Continue to be *inclusive,* listing less than ideal options as well as those that you consider right on target. You're not ready yet to identify a first-choice Alternate Position.
- Continue to be *specific.* Be sure that every Alternate Position you list relates to your specific sales proposal, as it stands right now.
- Continue to *test* your Alternate Positions by making sure that each one capitalizes on a Strength, eliminates or reduces the impact of a Red Flag, or does both.

Since our current focus is Response Modes, you'll want to pay special attention to this Key Element as you assess your list. For example, consider the option we suggested you might employ to get to the hypothetical Dan Farley: getting your friendly User Buyer, Doris Green, to show him that you could increase his productivity by 15 percent. Remembering that this option has to be inclusive, specific, and testable, you might judge its current value to your strategy by asking yourself questions like these:

- Is productivity increase a high-priority item for Farley right now? I have him down as in moderate

(+2) Growth Mode; do I need to reassess that rating?

- Is Farley's reluctance to see me evidence that he's not in Growth Mode at all? Might he be in Even Keel—and therefore uninterested in the Growth points of my sale?
- Does Doris Green have all the information *she* needs to sell Farley on the 15 percent increase?
- If Farley is less enthusiastic about Growth than he appears to be, can I show him that ignoring my proposal will eventually get him into Trouble? Can I sell him my Growth proposal as a means of avoiding Trouble?
- What feedback do I need to get from Green to be sure she's the right person to sell Farley? Is *she* as enthusiastic about my proposal as I need her to be?

These questions, of course, are only samples. But they should give you the general idea we're stressing. *Every selling strategy is only as good as its most recent reassessment.* Our point in asking you to test all the items on your Alternate Positions list in this way is to ensure that that list— which will be so vital to your Action Plan—continues to be up to date.

In a sense the entire first half of this book can be seen as an analytical machine designed to produce one meticulously tested product. That product is your Alternate Positions list. By now you should have already begun to work out some of the bugs in its design. Put it away for the time being. You'll be testing it again very soon.

► 9 ◄

THE IMPORTANCE OF WINNING

We began this book by approaching your sales objective from the viewpoint of *your* needs. In a Personal Workshop on position in Chapter 3, we asked you to assess your current feelings about that objective and to begin considering Alternate Positions that would make you feel more certain about its outcome.

In the past several chapters, we've been approaching your sales objective from the viewpoint of your various Buyers' needs. We've given you a framework for analyzing *their* feelings and for predicting the likelihood of your sales proposal's success based on those feelings.

Now we're going to bring those two approaches together by considering the sale as a way of fulfilling both your own *and* the Buyers' needs. We're going to present a model of selling that takes *mutual satisfaction* as the foundation of long-term success.

The emphasis here is on "long term." By using the Win-

Win model we present in this chapter, you'll be able to increase your success predictably over time.

Getting an individual piece of business can be a relatively simple task—if all you want is that one contract. The career professional in the Complex Sale, however, isn't content with pocketing the immediate commission. Such a salesperson wants:

- The order
- Satisfied customers
- Long-term relationships
- Repeat business
- Strong referrals

As a Strategic Selling professional, you want every sales objective, no matter how large or how small, to move predictably toward an outcome that delivers on *all* of these goals.

The key to getting all your sales objectives to do that lies in understanding the concept of Winning.

Winning: A Key to Long-Term Success

A lot of nonsense has been written about Winning, and much of it can be fatal to the sales representative. If you think, for example, that Winning has anything to do with intimidating your Buying Influences, you're likely to get a rude shock when you look for new leads and repeat business. Or if you think that a Win can be measured in simple monetary terms, you're going to be shortchanging your customers—and eventually yourself as well.

Our definition of Winning is different from the others you've encountered. The heart of it is the notion of *self-interest*. We've said that you Win in a buy/sell encounter when you come out of it feeling positive. The *reason* you feel positive is that you perceive that encounter as having served your personal self-interest.

Self-interest is misunderstood and criticized by many well-meaning people. Many sales representatives, even though they strive energetically to Win, are still reluctant to admit the importance of Winning in their lives, and some actually feel guilty about Winning. This happens because they confuse self-interest with selfishness, and conclude that looking out for your own self-interest is morally wrong.

People who view self-interest in this way, however, are distorting its true meaning. Actually, self-interest is an absolutely necessary, and in the long run very beneficial, natural instinct. It's this simple: All living things must serve their own self-interest or die.

Serving one's self-interest is equally crucial in the broad social order, and in that microcosm of the social order that is selling. Human beings in all social situations serve their own self-interest by attaining what they see as personal Wins. In selling, they do this by agreeing to business transactions that they feel will be to their *personal* advantage.

You already know this about yourself. You know that the sales that leave you feeling satisfied are those in which you have Won because some aspect of your self-interest— financial, personal, social—has been served by the transaction.

The same thing is true of your Buying Influences. They enter the buying-selling encounter hoping to Win too. And they leave the encounter satisfied when, and *only* when, they feel that it has served their personal self-interest.

The Four Quadrants of the Win-Win Matrix

Even though both you and the Buyer enter your sales encounters hoping that you will Win, that isn't always the way things turn out. Every buy/sell encounter can have one of four possible outcomes. These four outcomes are represented in the quadrants of what we call the Win-Win Matrix, shown on page 145. You're always positioned in one of these quadrants at the conclusion of any face-to-face buy/sell encounter.

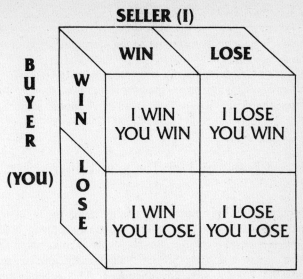

Win-Win Matrix

As we describe these quadrants, keep two interrelated points in mind:

First: Each quadrant of the matrix describes a relationship between you and *each* of your Buyers—not between you and "the account" or "the sale" as a whole. You cannot manage a sale so that any given buying company Wins. You can—and must—manage each sales objective so that every one of the Buying Influences for that objective sees a personal Win in the sale. Your goal in utilizing the Win-Win design is to achieve mutual satisfaction between you and *all* of your Buyers; if you leave even one of them with the feeling of losing, you'll be severely hampering your chances of maintaining good relations with that person and therefore the account over time.

Second: The matrix describes not only how you're *currently* positioned with each Buyer (during the selling cycle), but also how you're positioned with each Buyer *after the sale is made*. The assumption behind each quadrant of the matrix is that you've gotten, or will get, the business. But making *this* sale is not enough. Every *closed* sale can be a Lose as well as a Win, both for you and for your Buyers. Therefore, we use the Win-Win Matrix to describe the probable *long-term* outcome of a sale, assuming the order is received.

For optimum sales results over time, you have to try to direct every sales objective into the same quadrant of that matrix—the Win-Win, or "joint-venture," quadrant.

I Win–You Win: The Joint-Venture Quadrant

Webster defines adventure as "an undertaking involving danger and unknown risks." The naïve salesperson often welcomes adventure, seeing the Buyer as an adversary, the order as a prize, and the selling cycle as a fascinating, unpredictable contest with the customer. This adventurous approach to selling frequently leads to trouble, because it intensifies uncertainty—precisely the element that the good strategist wants to reduce.

We tell the participants in our programs that, rather than seeking *ad*venture, they should strive to develop *joint* ventures in which their Buying Influences are seen not as threats from the outside but as members of their own teams. Those of us who have prospered by using Strategic Selling know that good selling is never an adversarial game in which the Buyers' Losses are our Wins, but one in which the Buyers' Losses are our Losses too, and their Wins always serve our self-interest as well as theirs. We understand that only by enlisting our Buyers as *partners* in mutually supportive joint ventures can we hope to achieve mutual satisfaction over time.

Mutuality of Dependence

You know this isn't true of all social situations. Certain inherently adversarial encounters cannot be managed as joint ventures. In a baseball game or a divorce proceeding, for example, you can't expect the opposing sides to cooperate. But in any situation where *mutuality of dependence* is important, you must learn to hang together, or you will, as Ben Franklin observed of the bickering colonies, certainly hang separately. American labor and management have recently (and belatedly) begun to apply this fact in their dealings with each other—thus changing the traditionally bitter atmosphere of collective bargaining. Unfortunately, up to this point American labor and management have tended to see each other as enemies. Japanese business, of course, thrives on the opposite assumption—and we're now catching on to how well that assumption works.

Think about your own best sales: the ones from which you've come away feeling both emotionally and financially satisfied. Think about a sale in which (a) you satisfactorily served your *own* self-interest, (b) you also served the self-interest of your *Buyers,* and (c) those Buyers *knew* that you'd done this. That sale was by definition one with a Win-Win outcome.

There's nothing more satisfying to a sales professional than managing a difficult sale into the partnership, or Win-Win, quadrant of the matrix. Every real professional wants *all* of his or her sales to end up there.

There's nothing altruistic about this. We're not advising you to adopt a joint-venture approach to your customers out of politeness or ethics. Our reason is purely pragmatic. When your Buyers Win, you Win, because you get the repeat business and new leads you need to make both current and future sales quality sales. Thus, serving your Buyers' self-interests is ultimately the best way of serving your own.

I Win–You Lose: Beating the Buyer

The general public seems to think that everyone in sales wants to manipulate prospects into this second quadrant of the Win-Win Matrix.

Examples of the I Win–You Lose scenario abound in popular stories—from the used-car salesman who sets the odometer back to the appliance dealer who reneges on his warranty, from the messenger service that delivers your package two days late to the mail-order house that doesn't deliver it at all. The Federal Trade Commission and the post office are continually tracking down and restraining those lovers of the Win-Lose approach who have actually broken the law. But it's easy to play I Win–You Lose without ever breaking the law.

You can, for example, play Win-Lose in one of the following ways:

1. You can sell someone something at an inflated price at a time when that person's urgent business needs make it impossible to refuse.

2. You can describe the service capabilities of your firm unrealistically, leading the customer to believe that you'll correct any problem with your product instantly.

3. You can place a model in the Buyer's firm that's more (or less) sophisticated than what's really needed.

In each of these adversarial, and adventurist, scenarios, you're setting the Buyer up for a fall in return for a quick commission.

In spite of what the public has been led to believe, this "common" and "traditional" approach to sales is neither common nor traditional—at least not among successful salespeople. The *best* companies and the *best* sales representatives have always understood that, wherever repeat business is important, playing I Win–You Lose is a disastrous policy. The only positive thing it can get you is an initial order. It also gets you the last thing any salesperson wants: a customer out for revenge.

Buyer's Revenge

The principal reason that you should avoid playing I Win–You Lose is that the Win-Lose quadrant is short-term and *unstable;* given enough time, it always degenerates into Lose-Lose. So playing Win-Lose with anyone with whom you expect to have future business contacts isn't in your *own* self-interest.

Sooner or later, the people you've forced to Lose are going to discover that you've done them wrong. To refer back to the examples we've just given, they'll discover:

1. That the competition's price was 35 percent lower than yours for a similar product
2. That service requests aren't being answered as you promised they would be
3. That your product, in spite of its technical capabilities, isn't suited to the buying firm's particular needs

These things may not happen right away, but if you've really ignored a Buyer's self-interest, eventually that person is going to find out. The *best* you can hope for, when that happens, is that the Buyer will simply walk away and forget about you. A counterattack, by spreading the word around that you can't be trusted, is much more likely. Either way, you too will eventually Lose.

We've already mentioned one classic example of Buyer's Revenge: the sale to a textile company of the trouble-shooting program that never made it past the trial period because the sales representative had ignored the User Buyers. Ignoring them in this case was tantamount to saying, "I don't care about your self-interest. I can Win here even if you Lose." As subsequent events showed, that was a reckless assumption. The User Buyers simply saw to it that the sales representative's program didn't do the job. And the ultimate outcome of the sale wasn't even the unsatisfactory Win-Lose, but the worst of all possible outcomes Lose-Lose.

I Lose–You Win: Doing the Buyer a "Favor"

Every professional knows that playing I Win–You Lose is actually far less common that playing I Lose–You Win. Here the sales representative plays martyr, doing the Buyer a "favor" at the selling organization's expense. "I will deliberately Lose," the sales representative says in effect, "so that you, Mr. Customer, can Win." You've seen this many times in your work. One of our program participants complained that it was so common in his firm that it was "practically a company policy." Every time a sales representative gets an initial order by selling at a ridiculously low price, every time an extraordinary discount for bulk sales is offered, every time free service, free samples, or some other fringe benefit is thrown in with the order, the game being played is I Lose–You Win.

The rationale behind this approach is that the customer will be impressed with the representative's generosity and reciprocate in the future. "I'll scratch your back now," the sales representative implies, "and you can scratch mine later." Unfortunately it doesn't always work out that way.

The problem here is one of perception. When you play Lose-Win, you give the Buyer *a false sense of reality,* one that cannot be maintained indefinitely but that appears to be the norm. When you "buy the business" by giving away your product, services, or time, *you set your Buyer up to Lose* in the future by unrealistically raising his expectations.

No company is going to keep giving away its products or services forever. When your company decides it's time for the devil to be paid, you're going to have to give your "Win" customer the decidedly unpleasant message "Now it's your turn to Lose." Typically, the Buyer who hears that message forgets all about the "favors" you did him. He sees you playing Win-Lose with him *now,* and sets out to take revenge. When that happens, you both Lose.

Ultimately the Lose-Win quadrant, like the Win-Lose quadrant, is *unstable;* it too always *degenerates* into Lose-Lose, and therefore isn't in your own self-interest.

When—and How—to Play Lose-Win

We're not saying that you should *never* play Lose-Win. In certain situations it can be a useful *short-term* strategy. There's nothing like an introductory discount, for example, to interest a Buyer in a new product. But if you play Lose-Win, *let the Buyer know it.* And make sure its understood as well that the supposedly free lunch you're offering is a strictly limited offer.

The most common uses of the Lose-Win strategy in our society occur in the consumer products market. There the manufacturers who employ it don't have to explain to their customers what they're doing, because it's common knowledge. When the local supermarket stops using Barko dog food as a loss leader and reverts to the normal price, nobody cries, "Why are you trying to scalp us?" When the Super Sudzee Soap Company hangs a free sample of a new product on your front door in January, you don't call up a month later and say, "Where's my February freebie?" In the consumer products field, it's generally understood that playing Lose-Win by means of sampling or loss leaders is only a short-term gambit.

That may not be generally understood in your field of business. Never assume that your Buyers understand it. The most serious mistake you can make in playing Lose-Win is *failing to tell your Buyers that they're getting a special deal.* This leads to constant misunderstandings and resentment among Buyers who thought the special was the norm—and who therefore react to the real norm, when it's introduced, as if it were inflated or unfair. You can avoid this unwelcome situation by spelling out clearly what you're doing.

Put it in writing too. Don't rely on "friendship" to keep things on a sound footing when you know that, somewhere down the line, you're going to have to reintroduce your favored Buyer to reality. Unless the specialness of the Lose-Win scenario is stipulated on paper—either in the contract, on the invoice, or in a separate letter of understanding—it will be extremely easy for your Buyer to balk at your future terms.

Even if you play Lose-Win "properly," however, it's still only a short-term strategy. Your ultimate goal remains to position yourself in the Win-Win quadrant with all your Buying Influences.

I Lose–You Lose: The Catchall Quadrant

We call the Lose-Lose quadrant a catchall quadrant because it catches all the sales that you don't consciously and
actively *manage* into a Win-Win outcome. We've said that
each quadrant of the matrix describes a situation both during the selling cycle and at the sale's end, *after* the order is
taken. Unless you ensure that all of your Buyers see personal Wins in the sale, it will inevitably degenerate into a
long-term Lose-Lose outcome—no matter what it looks
like at the time the order is taken.

This is true for Win-Lose situations and Lose-Win situations, for the reasons we've explained above. It's also true
for that very small number of sales that, at some point in
the selling cycle, are already operating in the Lose-Lose
quadrant. For example, a customer who desperately needs
a product he sees as overpriced might insist on extraordinary delivery schedules as a way of justifying the expense.
The schedules might make the seller feel *he's* Losing, while
the high price would make the customer feel he's losing
also.

Such scenarios, however, are rare. Only a minuscule pro-
portion of the selling population *sets out* to play Lose-Lose.
Except for a few masochists and wackos, people in sales
generally understand that nobody has anything to gain from
working toward mutual destruction.

Your Buyers understand this too, which is why, if you
find yourself in an obvious Lose-Lose situation, you should
let your Buyers know that you're not any happier about it
than they are. Once Buyers in this situation understand
that you're not trying to beat them, they'll usually be willing to work *with* you, so that no one Loses.

The bottom line is this. Even though almost no one *sets
out* to play Lose-Lose, virtually every sale can still *end up*
as a mutual Lose unless it's effectively *managed* into a Win-
Win outcome for you and all your Buyers.

Your Joint-Venture Team

The best sales professionals understand intuitively the importance of the Win-Win dynamic. We all know people who seem to have a gift for making things happen: people who are always in the *right* place at the *right* time, who always know the *right* players to contact for a given objective, who always know what to say to each player—and whose revenue figures reflect their uncannily consistent good luck. When you examine how they operate, though, you find that their success has nothing to do with luck. They're successful because they understand the fundamental biological and psychological law that *everyone must serve his or her self-interest.* They put that law into practice by striving constantly to serve their own *and* their Buyers' self-interest. And they make sure that every Buyer knows it.

Each time you serve a Buyer's self-interest, you enlist that person as a member of a joint-venture team whose basic goal is mutual satisfaction. When you and your Buyers practice teamwork in this way, you make it that much easier for all of you to Win together. After that has happened once, you've established the expectations and necessary conditions for it to happen again, in every new sale you undertake.

Your Current Win-Win Position

This is an ongoing process. Your position in the Win-Win Matrix must be constantly reassessed throughout the selling cycle to ensure that, as business conditions and key players change, you're continually moving toward Win-Win outcomes with all your Buying Influences.

You may begin this process of assessment now, by making a preliminary survey of the Buying Influences for your chosen sales objective. We've said that you serve your own self-interest best when you serve the self-interest of each of your Buying Influences. Test whether or not you're doing that by assessing each one in turn. Start, for example, with the Economic Buyer (Dan Farley on our sample Buying Influences Chart) and ask yourself these questions:

- Am I sincerely and earnestly trying to serve Farley's self-interest in this sale? That is, do I really *want* him to Win?
- Does Farley understand that I'm trying to serve his self-interest? That is, does he *know* I want him to Win?

Then ask the same questions about each of the other Buying Influences on your chart.

If the answers here are negative, or if you're not *sure* of the answers, note that as an element of risk—a Red Flag area—of the sale. Perhaps you aren't yet in the Win-Win quadrant of the matrix with this Buying Influence and you need to *manage* your relationship with him or her toward a Win-Win outcome.

Even if the answers are clear and positive, you still need to remember that your current Win-Win position is only that—a current position. You need to *maintain* that position, so that you're still in the Win-Win quadrant through the end of the selling cycle.

You can manage your sales into the Win-Win quadrant and maintain your Win-Win position with each Buying Influence by using a Key Element of strategy that we'll introduce now: the concept of Win-Results.

► 10 ◄
KEY ELEMENT 4: WIN-RESULTS

Many of our Fortune 500 clients—including Coca-Cola, Hewlett-Packard, and Wilson Sporting Goods find our Win-Win concept so useful that they incorporate it into their own selling philosophies. Some companies have even adopted the Win-Win Matrix itself into their sales presentations. As a marketing executive for one of them told us recently, "We've made your matrix a standard visual aid in our presentations; it's an ideal tool for showing our customers that we're on their side."

To use the Win-Win concept as effectively as these corporate giants do, you need the same philosophical commitment—and something more. You need a practical, tested method for implementing the Win-Win philosophy in the real world. We're going to present that method now.

Implementing the Win-Win philosophy means making the Win-Win quadrant of the Matrix *operational* for each and every one of your Buying Influences—in other words, making each one realize that he or she has Won. How, speaking in practical terms, do you accomplish this?

The answer is that you give each Buying Influence something which will demonstrate that you've served that person's self-interest. That something is *Win-Results*.

What Are Win-Results?

"Win-Results" is a term that we coined early in the development of our Strategic Selling programs. In the several years we've been presenting those programs, we've found that the Win-Results concept always generates more discussion, more confusion, and more ultimate enlightenment than any other single concept. We've also found that the participants in our programs grasp the concept most quickly if we begin with a few definitions. The Win-Results concept derives from the following terms:

- *Selling:* Selling is a professional exercise in showing all your Buying Influences how your product or service serves their individual self-interest.
- *Product:* A product is designed to improve or fix some business process of your customer. In Strategic Selling, "product" is taken to mean either a product or a service—whatever *you* are selling.
- *Process:* A process is an activity or series of activities that converts what exists right now into something else. Examples of business processes would be shipping, invoicing, production, research and development, quality control.
- *Result:* A Result is the *impact* of a product on one or more of your customer's processes. Results are objective and corporate—that is, they generally affect many people at the same time, although they don't affect those people in the same *way*.
- *Win:* A Win is the fulfillment of a subjective, personal promise made to oneself to serve one's self-interest in some special way. Wins are always *different* for different people.

- *Win-Result:* A Win-Result is an objective business Result that gives one or more of your Buying Influences a subjective, personal Win.

Since you can position yourself in the Win-Win quadrant of the matrix only by delivering Win-Results, it's essential to understand both halves of the Win-Results concept. You can't ignore Results because a Result must take place *before* a Buyer will perceive a Win; it's a *precondition* to any Win. On the other hand, you can't ignore your individual Buyers' Wins either. If you concentrate *only* on Results, sooner or later you're going to deliver one of your Buyers a Result that's irrelevant—or, even worse, that's interpreted as a personal Lose.

This happens *constantly* in the Complex Sale. We'll give you just one example to demonstrate the problems it can create.

A program participant told us recently that he was having a difficult time understanding why he couldn't push a certain sale through. It was an "ideal" sales possibility, but, for reasons he couldn't fathom, it was being blocked by the president of the buying firm. "It's a perfect fit with their needs," we were told. "We've got a solid, approved payment schedule. We're even giving the lowest bid. If I were that guy, I would have signed three months ago. But he just won't budge."

"Tell us about the president," we said. "What's he like?"

"You mean personally?" our participant asked.

"Yes," we told him. "Personally."

He proceeded to describe someone who had built up a company from nothing, who had directed it energetically for thirty years, and who in another two months was about to begin a long-postponed retirement. As he talked, we got the picture of a tired, preoccupied executive who had to force himself to come to work in the morning. It gradually became apparent that, however good the Results our participant was offering him, they were unlikely to have an effect on the man, because in a sense he'd already stepped down. "It sounds like all this guy wants," we suggested, "is to be left alone. Is there a Win in this sale for him?"

No, our program participant suddenly realized. And once he realized that, he adopted a strategy which, given the president's intransigence, was the only reasonable one for the situation. He decided to wait the old man out.

In three months, the sales representative knew, the company would have a new president—and the sale would have a new Economic Buyer. So the salesman bided his time, adopting the strategy we recommended for dealing with an Even Keel Buyer, and kept up regular, low-profile contacts with the buying firm.

When the new president came in, this patience paid off. The new president, eager to start off with a success, was delighted to approve a low-bid, perfect-fit order. Approving that order not only got his company the Result he wanted, it also served his personal self-interest in a way it couldn't have served that of the retiring president: It made him look immediately like a go-getter and problem solver.

Same Result, different Wins. The lesson is clear. Although a given Result may have a single, clearly defined impact on a business process, it will always have different impacts on the Buying Influences involved in that process. And the personal impact can be negative even when the Result is positive.

We can put this lesson in the form of a Strategic Selling axiom: *Companies get Results, but only people Win.* Since your basic selling goal is to show each of your Buyers how your product or service serves his or her self-interest, delivering Results alone obviously isn't enough. You've got to understand how each of them, *personally*, Wins, because understanding that is what will put you in the Win-Win quadrant.

To make the distinction between Results and Wins more visible to you, the chart below presents the basic characteristics of each.

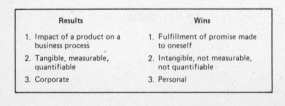

Results	Wins
1. Impact of a product on a business process	1. Fulfillment of promise made to oneself
2. Tangible, measurable, quantifiable	2. Intangible, not measurable, not quantifiable
3. Corporate	3. Personal

Using this chart as an overview, we'll explain the two halves of the Win-Results concept more fully. Since Results must happen *before* any Buyer perceives a Win, we start with Results.

Characteristics of Results

1. A Result is the impact of your product or service on one or more of your customer's business processes.

You need to affect your customers' business processes positively because process is the ultimate reason that anything happens, in or out of business; process is what *changes* one set of conditions into another. As the cooking process converts uncooked meat and potatoes into a prime rib dinner, as the exercise process transforms body fat into muscle, so too your customers' business processes are designed to convert one situation into another.

We've mentioned that such activities as shipping, invoicing, and quality control can all be seen as processes. In fact, virtually any business activity, from the sweeping out of a stockroom to the highest-level boardroom debates, can be viewed as a process, designed to convert some "raw material" into something of use.

Naturally everyone involved in the conversation would like that something of use to be something better as well. That's where you come in. *You are important to your Buyers when, and only when, your product or service impacts positively on one or more of their processes.* You can do this in one of two ways:

- You can *improve* an already good process.
- You can *fix* something that has gone wrong.

This relates back to our discussion of Response Modes in Chapter 8. We said there that Buyers are receptive to change, and therefore likely to buy, when they're in either Growth or Trouble Mode. In each of those modes, they're looking for a specific impact on their processes. In Growth, they want you to *improve* things. In Trouble, they want you to *fix* something. In either case, you become valuable to them because your product or service positively affects their business processes.

2. A Result is tangible, measurable, and quantifiable.

If you sell Doris Green an inventory control system to reduce her overtime by 16 percent, you don't have to know anything about her, or about her perception of reality, to determine the Result you've delivered: By definition the Result here is 16 percent overtime reduction.

Green, of course, may not *want* this reduction, and if she doesn't, then you'd be foolish to deliver this particular Result to her. But for the purposes of objective definition, her *impressions* of the Result don't matter. Results are impersonal and value free; they exist "out there," objectively.

3. Results are corporate.

By "corporate" here we don't mean that they're necessarily seen as Results on the corporation level (although that's often the case), but simply that they're *shared* by various people in the buying organization. Since processes are interrelated in the modern corporation—and therefore in the Complex Sale—any Result you deliver is likely to influence more than one process at the same time. Even when it alters only one process (say, Green's inventory control), there will still be *many people* involved in that process (Green's whole department), and all of those people will share the Result that you've contributed.

Characteristics of Wins

1. A Win is the fulfillment of a promise made to oneself.

The need to Win is essential for survival. When people feel they've Won, it's because they've fulfilled conscious or unconscious promises to themselves to serve their own self-interest. Two further points should be made about such promises.

First, promises to oneself aren't fabricated out of thin

air. They evolve for each person from the general *culture,* and the many specific *subcultures,* in which the individual grows up; the dreams and designs each of us has reflect our basic *values and attitudes* toward life—and these values and attitudes are, to a great extent, culturally determined. You wouldn't expect a Laotian mountain dweller, living largely on the subsistence level, to see a Win in the gift of a dishwasher or a library card. We all Win within the context of specific cultural environments.

Second, promises to oneself *change* as values and attitudes change, and in some instances they become outmoded before they're actually fulfilled. This is especially true in a culture such as ours, where change and future shock are such constant presences. The middle-aged man who in his youth promised himself a Florida condominium and a Bentley may find, once he's in a position to get them, that they've lost their importance to him: They're no longer seen as Wins. In assessing Wins, therefore, you always have to be attentive to the *current* perceptions of the potential Winner involved.

2. Wins are intangible, not measurable, and not quantifiable.

For most human beings, the most important things in life are subjective rewards such as family feeling, a sense of security, and the pleasure of knowing you've done your best. Satisfying and enriching those feelings are the ultimate Wins.

Psychologists are always "discovering" this about people in the sales profession. You've probably seen the attitude surveys that these social scientists give members of our profession. In every one we've seen, the researchers reach the same "surprising" conclusion that what really turns good sales representatives on is not their six-figure commissions but job satisfaction, recognition and challenge. The popular belief that the top salespeople are in it just for the money always turns out to be a misconception. In every assessment of "sales motivators" we've seen, sales representatives put money pretty far down the list, behind a host of less tangible, less concrete rewards.

The same thing is true of people on the "other side" of the buy/sell encounter. Your Buyers, like you, remain in their profession largely because it allows them to achieve the intangible recognition and satisfactions they need to Win.

The intangible rewards that may serve as Wins for individuals are enormously varied. The following list of sample Wins suggests their range and variety.

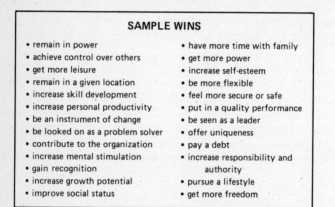

SAMPLE WINS

- remain in power
- achieve control over others
- get more leisure
- remain in a given location
- increase skill development
- increase personal productivity
- be an instrument of change
- be looked on as a problem solver
- contribute to the organization
- increase mental stimulation
- gain recognition
- increase growth potential
- improve social status

- have more time with family
- get more power
- increase self-esteem
- be more flexible
- feel more secure or safe
- put in a quality performance
- be seen as a leader
- offer uniqueness
- pay a debt
- increase responsibility and authority
- pursue a lifestyle
- get more freedom

Of course, this list is only a sampling. *People Win in countless ways.* One of your responsibilities as the manager of your sales objectives is to determine what those ways are for each of your Buying Influences.

3. Wins are personal.
We said that Results are corporate, or shared, and used the example of Doris Green's inventory control department to show how a single objective Result can benefit many people. But those people *won't all benefit in the same way.* This is perhaps the most important single distinction between Wins and Results. Even though an objective Result can generate Wins for many people, no two of those Wins will be identical. Each one will be linked to the *personal* perceptions of an individual Buying Influence.

Take the hypothetical Result that we're delivering to Green's department: a 16 percent reduction in overtime. Green herself may see this Result as a Win because it will help her run a tighter ship and thus satisfy a need for control. A member of Green's staff, though, may see this same Result as a Win for an entirely different reason: To him, the overtime reduction may be seen as a Win because it enables him to spend more time with his family. Same Result, different Wins.

Furthermore, another member of Green's staff may not see the Result as a Win at all. A staff member who *needs* the overtime to pay her bills won't see her self-interest being served by a 16 percent reduction; for her, this Result will translate into a Lose.

This basic distinction between corporate Results and personal Wins underscores a fundamental Strategic Selling lesson: *It's never enough to sell Results alone.* To manage each Complex Sale into the Win-Win quadrant with each Buying Influence, you *have* to determine how each one Wins.

Determining Your Buyer's Wins

To make the Win-Win quadrant of the matrix operational, you need to do two things: You need to be able to identify which Result or Results each of your Buyers needs to get from your sales proposal, and then show each of them how that Result can bring a personal Win. When you accomplish these two tasks, you're selling Win-Results.

It isn't always a straightforward task to understand and address your Buyers' subjective needs in this way. But determining their Win-Results needn't be all guesswork. Years of working with sales representatives in various fields have taught us that there are three reliable methods for identifying them:

1. You can *infer* your individual Buyers' Wins, either from the Results they're likely to want or from what you know about their attitudes and lifestyles.
2. You can *ask* them directly what's in the sale for them.
3. You can get *Coaching*.

Inferring the Win

Even though each of your Buyers Wins in an individual way, *categories* of Buyers tend to look for similar Results for their organizations. Knowing this can help you assess whether or not a particular Buying Influence is *likely* to Win with a particular Result.

True, determining Results alone is never enough. But if you *start* with the Results that Harry Barnes wants in a given situation, you'll be in a better position to *infer* the different Wins that each of those Results can give him.

The chart below, listing a number of sample Results, has been useful to many of our program participants in getting a handle on typical Results that produce Wins for people in each of the four Buying Influence categories.

SAMPLE RESULTS

Economic	User
• low cost of ownership • good budget fit • ROI • financial responsibility • increased productivity • profitability • smooth out cash flow • flexibility	• reliability • increased efficiency • upgrade skills • fulfill performance requirements • best problem solution • do job better/faster/easier • versatility • super-service • easy to learn & use
Technical	**Coach (Wins)**
• specs best and product meets them • delivery timely • best technical solution • discounts/low bids/price • reliability	• recognition • visability • get strokes • make contribution • be seen as problem-solver

Notice that the Results in each case relate directly to the Buyer's business concerns as outlined in Chapter 5 on Buying Influences. Economic Buyers, for example, look for Results addressed to the bottom line and organizational stability, such as ROI (return on investment). User Buyers concentrate on on-the-job performance; the Results they usually want for a Win enhance that performance. Technical Buyers are interested in having the product pass their screening tests; they're most likely to Win when you deliver Results that meet or surpass those tests.

Notice too that Coaches don't have their own Results, only Wins. *Your success in the sale* is what is going to give your Coach a Win.

There's an element of speculation in inferring Wins from Results, so you need to double-check your inference by looking at other data. It's likely that you already have access to that data. If you've called on Farley three times, you already know something about his Wins. If his office is overflowing with golf trophies and community plaques, he's probably got a strong need for achievement and recognition. If pictures of his children dominate the walls, security or family approval might be the key. If his appointment schedule is a model of regularity—if your one-hour meeting scheduled for 10 A.M. begins promptly at 10 and ends precisely at 11—then he probably values precision and efficiency. The more you know about your Buyers' lifestyles and attitudes, the better you'll be able to infer their Wins.

You can pick up other data from the company culture in which your Buyer works. As numerous observers of the American corporation have pointed out, each large company today has its own internal culture, comprising attitudes and values that both reflect and influence those of its individual employees.

For example, recognition for public service is more likely to be seen as a Win by Buyers in a company that projects a high community profile than by Buyers in one that prefers isolation. Being seen as an innovator or a maverick is more likely to be appreciated as a Win in a company that sees itself as the leading edge of an industry than in one that has been doing business the same old reliable way for fifty years.

We're not saying that individual Buyers' values are ever *merely* a reflection of their companies' values. But company cultures are still a valid standard against which to check your impressions of a given Buyer's Wins.

One caution: Remember that inferring is only a sophisticated form of guessing. Your inferences should always be *checked* by asking the Buyer directly, and/or by Coaching.

Asking the Buyer Directly

The second way to discover your Buyer's Wins is simply to ask. We don't mean you should sit the inscrutable Mr. Smithers down and blurt out, "What are your Wins in this sale?" Instead, you should ask what we call attitudinal, rather than objective, questions.

An *objective* question seeks to find out what the Buyer wants or needs. Most sales representatives concentrate on objective questions—or, worse, try to guess the Buyer's Wins—because they don't like to "pry," they want to stick to the facts, or they just don't want to hear the answer that they expect to get to a question about attitude. Whatever reason they may have for limiting themselves to objective questions, they get out of them just what they put in: the facts. And the facts are never enough to make a quality Complex Sale.

Attitudinal questions, on the other hand, seek to find out how the Buyer *feels* about the situation: "What's your opinion of this system?" Or, even more directly, "How do you feel about this proposal? How can I improve it to make you feel more comfortable?"

Questions about attitude are always appropriate; they should never be regarded as prying. Because they help you to probe beyond the product to each individual Buyer's Wins, they can help you check your own reactions to the changing sales situation, and also track your Buyers' changing needs.

They can give you valuable feedback, for example, on the numerical ratings that you gave your Buyers in Chapter 8. If you've identified Doris Green as a $+3$ User Buyer and a subsequent attitudinal question reveals that she feels "uneasy" about the pending sale, then you've uncovered the fact that she's not really a $+3$. Such questions are extremely useful in providing continual assessment of the "inner sales" you need to make before any papers will be signed.

One reason that many sales representatives feel uneasy

about asking attitudinal questions is that they realize getting honest answers to them can present difficulties. The smart strategist is alert to these difficulties and doesn't back away from them. A main thrust of Strategic Selling—and particularly of our Red Flag highlighting system—is to *uncover* difficulties in achieving your sales objective so they can be dealt with. Attitudinal questions are a means of helping you do that.

When you ask your Buyers about their Wins, you'll find both *ignorance* and *deception* to be occasional Red Flag areas. Some people who would like to tell you how they Win just don't know themselves. And others don't want *you* to know: They're happy to talk about Results, but they feel that their *personal* feelings about the sale are really none of your business.

In such cases you may be able to interpret the visible Results by reading between the lines to find the hidden Win. For example, a friend of ours just bought a new Porsche. When we asked him why he bought the car, he went on and on about its being a great investment; he was particularly impressed, he said, with the 3.2 liter engine, the acceleration from 0 to 60 in 5.6 seconds, and the high Porsche resale value. You'll recognize these things as Results. They may have been factors in the sale, but they certainly weren't as important as the less measurable, intangible fact that driving the car made him feel like Al Unser. You only had to see him behind the wheel to realize that *that* was the Win—and the decisive reason for the purchase.

Or take the example of the Economic Buyer who has a need to play it safe, but wants you to interpret his timidity as prudence. We know of one such person who consistently buys everything he needs from the sales leader in the field. Often the leader is a little higher in price than the competition, but he feels that he can't get in trouble if he sticks with number one. If you ask him why he takes the price beating, he doesn't say, "I'm afraid to make a change. Security is my Win." He tells you how reliable number one's service record is, and claims he can't get such service anywhere else. This is an example in which you may have to infer his Wins from what he says about the Results.

Because Buyers often disguise their Wins like this, we advise our program participants to *beware* and *compare* whenever they ask for a Buyer's feelings about a sale. *Beware* of answers that focus only on Results. *Compare* what you're told with other information you have about this individual's needs—both business and personal needs. And in reading between the lines to get at Wins, be careful not to guess.

Getting Coaching

One way of avoiding guesswork—or at least of double-checking your speculations—is to utilize your Coach. Since a good Coach is by definition credible to the other Buyers, they may entrust information to this person—both objective and subjective—that they wouldn't entrust to you. So if a Buyer is difficult to read, your Coach might be the key.

Remember, your basic selling goal should be to serve each Buyer's perceived self-interest. Zero in on that self-interest by asking your Coach, *"What Results should I be stressing with Dan Farley to show him what's in this sale for him?"*

In Chapter 12 we'll discuss your Coach in more detail and explain a number of ways in which this critical and unique Buying Influence can help make your management of the Complex Sale more predictable. One of the most important of those ways is in helping you to find out how each of your individual Buying Influences will Win.

Two Ways *Not* to Determine Wins

The three methods of determining Wins that we've just described—inferring the Win, asking the Buyer, and getting Coaching—have been used reliably by thousands of sales representatives and managers, in countless business situations. Two other common "methods" are *not* reliable, and you should avoid them both. They are:

- To interpret the Results as the Win
- To assume that your own Win is the same as your Buyer's

Interpreting Results as Wins

Examine Results first, by all means. You can't deliver a Win without a Result. But it doesn't follow that a good Result *equals* a Win; it's a precondition, *not* an equivalent.

You'll recall the story we told earlier in this chapter about the sales representative who had such trouble convincing an aging president to buy. The sales representative had a whole string of good Results. His product would save the buying firm money, it would raise productivity—it was, as the salesman complained, "a perfect fit with their needs." But the president still wouldn't buy, because the salesman had failed to demonstrate to him that the sale was in *his* self-interest.

The lesson is clear. Always start, but never *stop,* with Results. Unless you understand each individual's personal reasons for buying, you can easily find yourself, even after you've sold a Buyer many times, presenting a great Result in a situation where the Buyer sees only a personal Lose.

Confusing your Wins with the Buyer's Wins

When the salesman who had such trouble with the retiring president told us about his plight, one phrase stuck in our minds. *"If I were that guy,"* he said, "I would have signed months ago."

True, maybe, but irrelevant. In fact, it was worse than irrelevant. Realizing that he himself would have signed caused the sales representative here to make what is probably the single most common error among people just beginning to use the concept of Win-Results. That error is in *projecting their own Wins onto their Buyers*—in assuming that the way the Buyer will Win is the same way the sales representative would Win in the same situation. Making this assumption almost always leads you to misidentify your Buyers' Wins.

Sales representatives who make this miscalculation do so for a logical enough reason. They confuse their own self-interest with that of the Buyer by asking themselves, with all the empathy in the world, "How would I Win if I were Doris Green?" But empathy won't give you the answer you need in this kind of situation. What you always have to do, therefore, is to focus *first* on Results, and then ask, "How can this Buyer Win?" given the Results you can offer.

Personal Workshop 5: Win-Results

In applying the Key Element of Win-Results to your chosen sales objective, we suggest you first develop a list of corporate Results that you can use to give each of your Buyers a Win, and then use those Results to identify the Wins for each Buyer.

Step 1: Identify Results for your type of business.

The purpose of this step is to give you a fix on the Results concept as it operates *generally* in your field of business. You can get that fix by first going back to the sample Results that we listed earlier in the chapter, and then making up your own chart, using that one as a guide.

Open your notebook flat, so that you have two blank facing pages in front of you. Working first on the left-hand page, write the heading "Results" at the top. Then divide the page into three columns, under the subheads "Economic Buyer," "Technical Buyer," and "User Buyer." In each column write down as many Results as you can that those Buying Influences typically look for *in your business*.

In identifying these corporate Results, remember that Economic Buyers focus on the bottom line and organizational stability, that User Buyers want to know how you can improve their on-the-job performance, and that Technical Buyers are most interested in the product per se. You don't need a Coach column since, as we've mentioned, Coaches don't have their own Results.

If you're like our program participants, many of the Results you write down will be identical to our sample Results. Start with our chart, but don't stop there. Add to the list whatever Results you can think of that are specific to *your* industry or product line. Your goal here is to generate a list of Results that tend to be typical for the Buyers in *your* selling arena. If you spend about five or ten minutes on this step, you should be able to come up with at least six or eight typical Results for each of the three categories of Buying Influences.

Step 2: Test these Results.

The next step is to test this list objectively. You can do that by asking yourself the following questions about each item on the list:

- Is this Result measurable, tangible, and quantifiable?
- Is it corporate—that is, can it be shared by more than one Buying Influence?
- Is it business related—that is, does it positively affect a business process of my customers?

Step 3: Identify Results for your current sales objective.

You now know what Results each of the three categories of Buyers generally look for in your business. Now we suggest you get more specific and generate a list of Results that the individual Buying Influences want or need with regard to *the particular sales objective* you've been working on in this book.

Use the right-hand page of the open notebook to make out this list. At the top of the page write "Win-Results Chart," and then divide the page into three columns, under the subheads "Buyers," "Results," and "Wins." Take out your Buying Influences Chart and copy down the names of all your Buyers in the left-hand column. As you know, you may have four of these, or fourteen. Then, in the middle column, next to the name of each Buyer write down only the one or two *key* Results he or she wants from this particular sale.

You can use the Results list that you just drew up as a bank from which to draw out this new list. You're performing a process of distillation—starting with the Results that are universal in your business by Buyer type, and narrowing the focus to identify the Results relevant to *this* sale, and *these* Buying Influences, right now.

Step 4: Test your individual Buyers' Results.

Once you've listed the one or two most important Results for each Buyer, test them *objectively*. Your goal here is to see that you've identified Results that are *specific* and *relevant* to each Buyer's situation. It's not enough to say that one Result you can give to Dan Farley is to make his job "go easier." Look at the Result you've identified for Farley and ask yourself the following test questions:

- What business *process* of Farley's does this Result address?
- How does the Result *improve* or *fix* that process?
- How does the Result relate to *the specific business concerns* of Farley's category of Buying Influence? Since Farley is your Economic Buyer, this means, for him, how will your Result change his organizational growth and stability?

Then ask the same questions for each of the other Results, and all the other Buyers, on your chart. Remember that the specific business concerns of your User Buyers will be linked to on-the-job performance and that those of your Technical Buyers will be linked to their screening tests of your product or service.

In testing the Results you expect to be able to deliver to your Buyers, be sure too that each suggested Result refers to today's reality, not yesterday's. The strategic representative, aware that reality is always changing, tracks the Buyers' needs from sale to sale.

It should take you a minute or two for each Buyer to complete this step of the exercise. If you're uncertain about a given Buyer's Results, put a Red Flag in the middle column near that person's name.

Step 5: Identify your Buyers' Wins.

Because Results alone are never enough to establish long-term success with your Buyers, focus now on the other half of the Win-Results concept, and identify your individual Buyers' personal Wins.

Turn back to the sample Wins that we presented earlier in the chapter. Using that chart as a guide—but *only* as a guide, not as a definitive catalog—go down the list of Buyers on your Win-Results Chart again, this time trying to identify the Wins that the Buyers will get from the Result or Results that you've recognized as important to each person. For each Result, ask yourself the following question:

> *How will this Buyer Win if my product or service delivers this Result?*

The answers you get should provide the linkage you need between each person's Wins and Results.

For example, consider the Result that we're going to deliver to Doris Green: the 16 percent reduction in overtime. If you know she wants this reduction to maintain control over her department, you have a clear statement of her Win-Results: "Doris Green wants an overtime reduction (Result) so she can maintain control (Win)."

Or say you have a product that will ensure the continued reliability of one of Harry Barnes's processes—and you also know that Barnes puts a high premium on reliability and stability. A statement of his Win-Results might be "Harry Barnes needs reliability of his system (Result) to maintain a sense of security (Win)."

In this exercise, you'll probably come up against one or more Buyers whose Wins you can't readily determine. If that happens, put a Red Flag in the Wins column of your Win-Results Chart. If you know that Gary Steinberg is anxious to move his inventory faster, for example, but you don't know his *personal* reasons for wanting to do so, then you understand his Results but not his Wins. You should put a Red Flag in the Wins column to remind yourself that you need more information on this point.

When you're finished with this step, your Win-Results Chart should look something like the example on page 174.

Step 6: Analyze your current position.
Now investigate both your Win-Results Chart and your

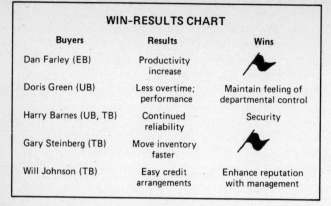

WIN-RESULTS CHART

Buyers	Results	Wins
Dan Farley (EB)	Productivity increase	🚩
Doris Green (UB)	Less overtime; performance	Maintain feeling of departmental control
Harry Barnes (UB, TB)	Continued reliability	Security
Gary Steinberg (TB)	Move inventory faster	🏴
Will Johnson (TB)	Easy credit arrangements	Enhance reputation with management

Buying Influences Chart with an eye to discovering what further information you need to improve your position. Look at each Buyer in turn, assessing your areas of Strength and your Red Flags. Test whether or not there's information you haven't yet uncovered, but can, by asking yourself questions like these:

- What *else* do I know about Steinberg—aside from his Results—that can help me understand how those Results can help him Win?
- What do Steinberg's lifestyle, values, and attitudes tell me about how he might Win?
- Have I asked Farley both objective and attitudinal questions to determine his Wins?
- If I haven't seen Farley myself, have I arranged for someone else to do so?
- Can my Coaches help? Have I asked *them* to explain to me how Farley and Steinberg Win?

Use the answers to these questions to consider revisions of your Alternate Positions list. Remember especially that, wherever you have *a lack of data* about a given Buying Influence, you have a significant Red Flag. Always make the uncovering of such data a new option on that list.

Step 7: Determine your present Win-Win status.
Knowing something about your various Buyers' Win-Results, you can now start managing your sales objective into

the Win-Win quadrant of the matrix. First, test whether or not you're currently working with each Buyer in that quadrant by asking yourself:

- Have I delivered or can I deliver the Results that each Buyer needs to Win?
- Does every Buyer have confidence that I can do this? In other words, do they all *know* I'm playing Win-Win with them?

If the answer to either of these questions is no, then you can't really count on stability in your position. You may or may not be in the Win-Win quadrant.

For example, if you deliver Barnes a Result but don't really know how he Wins, you're setting yourself up for a Lose, if not in this sale, then in future ones. Or if Farley doesn't believe there's a Win in your sale for him, then as far as he's concerned you're playing Win-Lose with him—and you're therefore risking the loss of the sale.

Look at the Red Flags you've placed both on the Win-Results Chart that you prepared in this Personal Workshop and at those you placed on your Buying Influences Chart. Where are you solidly positioned and where do you still lack information that you need to serve each Buyer's self-interest? Answering such questions realistically will give you a firmer grasp on how close you actually are to the Win-Win strategy you want.

Step 8: Revise your Alternate Positions list.

The next step in managing your sale into the Win-Win quadrant of the matrix is to use what you've learned about Win-Results to revise your current position. As in previous workshops, you do that by sharpening, cutting, and adding to the options on your Alternate Positions list.

In Step 6 of this workshop we advised you to consider revisions of the Alternate Positions list based on your current position with regard to Win-Results. Incorporate any relevant revisions now and *test* each one against the concept of Win-Results. Ideally, you want every item on this developing list to help you *understand* the Win-Results of your Buyers better, to help you *deliver* those Win-Results more effectively, or to help you do both. Revise your list with this in mind.

For example, in getting rid of that Red Flag next to Gary Steinberg's name, the "position" of "Take Gary to lunch" may or may not get you any closer to the information you want. A good Alternate Position in this situation might be "Get Doris Green to explain to me why Gary is so person-ally concerned about inventory." That focuses in on the specific lack of data that you need to correct.

In previous workshops, we advised you to be *inclusive* about your Alternate Positions, to be *specific,* and to *test* them against the Strategic Selling rule that every good Al-ternate Position eliminates a Red Flag, leverages from a Strength, or does both. You should continue to be specific and to test your options. But it's time to get a little less inclusive and more discriminating. Since the concept of Win-Results is so central to an effective sales strategy, we urge you to look over all the items on your Alternate Posi-tions list with it in mind. Consider dropping any option that does not, directly or indirectly, help you deliver to at least one of your Buying Influences a Result which that person needs to Win.

Most important of all, remember *self-interest.* Because it determines all buying decisions, it will remain a benchmark for you in assessing all future Alternate Positions.

Summary of Win-Results

Since our fourth Key Element of strategy so often proves difficult for our program participants, we close this chapter with a summary of its major points. You should use it as a reference as you continue to refine your sales strategy.

- Any *product* (or service) provides the tools and knowledge needed to improve a *process.* The pro-cess, in turn, produces the *Results* through which a person Wins.
- Your Buyer *Wins* when his or her *self-interest* is served. That's why Winning is important and why

you need to understand how your Buyer Wins in order to sell him.

- People buy because they perceive a relationship between your sales proposal and their individual self-interest. The art and craft of selling is in demonstrating the connection between the proposal and self-interest.

- It's often difficult to *ask* someone how he or she Wins. Therefore, focus first (but not only) on the person's Results and then ask how the person will Win with those Results. *Coaching* helps you to understand the Win.

- The ideal buy/sell situation is a Win-Win scenario. *Serving your customers' self-interest is ultimately the best way of serving your own.*

▶ 11 ◀

STRATEGIES AND TACTICS FOR GETTING TO THE ECONOMIC BUYER

The heart of Strategic Selling is managing every one of your sales objectives so that you end up in the Win-Win quadrant of the matrix with all your Buyers. Frequently this proves to be most problematic with regard to Economic Buyers, because the Economic Buyer differs from the other Buying Influences in two significant ways:

- Economic Buyers are more difficult to *identify* than the other Buyers.
- Economic Buyers are more difficult to *reach,* both physically and psychologically, than User and Technical Buyers.

For these reasons, establishing a Win-Win outcome with the Economic Buyer is a common area of concern, even among sales representatives who are extremely competent in establishing such outcomes with other Buyers.

Yet failure to cover the Economic Buyer adequately, or to see to it that the Economic Buyer perceives a personal

Win in the sale, can undermine even the most "straightforward" sales scenario. Since the Economic Buyer can by definition *veto* the sale at any point in the selling cycle, it's only common sense to cover that key player as *thoroughly* as possible, and as *early* as possible in the selling cycle.

Problems in Getting to the Economic Buyer

What makes getting to the Economic Buyer so tough?

When we put this question to our program participants, we get a variety of answers. Some of the more common ones are:

- "I don't know who he is."
- "I don't know where to look in the buying organization for that kind of approval."
- "A purchasing agent is in my way—he says to deal just with him."
- "It's like talking to my father when I meet him."
- "She refuses to see me."
- "I don't have any credibility with people at that level."
- "No one wants to assume the authority to sign for the order."
- "All her calls are screened."
- "He makes me nervous—I don't know what to say to him."
- "I don't know what his needs are."
- "He's in Detroit and I'm not."
- "He just doesn't talk to salesmen."

You'll probably recognize some of the responses on this list as being relevant to your own situations. We'd be very surprised if you didn't—these are typical responses.

Just as typical is the fact that the responses we get can always be broken down into three root problems.

In the hundreds of programs we've presented, and in our own business as well, we always see this same pattern. No matter what industry our participants are in, and no matter what the average size of their sales, their complaints about getting to the Economic Buyer always fall into one of three categories:

Problem 1: They can't *identify* the Economic Buyer.
Problem 2: They're *blocked* from getting to the Economic Buyer.
Problem 3: They're *uncomfortable* talking to the Economic Buyer.

If you look at the responses given on the list above, you'll see that this pattern holds true:

- Responses such as "I don't know who he is" and "I don't know where to look" and "No one will assume the authority" decode as "I can't *identify* him."
- Responses such as "A purchasing agent is in my way" and "She refuses to see me" and "All her calls are screened" decode as "I'm being *blocked* from seeing her."
- Responses such as "He makes me nervous" and "I don't have any credibility" and "It's like talking to my father" decode as "I'm *uncomfortable* talking to him."

If you review your past sales and think about the problems you experienced in getting to your Economic Buyers, we're sure you'll see the same pattern.

Throughout the rest of this chapter, we'll be giving you strategies and tactics for overcoming each of these three basic problems. We'll begin by briefly reviewing who the Economic Buyer *is,* and what this person *does* in your sale.

Profile of the Economic Buyer

In helping our clients develop skill in identifying the Economic Buyer for each sales objective, we've found it useful to emphasize three concepts:

- The Economic Buyer, like all the other Buying Influences, is *sale specific.*

- The person playing the Economic Buyer role is often *highly placed* in the buying organization.
- People acting as Economic Buyers are generally paid very well for their ability to *see into the future*.

The "Sale-Specific" Economic Buyer

We call the Economic Buyer "sale specific" because that person plays the Economic Buyer role for a specific sales objective, *not* for an account. There's no such thing as "the Giant Soap Company's Economic Buyer," but only a number of key individuals in that company who can play the Economic Buyer role; there's no guarantee that the person who plays that role for one sale will play it for a second sale to the same company—even if the second sale involves the same product and dollar amount.

The Economic Buyer's Organizational Position

Because they have direct access to and discretionary use of needed funds, people playing the role of Economic Buyer are most often highly placed in their organizations. In smaller, entrepreneurial-type companies, the president of the firm himself or herself will often play the Economic Buyer role on many sales. But even in large conglomerates, most Economic Buyer decisions—that is, decisions to release necessary funds—are made by senior managers. Very few companies allow the Economic Buyer role for major purchases or policy decisions to be played by junior management. And the more money involved in the sale, the higher you have to look for the release-of-funds decision.

Reading the Future

Since Economic Buyers are often senior-level managers, they're typically highly paid; most of the Economic Buyers we hear about and deal with take home six-figure salaries. But they aren't paid solely for the day-to-day management of the business. That may be a *part* of their responsibility, but the real reason for their high salaries is the ability to plan ahead: to forecast future business conditions and see to it that their companies profit from them. They're paid their handsome salaries and bonuses chiefly for the clarity of their crystal balls.

The Economic Buyer can be considered analogous to the captain of a ship for a particular voyage. Like ship captains, most Economic Buyers aren't really paid to *do* anything. They don't navigate, manage the engine room, or hold the wheel themselves. But it's their direct responsibility to know exactly where the ship is going, and to make those management decisions that ensure it will arrive safely and on time.

Keeping these three elements of the Economic Buyer profile in mind, you can address the problems of *identifying* the Economic Buyer for your specific sales goal, of being *blocked* from seeing that person, and of overcoming your *discomfort* so that you cover the Economic Buyer effectively on every sale.

Solving Problem 1: Identification

In identifying the Economic Buyer accurately for each specific sales objective, you have to be attentive to what we call the *float factor* in Complex Sales. By "float factor" we mean the fact that the role of Economic Buyer shifts, or floats, up and down the corporate ladder, often between one sale and the next, or even *during* a sale. A common error even of experienced sales representatives is to be unaware of this factor and to assume that Farley, who gave final approval for the last sales objective, must also be the Economic Buyer for the next one. This makes the risk of misidentification a constant threat.

The Float Factor and Perceived Risk

In Chapter 5 on Buying Influences, we described five variables that can cause the role of Economic Buyer to shift up or down the corporate ladder. If you're having difficulty identifying the Economic Buyer for a given sale, you can often clarify the situation by asking yourself how that sale is likely to be perceived by the buying organization in terms of these five variables.

1. The Dollar Amount of the Sale.   Generally speaking, the higher the dollar amount of the sale, the higher the Economic Buyer role will float. Remember, though, that we mean dollar amount *relative to the size of the buying organization.* A ten-thousand-dollar sale to a small firm might bring in the president as Economic Buyer; the same size sale to General Motors probably would not.

2. Business Conditions.   Hard times cause the Economic Buyer role to float upward. When a firm is suffering setbacks or slow activity, buying decisions that are normally made by middle management pass to the managers at the top. The reverse happens when the economy is good.

3. Experience with You and Your Firm.   For first sales to a new account, you should look high up in the organization for final approval. Once you've established a history of Wins with at least some of the Buying Influences for a given company, approval for the same level of sale may pass down the corporate ladder.

4. Experience with Your Product or Service.   This variable illustrates the same principle. The less a company knows about the specific product or service involved in your sales goal, the more likely it is that approval will have to come from high up. With experience, the Economic Buyer role will float down.

5. Potential Organizational Impact.   Since Economic Buyers are generally concerned with long-range effects, the role of Economic Buyer will float upward if the buying organization feels that your sales proposal will have a significant long-term impact on organizational growth and stability.

All five of these variables have one thing in common. The reason that each of them is important in generating float is that behind all five is the same fundamental business factor. That factor is *perceived risk* on the buying organization's part.

More than any other category of Buying Influence, Economic Buyers are paid to take calculated risks that, they hope, will lead to financial and developmental rewards. The entire focus of their decision making can be seen as the balance between risk and reward. *And the greater the perceived risk, the higher the role of Economic Buyer floats.*

In identifying who is playing the role of Economic Buyer for your sale, therefore, we suggest that you ask yourself two test questions. The first one is the question we mentioned in our discussion of Buying Influences in Chapter 5:

> *At what level in my own organization would final approval for a sale of this type have to be made?*

The answer to this question will suggest to you the general level at which you should look in the buying organization for the person playing the Economic Buyer role. Remember, though, that the level at which final approval might be found is *relative to the size of the buying organization.* If your company and the buying company are the same size, approval will probably come at about the same level. But if your company is smaller than the buying organization, you may have to look *lower;* and if your company is larger, you may have to look *higher* in the buying organization.

The second question relates to the underlying element in our discussion of the float factor: the element of *perceived risk.* Once you know at which level of the buying organization you're likely to find your Economic Buyer, ask yourself:

> *Considering the level of perceived risk involved in my sales proposal, should I be looking higher up the corporate ladder or lower?*

If the level of perceived risk is high, adjust your sights upward; if it's low, adjust them down.

As you go through this searching process, remember that we specified *perceived* risk. Just as it's your *Buyer's* perception of reality, not yours, that's critical in determining Response Modes, it's the *buying* firm's perception of risk, not yours, that will help you identify the probable organizational level of the Economic Buyer. You may be selling the Mammoth Company a fire prevention system that *you* know has never failed. But if Mammoth's people have never done business with you before, if the system would mean a major commitment of funds for them, or if the impact on their company would be profound, they still may want final approval for the purchase to come from the top echelons.

One caution: It's very common for the sales representative to look at too *low* a level. Many representatives are willing to talk to a plant manager when they really should go to a division manager, or to a director when they really need to see the president. No doubt this is a result of the discomfort many people feel in the presence of top management—a problem we'll discuss in a moment. For whatever reason, incorrectly identifying the Economic Buyer too far down the ladder is a common cause of mismanaged sales.

For this reason we encourage you to make it a rule of thumb that you cover the bases with your customers *one level above* where you believe the Economic Buyer to be. This is particularly important on an initial sale to an account. Identifying the Economic Buyer accurately as each new sale begins is basic to good strategy.

Zeroing In on the Economic Buyer

Once you've located the *level* in the buying organization from which approval must come for your sale, you need a way of finding whether or not the person you *think* is the Economic Buyer at that level will actually play that role for *this* sale.

There are three ways you can do this. You can:

- *Ask* the suspected Economic Buyer directly
- Get *Coaching*
- *Guess*

Only the first two ways are acceptable. Representatives who "think" they know who the Economic Buyer is for their sale, or who have a "pretty good idea" who controls the funds, very often guess wrong. If you don't *know* who the Economic Buyer is for the sale you're working on, put a Red Flag in the Economic Buyer box on your Buying Influences Chart. Then zero in on the actual Economic Buyer by asking and/or getting Coaching.

1. Asking the Buyer Directly. This is the most straightforward method. An abrupt colleague of ours zeroes in on the Economic Buyer by addressing the person he thinks is the Economic Buyer in the most blatant fashion. "Once I've covered the bases with all my other Buying Influences," he says, "I go to the guy I think is the Economic Buyer and put a close on him. If he signs the order, I know he's the Economic Buyer. If not, either I've got more work to do on him, or I've got to look someplace else."

If you prefer this direct method, by all means "put a close" on your suspected Economic Buyer and see if he or she comes up with the money for the sale. If you prefer a less blunt approach, you can still find out if you've got the right person for your sale by asking appropriate, if somewhat less direct, questions. In asking these questions, remember what the Economic Buyer actually *does*. By definition this is the person who releases the dollars *for your particular sale*. If you're fairly certain that Dan Farley has the authority to do that, but you want to test your perceptions, you might ask him questions like these:

- Are you recommending me, Dan, or will you give the final go-ahead yourself?
- Is there anybody who can veto this proposal?
- What's the approval *process*? After you give your OK, is that it? Or is there somebody else we need to see?

Such questions are designed to cut through the baloney of "referrals" and "tentative approvals" and "provisional orders" by focusing on the Economic Buyer's actual role in the sale.

2. Getting Coaching. Asking your suspected Economic Buyers if they really have the authority to release the needed funds may or may not get you a straight answer. We've explained how Technical Buyers will often try to pass themselves off as Economic Buyers, and that real Economic Buyers are adept at hiding within corporate structures. That's why you generally need Coaching to help you accurately identify the Economic Buyer. By asking a reliable Coach the above questions, you can often get clearer information than you will from the suspected Economic Buyer about who actually releases the money for your sale.

Solving Problem 2: When You're Blocked

It's not uncommon for an Economic Buyer whom you've correctly identified still to be out of your reach. The individual may, for example, be in a remote geographical location: the real approval for your sale may have to come from a home office located hundreds of miles from your territory. Or the Economic Buyer may be isolated from outside calls by a professional screen—the secretary who tells you, every time you try to get to the boss, "Mr. Farley is still out of town." Or you may be blocked by one of those Technical Buyers who specialize in masquerading as Economic Buyers.

Dealing with geographical remoteness and with protective secretaries often requires merely the employment of good proxies. You can often get to an "inaccessible" Economic Buyer by letting someone else in your organization cover that particular base for you. The best choice for that someone else is often a person at the *same organizational level* as the Economic Buyer.

Dealing with a *Buying Influence* who's actively trying to block you from seeing the Economic Buyer can be a more difficult scenario. And it's an extremely common one.

If you get to the Economic Buyer early enough in the selling cycle, you can often avoid this problem. No Technical Buyer is going to be able to throw an effective block at you if you've seen the Economic Buyer first. But let's assume you haven't already covered the Economic Buyer base. How do you handle the block?

Handling the Block: Three Methods

In handling a person who's actively blocking you from seeing the Economic Buyer—often this will be one or more Technical Buyers—you should begin by understanding *why* another Buying Influence would want to do this.

When we ask our program participants who have been blocked from getting to the Economic Buyer to explain why they were blocked, they give answers like the following:

- "The Technical Buyer wants to handle everything personally."
- "He's strong for my competition."
- "The boss says she won't see salesmen."
- "He's afraid I'll hustle the old man."
- "She says the Economic Buyer wants her to make the final decision."
- "He doesn't like my company—he just doesn't want me to make the sale."

When you examine these answers closely, you find that there's an underlying theme. No matter what the *given* reason is—no matter what the apparent motivation of the blocking Buyer—there's always the *same* root cause.

That cause relates back to what we said in the last chapter about the importance of giving *all* of your Buyers individual Wins. When another Buyer attempts to block your access to the Economic Buyer, it's often because the blocker sees the proposal you're offering as a personal *Lose,* not a Win.

There are three ways you can deal with this root cause. You can:

- Show the blocking Buyer how to *Win* in the sale by getting you to the Economic Buyer
- Go *around* the blocker to get to the Economic Buyer
- Go *along* with the block

Each of these three choices could be valid, depending on the situation.

1. Showing the Blocker How to Win. Showing the blocker how to Win is by far the best of the three strategies and you should always try it *first,* resorting to the other two strategies only if it fails. Since the blocking Buyer's perception that he or she will Lose if you make the sale is the reason for standing in your way, you can sometimes turn the situation around by demonstrating that this perception is mistaken. In order to become a sponsor rather than an antisponsor of your proposal, the blocker has to see that it's *in his or her self-interest* for you to get to the Economic Buyer.

Ideally, you want to go one step beyond this. You want to show the blocker how to Win not just by *letting* you get to the Economic Buyer, but by *taking* you there personally. The best way of handling a blocking Buying Influence is to show that you have something the Economic Buyer needs—and that the blocker can get the credit and recognition for bringing it to the Economic Buyer's attention by helping you. If you can show the Technical Buyer that you have something of *value* to the Economic Buyer, you'll very likely be able to convert a "Lose" perception into a "Win" perception, because there will be a realization that cooperating with you will enhance the Technical Buyer's *own* value to the Economic Buyer.

The something of value that the Technical Buyer can help you give the Economic Buyer is always the same thing. The single most valuable contribution you can bring to any Economic Buyer is *knowledge.*

Specifically, it's knowledge that will help the Economic Buyer do what he or she is paid to do: predict the future and set appropriate organizational plans. If you and the blocking Buyer together can increase the Economic Buyer's *predictive capability,* everybody will Win. We'll speak more about this critical type of knowledge, and how you can deliver it, in a minute.

2. Getting Around the Block. No matter how earnestly you work to show a blocking Buying Influence how to Win by helping you in your sale, you may still come up against a Buyer who simply won't be moved. When you confront a

User or Technical Buyer whose Lose perception can't be turned around, you'll be forced to consider the second option—getting around the block.

We've mentioned the advantage of using proxies in getting to an Economic Buyer whom you can't reach personally. This technique can often effectively circumvent a blocking Buyer. But there's a real danger here. In fact, in spite of its apparent elegance, this end-run approach to a blocked sale is actually a high-risk strategy.

The risk is that, in your eagerness to reach the Economic Buyer, you'll simply *ignore* the blocking Buyer's resistance as irrelevant or at least unimportant. We pointed out, in our story of the mismanaged textile-plant sale, what serious long-term repercussions this approach can have. The danger is simply stated: Whenever you make a sale *in spite of* a key player's disapproval, you're perceived as playing Win-Lose with that person. You turn the player into an enemy because you're seen as serving your own self-interest at the other's expense.

Circumvented blockers have the memory of an elephant. Ten or twenty years later they'll remember your going over their heads, and get even. Therefore, we advise our clients that they should employ this damn-the-torpedoes strategy *only when they have little or nothing to lose.* If your position with the Smith account isn't very solid anyway, or if the potential Win for you is huge, you may be justified in alienating a blocking Buyer and of making the sale over objections. But, since *any Buyer ignored is a threat,* watch out for revenge down the line. We always advise our program participants that, even when they feel such a strategy is the only choice left, they still discuss the sales objective and strategy in question first with their district or regional sales managers, and with their Coaches.

3. *Going Along with the Block.* Going along with someone who's keeping you from getting to the Economic Buyer can often cause you to lose the immediate business. Therefore, it may look like a very bad strategy. Admittedly, it's not attractive. But there are situations that warrant it.

A friend of ours in advertising sales, a man we'll call

Gary, had to make this difficult choice last year. He was the account executive for a firm that brought in five million dollars a year; that one firm accounted for about half of Gary's own income. To tie in with the holiday season, Gary suggested a promotional package to this firm that one of its middle managers found offensive. Gary had excellent relations with that manager's superior, and the manager's approval wasn't essential to the closing of the promotional deal. But Gary knew that if he went around the blocker to his boss (who was the Economic Buyer), he would jeopardize future sales.

So he withdrew the proposal. It cost him a ten-thousand-dollar commission but, as he told us some months later, he never regretted the decision. "I had learned in your programs," he explained, "never to leave a Buyer feeling beaten. I just couldn't afford to gamble half my income on that one campaign. And you know something? That guy really appreciated my respecting his feelings. He's become my best ally in that account. I'm doing a promotion for them this year that will let me double the ten thousand I lost."

The lesson is, if you already have a good relationship with the buying organization and if your current sales objective doesn't warrant alienating one of your Buying Influences, you may want to let the immediate order go in favor of protecting the business you already have—and of keeping open the possibility of larger future sales. Behind such a decision would be a basic goal of Strategic Selling: ensuring *long-term* account success.

Of course, this is still at best only a temporary solution—like waiting at a roadblock until the road ahead is fixed. You can't manage an account over time by acquiescing in Buyers' blocks. *Your first plan should always be to show all your Buyers how they can Win.*

Solving Problem 3: Discomfort/Fear

An eager but green sales representative decided to make a "cold call"—without an appointment—on a vice-president

in an account he'd recently acquired. He hadn't sold anything to the account yet, but he'd heard that the vice-president's approval was essential to virtually all sales. So, to
"save time," he went straight to the top, determined to feel
out the terrain. He was extremely nervous about meeting
the high-level executive, but he decided to adopt a positive
mental attitude and just do his best in the lion's den.

The vice-president, who was part of a company that valued ready access to its executives, was at his desk when the
young man arrived.

"Hello, there," he said. "I'm George Grant. From the
Webster Group? I just happened to be in the neighborhood
and thought I'd see how you were. Do you have any orders
for me?"

The vice-president looked up from his papers, gave
George a quick, astonished once-over, and replied drily,
"Yes, I have two orders for you. Get out and stay out."

You'll recognize this as almost a textbook case of selling
blunders. Not only didn't George have an appointment, he
didn't even call before dropping in. And, when he did drop
in, he had no particular reason to be there: no sales proposal to follow up, no referral, no question that needed
answering. No wonder he was nervous. He had good reason to be.

The story illustrates not only the fact that preparation
before the selling event is critical to strategic success, but
also the related fact that, in preparing yourself to meet an
Economic Buyer, your *psychological readiness* is just as important as your knowledge of your product or your obser-
vance of the common amenities such as making an
appointment before you drop in.

There were two related reasons that George felt uncomfortable with the vice-president. They are the same reasons
that you or any other sales professional might feel uncomfortable in the presence of your Economic Buyers:

- You might feel *intimidated* by someone who appears too busy or too successful to care about
  what you have to say.
- You might feel *uncertain* about what an Economic

Buyer wants or needs to hear—uncertain, in other words, about what you're doing there.

When You're Intimidated

There's only one sure way we've found to overcome feelings of intimidation when you confront a high-level executive. That's to remember that, although the Economic Buyer for your sale might have a three-inch carpet and a four-car garage, he's still a *human being*—and it's to that human being that you're selling.

We don't mean that he's "just an ordinary Joe." He's not. Typically, people who play the role of Economic Buyer *are* different, if only because they make more money than the rest of us. But if you focus on their differences, you'll only intensify your feelings of discomfort. You want to minimize those feelings. One way to do that is to remember that Farley, aside from being the person who will release the funds for your sale, is probably also a husband, a father, a golf player, a man who may water the lawn and watch TV and order in Chinese food, just like people in less glamorous occupations. Just like you, he's got regrets about the past and hopes for the future and needs, both business and personal, that have to be met right now.

What you always have to remember is that, since you're offering him a proposal, *you are in a position to fulfill some of those needs*.

In order to do that, though, you have to learn whatever you can about the Economic Buyer as an *individual*.

Again, as is so often the case when you're clearing away difficulties that stand in the way of your sales objective, a reliable Coach can be a valuable asset here. A good Coach can help you turn those difficulties into opportunities by providing answers to questions about the Economic Buyer's business needs, and about personal interests as well.

Answers to the first type of question will help you identify which corporate Results your product or service can provide to the buying company. Answers to the second type of question will help you determine the Economic Buyer's personal Wins. Having your Coach brief you *before* you make that first call on what your Economic Buyer is like as a person is an excellent way of zeroing in on likely Win-Results—and thus of reducing your discomfort in this key player's presence.

When You're Uncertain

The ultimate reason you want to talk to an Economic Buyer, naturally, is to get approval of your sale. But that's not necessarily the reason this person will want to see you. It's up to you to make sure that the Economic Buyer has as good a reason as you do for wanting you to get together.

It's the Buyer's perception, not yours, that we're talking about now. Every time you call on an Economic Buyer, the unspoken question is always going to be "What reason do you have for taking up my valuable time?" If you can't answer that question to the Economic Buyer's satisfaction before you go in, don't count on remaining comfortable after you get there.

Therefore, if you want to further reduce your discomfort with an Economic Buyer, you have to make sure, every time you call on such a Buying Influence, that you have a *valid business reason* for doing so.

What the Economic Buyer Always Wants: Knowledge

What does the Economic Buyer consider a valid business reason? We've observed that the one thing the Economic Buyer always wants is *knowledge* that will increase predictive capability—the ability to plan ahead for the business. This fact leads to the following Strategic Selling axiom:

> *You have a valid business reason for contacting an Economic Buyer when you can present knowledge that will make a contribution to the way he or she is doing business.*

This observation surprises many people who are new to selling. Sales representatives who have had limited experience with Economic Buyers often tend to place these top executives on a pedestal, assuming they know *everything*. This is a misconception. In fact, Economic Buyers almost always know *less* than you do about many areas of your industry. Such Buyers are by nature generalists. They don't have time to keep up with all the day-to-day developments in their business, and they therefore often lack relevant details because they've got their eyes on the big picture. *That's why they need you.* You can provide the details they need to make that picture clearer.

Top-management Economic Buyers are paid for the clarity of their crystal balls. Knowledge that increases their ability to predict the future, and thus decreases their perceived risk and uncertainty, is held in the *highest* regard: That kind of knowledge is more important to the Economic Buyer than anything of material value. The ideal situation for you is to bring the Economic Buyer information that can serve as Windex for a clouded crystal ball.

This information may or may not be related to your immediate sales objective. Naturally, if the information you present demonstrates how to be in the forefront of an industry trend by buying *your* product now, so much the better. But you can still get the Economic Buyer on your side—and therefore increase the probability of approval for your sale—if you bring general, industry-wide information, whether or not it's part of your own presentation.

The importance of bringing the Economic Buyer this kind of information was demonstrated by one of our clients, a major manufacturer of snack foods, a few years ago, when the company's national sales manager gave a joint presentation to the heads of several supermarket chains.

The occasion wasn't a specific-product presentation. That is, the manager wasn't pushing *his* brand, but simply presenting some general information that could be useful to the assembled Economic Buyers in their industry. Among the pieces of information he gave them, though, was the fact that the average profit margin for snack foods—no matter whose label they carried—was extremely high as compared to grocery items overall. The results of this information session were dramatic. Although our client made no claim that his products' specific profit margins were any better than those of his competitors, within a matter of months the company had significantly increased its shelf space in all of the affected stores. This was the Economic Buyers' way of saying, "Thanks for the information," and of increasing their own profit in the bargain.

Knowledge the Economic Buyer *Doesn't* Want

The snack food manufacturer was successful in increasing his penetration in the food accounts because he understood the Economic Buyers' real business needs. He understood that the knowledge they could use had to relate to *long-term* increased profitability. People who forget this point often attempt to bring the Economic Buyer the *wrong kind* of information. This clouds rather than clarifies their crystal balls. The net result is that the person who brings the Economic Buyer this kind of knowledge undermines his own position.

We've mentioned the "features and benefits" or "bells and whistles" bias that many sales representatives still bring to their work. This bias has a provisional usefulness when you're selling to User Buyers and certain Technical Buyers, but it's almost always a drawback when you're trying to sell the Economic Buyer. Knowledge about bits and bytes in computers, about torque and compression ratios in machinery, or about trace ingredients in food products isn't of immediate value to a person whose eye is on long-range planning, institutional stability, and return on investment. Don't waste your time, or your Economic Buyer's, selling him these nuts-and-bolts features.

Think back to the analogy we used earlier about the Economic Buyer being the captain of the ship. As a salesperson, you're like a marine instruments specialist trying to sell a new navigational system. Considering the captain's needs and interests, it would be a mistake to emphasize the size of the computerized system's memory, or to boast about how your product will do for this century what the sextant did for the eighteenth. The navigator wants to hear those details. The captain doesn't. He just wants you to answer one question: "Will this product help me plan my ship's course better?"

Selling a Concept

The distinction between the knowledge that the Economic Buyer wants and doesn't want can be stated in another way. Generally, when you're talking to Economic Buyers, you're selling a concept, or making a *concept sale*. Those who do best with Economic Buyers remember that. Those who wonder why "Farley just isn't paying any attention to me" are usually trying to make a *product sale* instead.

The difference between a concept sale and a product sale can be understood readily if you consider two types of decisions that go into automating a plant or series of plants. The decision to automate in the first place has major implications for the business as a whole, and long-term effects on its organizational stability and growth. That's an example of a concept decision. If you're selling robotics to a growing company, the *first* sale you have to make is the concept sale that convinces the relevant players that automation is necessary. You always make *that* sale to an Economic Buyer.

But once the Economic Buyer has decided to automate, you have to convince a whole range of other players that your particular product line is best equipped to do the job. That's a product sale, and it's usually taken up chiefly with User and Technical Buyers. It always comes *after* the concept sale has been made, never before.

Concept and product sales are interrelated, of course, but in most cases you'll be better off presenting the *end* results to your Economic Buyers, and filling them in on how you *get* those results only if they ask. Top managers seldom want to know "what is this feature called?" They want to know "what will this do for my company (or division or department)?"

Selling the Economic Buyer on the concept behind your

product is so important that we consider it one of the sales representative's chief responsibilities in dealing with these key Buying Influences. But there's another, related, responsibility that's just as important. In addition to selling a concept, you have to sell your own *credibility*.

Establishing Credibility

This means not only your personal credibility, but also that of your company. Ideally, you should make your concept indispensable to the Economic Buyer—and at the same time make it clear that only you and your company can make it possible to implement it. Even if the *immediate* sales objective you have in mind isn't approved, delivering this combination of concept and credibility will establish the reliability you need to make *future* sales.

Four techniques that we've found effective in this regard are to use:

1. Like-rank selling
2. Advertisement of past successes
3. Executive briefings
4. The services of a "guru"

1. Like-Rank Selling

Although it's your responsibility as manager of your sale to see that every base is adequately covered, you may not always be the best person to sell to each of your Buying Influences. Arranging a meeting between buyers and sellers of *like rank* often solves this difficulty. Since executives and other business people are often most comfortable talking to their peers, your own boss (to use just one example) might find it a lot easier to establish credibility with your Economic Buyer than you would.

Your job is to cover each Buying Influence base with the person *best qualified* to do so. Economic Buyers are seldom reluctant to exchange ideas with management peers. If you can arrange for your Economic Buyer to visit one of your company facilities where that's possible, you'll be using like-rank selling effectively.

2. Advertising Past Successes

You can also arrange for your Economic Buyers to visit a customer installation where you have a successful track record, and where by definition you'll be immediately distinguished from the competition. By showing how your product or service has worked well for another client, you demonstrate concept and credibility, and also bring the Economic Buyers the one thing they can't do without: information about how to improve their *own* businesses.

3. The Executive Briefing

The executive briefing, which is really a special case of advertising past successes, is a common tactical approach in the fields of packaged goods and consumer products. Many of our Fortune 500 clients in these fields give such briefings once or twice a year to executives in their principal accounts.

At these periodic presentations, they review with their Economic Buyers the Results and Wins they've provided in the recent past, and suggest future joint ventures that will ensure that the customers will continue to Win. Even when there's no specific proposal on the table, the selling firm is thus still able to reinforce the satisfactions that its customers have enjoyed as a result of their previous associations.

4. Using a "Guru"

A guru, in Strategic Selling terminology, is someone with expertise in an area that exerts influence on business trends. This expert may or may not be from your company, and may or may not be well versed in your particular business.

Economic Buyers achieve their positions of authority in part because they're receptive to new ideas. The advantage to you of arranging a meeting between a guru and your Economic Buyer is that it will introduce the latter to new ideas—and the credit will go to you, as well as the guru, for bringing them to the Economic Buyer's attention.

In addition, employing a guru as a kind of middleman can allow you to get to the Economic Buyer knowledge that *you* have, but that you know will be more believable coming from an impartial expert. For example, having an R&D expert tell an Economic Buyer that your company is at the cutting edge of a certain technology may be a much more effective way of getting your message through than your saying, as a sales representative, "We've got the best stuff on the market."

The guru technique is used with some frequency—and with extraordinary effectiveness—in dealings between major firms. It's a way not so much of facilitating specific sales as of establishing a history of healthy interaction, in which both the firm that supplies the guru and the firm that receives new knowledge see themselves as having Won.

We were called in as gurus ourselves late last year, when one of our clients bought one of our Strategic Selling programs not for itself, but for one of *its* clients. Our new participants were very pleased with the program, and their appreciation extended not just to us, the gurus, for having presented it, but also to the company that had made it possible. So everybody Won.

These four techniques are only samples. You may come up with other techniques that are also effective in improving your position with Economic Buyers. Use anything that works, of course, as long as you're sure that you're delivering what the Economic Buyer always needs—knowledge to improve forecasting ability—and that you're delivering it in a Win-Win manner.

It's true that you'll have to assume the immediate burden here, since typically the company delivering the knowledge picks up the tab. But you'll almost certainly be repaid in future business. Delivering knowledge to an Economic Buyer is not a gift. It's an investment.

Keeping in Touch

It's especially crucial to cover the Economic Buyer on an initial sale to a new account—and to do this early in the selling cycle. But that's not enough. Maintaining *regular* contact with all the potential Economic Buyers in every account is critically important to long-term account strategy.

One of the most common questions we're asked in our seminars is "How often do I have to see the Economic Buyer after I make that first sale?" Even among experienced sales representatives, there's a high degree of uncertainty about how frequently Economic Buyers should be contacted to maintain healthy business relations.

The question has a two-part answer, which ties in everything we've said about bringing what the Economic Buyer needs, about reducing your own discomfort, and about preparation:

- Contact with the Economic Buyer must be *periodic,* not sporadic.
- Whenever you contact the Economic Buyer, you should have a *valid business reason* for doing so.

You don't have to contact the Economic Buyer on *every* repeat sale, but contact after the first order should still be *periodic* rather than haphazard. If you don't schedule meetings with your Economic Buyers on a regular basis, it's easy to fall back into the old discomfort trap and to let contact with these key players slide until your position in their accounts has eroded.

Since they know that they'll be seeing their Economic Buyers in another month, or three months, the best sales strategists are always looking for valid business reasons to do so—that is, for contributions they can make to the way the Economic Buyer is doing business.

These contributions can be as major as showing the Economic Buyer that your company's new refining process can save 18 percent in materials cost—or as "minor" as bringing an article on Japanese management techniques, a news clipping on stock price fluctuations, or a brochure on an upcoming management seminar. As long as they highlight future trends that might, directly or indirectly, have an impact on the company's business, such contributions will always be appreciated—*even if the Economic Buyer has already seen them.* The point is for you to demonstrate that *you* want the Buyer to Win. An Economic Buyer who understands that can be an invaluable ally in any sale.

Personal Workshop 6: Testing Your Position with the Economic Buyer

Take out your Buying Influences Chart, your Win-Results Chart, your Alternate Positions list, your notebook, and your Red Flags. You'll need about twenty minutes to test your position with the Economic Buyer for your chosen sales objective.

Step 1: Who is the Economic Buyer for this sale?

In defining exactly who the Economic Buyer is for your sale, remember that this *single* individual has *final* authority to *release the needed funds*. Look at the name you've placed in the Economic Buyer box of your Buying Influences Chart, and ask yourself whether or not you *know* for certain that this person controls the funds for *this* sale. If you're not certain who the Economic Buyer is, look over your Buying Influences Chart again and see if you can uncover a "hidden" Economic Buyer in one of the other key players. Think also about all the rest of the account, to see if you've overlooked a "mere rubber stamp" high up in the buying organization who will actually give final approval to spend the money.

Once you've come up with the name of the person who you believe controls the funds you need, even if you're certain that you've got the right person, test yourself by asking these further questions about your equivalent of Dan Farley:

- Is Farley at the right *level* in the buying organization to make such a buying decision? If such a decision were being made in *my* company, would the Economic Buyer approval come from the same level? (Remember to take into account the relative size of the two companies.)
- Have I considered the *risk* factors that might

cause the Economic Buyer role to float upward or downward from this level?

- Am I focusing on the Economic Buyer for *this* sales objective?
- Is Farley's approval *final*? Can I honestly take his yes as a release of funds, or is it only a recommendation?
- Is there anybody else in the buying organization who can *veto* Farley's approval?

In asking these critical questions, remember that you have several sources of information to tap. Don't rely only on your *own* impressions of the sales situation. If possible, ask the Economic Buyer himself, in direct or indirect questions. And double-check the answers by asking the same questions of your Coach.

Step 2: How well is the Economic Buyer covered?
Keeping in mind that *any uncovered Buyer is a threat,* determine how well you've covered the Economic Buyer by asking yourself questions like these:

- Have I personally seen Dan Farley myself, or have I arranged for him to be contacted by someone better qualified to do so? (Until you've seen to it that the *best qualified* member of your selling team has contacted the Economic Buyer, you have to consider that Buying Influence base a Red Flag.)
- If Farley hasn't yet been contacted, why not? If he's geographically distant or being screened by a secretary, can I use good proxies or *like-rank selling* to get through?
- If I'm being *blocked* from getting to Farley, what's my best strategy for dealing with the blocker? In this specific sales situation, is the best strategy to go *along,* go *around,* or show the blocking Buyer how to *Win?*

Step 3: How receptive is the Economic Buyer to my proposal?

We've said that each Response Mode dictates a different selling strategy. In this step of the workshop, test the assessment you made in Chapter 8 of your Economic Buyer's Response Mode, to assure yourself that, at this point in the selling cycle, you're approaching this player with the appropriate strategy.

Do that by asking yourself these questions:

- If Farley is in Growth Mode, does he understand that my proposal will help him *improve* the business process or processes that he wants improved?
- If he's in Trouble Mode, does he understand that my proposal will *fix* whatever's wrong? Is he convinced that I understand the *urgency* of his problem?
- If he's in Even Keel Mode, can I demonstrate to him that there's a *discrepancy* he hasn't perceived between his current reality and desired results? Can I arrange for another Buying Influence to warn him about Trouble on the horizon?
- If he's in Overconfident Mode, is it wise for me to try to sell him at this time—or should I lie low until he cycles into Trouble? Have I made the necessary *preparations* to solve his problem when it eventually arises?

Step 4: Am I playing Win-Win with the Economic Buyer?

You know you're playing Win-Win with your Economic Buyer when you can give positive answers to the following questions:

- Have I delivered, or can I deliver, to Dan Farley's company a Result that will create a positive impact on one or more of its processes?
- Does this Result translate for Farley as a personal Win that will satisfy his self-interest? (Remember here that Wins are individual and intangible, and that you can often use Coaching to give you reli-

able information on how a given Buying Influence Wins.)
- Does he *understand* that I've been responsible, and will continue to be responsible, for delivering Win-Results to him? In other words, does he *know* that I'm eager to play Win-Win?

If you can't give yourself concrete, positive answers to these questions, you need to reconsider your position. Look over your Buying Influences Chart and your Win-Results Chart again, concentrating on the Economic Buyer. Place Red Flags anyplace on those charts where the answers to the above questions weren't satisfactory. What questions do you need to ask your *Coach* to help you eliminate these Red Flags?

Step 5: Do I have a Valid Business Reason for seeing the Economic Buyer?

No matter how solid your position with your Economic Buyer may look to you, it's always in jeopardy unless, every time you see the Economic Buyer, you have a valid business reason for doing so. Test whether or not you have such a reason for seeing your Economic Buyer by asking yourself these questions:

- What *knowledge* do I have that Farley can use to forecast future trends in his business? How will this knowledge help him put Windex on his crystal ball?
- How is this knowledge concept related rather than product related? How will the contribution that I can make to his business influence organizational stability and growth, and not just the nuts and bolts of daily operation?
- How does my contribution not only help Farley in *his* business, but also establish the credibility of *my* firm? Whether or not it leads to an acceptance of my immediate sales proposal, how does it distinguish me from the competition?

Step 6: Revise your Alternate Positions list.

Throughout this workshop, you've been asking yourself questions designed to clarify your current position with your Economic Buyer. Use the answers to those questions now to improve that position. Take out your Alternate Positions list and add to it any strategy options that this workshop has suggested.

As you revise the list, work only on those Alternate Positions that relate to the Economic Buyer. Continue to be *specific,* and continue to *test* each entry against the rule of thumb that every good Alternate Position eliminates a Red Flag, leverages from a Strength, or does both.

For example, if in Step 2 of this workshop you noticed that Gary Steinberg was blocking you from getting to Farley, it's not sufficient to list "Get past Steinberg" as an Alternate Position. A more specific Alternate Position would read something like this: "Show Steinberg how he can Win by sponsoring my productivity-increasing proposal to Farley."

Or, if in Step 4 you noticed that you still don't understand how Farley is going to Win in the sale, you can't just list "Get Farley to Win." A sound Alternate Position—one that employs a Strength to eliminate a Red Flag—would be "Ask Doris Green to explain how a 15 percent productivity increase would translate into a Win for Farley."

A Final Check of Your Position with the Economic Buyer

Your continual revision of your Alternate Positions list is a way of remaining *prepared,* and thus of *reducing discomfort,* each time you meet your Economic Buyer. But you won't be able to carry this list around with you, and to review it in detail, every time you knock on Farley's door. To reduce your discomfort before each individual meeting, you need a "short form" test, to gauge the most important features of your upcoming interaction.

We've found that you can efficiently and quickly reduce

your discomfort in the face of meeting an Economic Buyer if, just before you go in, you ask yourself four key questions:

1. *What do I need to FIND OUT?* That is, what *information* do I need to get from this Economic Buyer, or from someone else, to help me better address the required Results and personal Wins?

2. *What do I want the Economic Buyer to KNOW?* That is, what contribution can I make to long-range business planning?

3. *What do I want the Economic Buyer to DO?* That is, how will that contribution provide Results that will have a positive impact on both the buying business and mine?

4. *What do I want the Economic Buyer to FEEL?* That is, how will those Results translate into a personal Win that the Economic Buyer will attribute to me?

When you can answer these questions clearly, and when you know how you'll get the Economic Buyer to know, do, and feel what you want, you'll automatically feel more relaxed about facing this key Buying Influence, and will be able to go in to your meeting with confidence.

▶ 12 ◀

YOUR COACH: A KEY TO THE OTHER BUYING INFLUENCES

Clearly, understanding the identities of the people who play the Buying Influence roles for each of your sales objectives is at the foundation of good sales strategy. Using the first four Key Elements of strategy (Buying Influences, Red Flags/Leverage from Strength, Response Modes, and Win-Results), you've been making your positions with the Buying Influences for your current sales objective clear to yourself, and improving them, throughout this book. By now you should have eliminated many of the Red Flags in those positions, gotten a better understanding of what each of your key players needs to Win, and have a picture of how the Results your product will deliver can provide those Wins.

Throughout our ongoing analysis of your current sales objective, we've stressed the importance of your Coach in improving your strategic position with the other Buying Influences. Beginning with the story of Greg, the computer salesman in the Introduction who utilized an outside consultant to reposition himself with the Economic Buyer, we've said that the use of effective Coaching can often be the difference between a sale that *almost* makes it to the close, and one that not only closes in your favor but also generates Win-Win sales for you far into the future.

Because a good Coach is so essential to good strategy, and because the Coach is significantly different in some respects from the other Buying Influences for your sale, we find it useful to bring together in one place all the information you need to know to develop and use Coaches wisely. A good Coach is often a key to your strategy with all the other Buying Influences; this chapter will show you how to use that key.

A Coach cannot only enable you to check the accuracy of your information and the viability of your position as the sale progresses, but also help you tie together everything that you know, or are still trying to find out, about your Buying Influences. More specifically:

1. As you begin your strategy, your Coach can help you find the *real* key players for your sales objective.

2. Your Coach can help you identify areas of Strength in your position that you can use to eliminate Red Flags as your strategy develops.

3. Your Coach can help you understand each Buyer's perception of reality—and thus gauge how each one is likely to react to your proposal in terms of the four Response Modes (Growth, Trouble, Even Keel, and Overconfident).

4. Your Coach can help you understand the Results each Buyer needs to Win—and how to deliver those Results so that your Buyers perceive themselves to be in a Win-Win scenario with you for this sale, and for all future ones.

Your Coach will only be able to help you in these areas, though, if he or she fits a very particular "job description." Not every person with grease on his hands knows how to fix a carburetor, and not everyone who looks like a Coach can necessarily meet the special qualifications of the Coaching role. Therefore, you need exact criteria to determine who is, and who is not, a potential Coach.

The Three Coaching Criteria

We've explained that a good Coach can be found *anywhere*—in your organization, in the buying organization, or somewhere outside both. It's not geography or organizational placement that determines whether or not a person can fill the Coaching role for you on a given sales objective, but rather how well the candidate fulfills three specific Coaching criteria:

- *Criterion 1: Your credibility.* A Coach is someone with whom you, the sales representative, have personal credibility. That is, your Coach has got to believe in you, to be convinced that you can be *trusted*. Generally, when you have this credibility with a potential Coach, it's because this person has *Won* with you in the past. So the first thing to ask yourself, when you're considering candidates for the Coaching role, is this: "Do I have a track record of performance with this person?"
- *Criterion 2: The Coach's credibility.* A good Coach must have credibility with the *buying organization*. That is, the organization must trust the *Coach* enough to give out reliable information. Since you need your Coach to explain to you how the buying organization works, this criterion is fundamental. So the second question to ask is "Does the buying organization trust this person?"
- *Criterion 3: Desiring your success.* The crucial distinction between your Coach and the other Buying Influences is that by definition the Coach *wants you to make this sale*. It doesn't matter why; the third criterion is fulfilled if the person you're considering as a Coach is eager for your success.

Therefore, the third question to ask is "Does this individual see a personal Win in this sale?"

The ideal Coach will fulfill all three of these criteria. Don't be surprised if the people you consider as Coaches don't measure up on all three counts. Just beware of people who are overflowing with "helpfulness," yet don't meet *any* of the criteria; they're definitely not Coaches. Concentrate on the people who come closest to passing this three-part test. Focusing on these three criteria is the only objective way you can assure yourself that the person you're considering as a Coach can give you the one thing you need: guidance in *this* sale.

People Mistaken for Coaches

In narrowing down the field of potential Coaches so you can focus on the best possible candidates, we've found it useful to identify at the outset certain common types of individuals who look like Coaches, but who cannot fulfill the Coaching role. Among these "false Coaches" are the following:

The "Friend"

Probably the most common single error made in identifying potential Coaches is to confuse the Coach's liking the sales representative *personally* with liking the *sales objective*. In the search for reliable Coaching, "He likes me" should *never* be taken as an equivalent of "He likes my proposal and wants me to make the sale."

You want your Coach to like you, of course. You're not going to get reliable data easily from someone with whom you have no rapport. But personal rapport isn't enough. You want your Coach to like you for a particular reason— because this individual has *Won* with you in the past. A person who has Won with you already is likely to believe that he or she can Win again with you now. That is, you'll have the necessary *credibility* with that person. Your credibility constitutes our first Coaching criterion.

But that's still only one criterion. Don't forget the other two. No matter how close you are to Doris Green, and no matter how great a guy she thinks you are, you still don't have a Coach in her unless she's trusted by the buying organization, and unless she perceives a Win in *this* sale for her. A Coach *must* like your proposal.

The Information Giver

It's true that your Coach's primary duty is to provide you with information. But not just *any* information. To be a reliable Coach, the person has to get you information that's *unique* and *useful* to you in this particular sale.

- By "unique" information we mean information that you can't readily get elsewhere.
- By "useful" information we mean information that will help you improve your position with the Buying Influences for this sale.

These two characteristics are interactive, and equally essential. The person who gives you production specs that were contained in the buying company's last stockholders' report may be giving you useful information—but it's hardly unique, since you could easily have gotten it yourself. On the other hand, the person who tells you that your Economic Buyer has a star-shaped mole on his shoulder is giving you unique information that's useless. The *unique* and *useful* information you want your Coaches to provide will tell you how the buying organization *really* works, how each of the Buying Influences *really* Wins—and how the Results *your proposal* delivers can help each of them to Win.

Ideally, your Coaches provide a "map" that guides you to the other Buying Influences. Beware of Coaches who offer you "rare" or "interesting" maps that don't show you where you want to go. There's no point in having the definitive map of New Jersey in your pocket if your sales objective is in Kansas.

The Inside Salesman

An inside salesman, as we use the term, is someone in the buying organization who does some of your selling for you, and who usually recommends you over the competition. In other words, he takes on some of your responsibilities—generally because he sees something in the sale for him. This means that he fulfills the third Coaching criterion: He sees your success as a Win for him.

But, again, that's only one criterion. By itself, it's not enough to make a person a good Coach. As important as inside salesmen are to many Complex Sales, not all of them make good Coaches.

Therefore, you have to test inside salesmen against the first two Coaching criteria as well: (1) They have to trust *you* and (2) the buying organization has to trust *them*. If they don't trust you, their desire for you to make the sale may prove unstable. And if they aren't trusted by the other Buying Influences, they may not get you accurate information.

There's an additional danger in seeking Coaching from inside salesmen. By definition an inside salesman *sells*. That's not at all what a Coach does. Ideally, you want to do your *own* selling, with the Coach's guidance. Coaches belong on the sidelines. You should no more want your Coach to sell for you than an NFL quarterback would want his Coach to take the snap from the center. In developing inside salesmen as Coaches, remember a cardinal rule: The more you let somebody else run the plays *for* you, the less control *you* have of the ball.

The Mentor

As you know, many executives today get their professional start under the wing of old-timers in their organizations (sometimes outside of their organizations) who take on an unofficial responsibility for showing the newcomers the ropes. The older person introduces the younger one to the "right" people, explains company protocol and procedure, and in general grooms the new executive to carry on the senior executive's personal brand of leadership.

It's true that you may find Coaches in your own organization. And it's true that a mentor such as we're describing here can be a valuable asset. But you shouldn't confuse a mentor with a Coach.

By definition a mentor wants you to succeed in your *career*. He grooms you to follow in his footsteps so that your success in business as a whole will reflect well on him. A Coach's desire for your success, while just as solid, is far more focused than that: Your Coach by definition wants you to succeed *in this sale*. Though committed to your success, the mentor *may* have nothing to contribute to the information you need to make this sale. Your Coach, on the other hand, may care little about your long-range plans. But a Coach who sees a personal Win in *this* sale can still be a reliable asset.

The Best Possible Coaching Situation

Although, as we've observed, good Coaches can be found almost anywhere, there is one ideal source. The best of all possible Coaching situations is to turn the Economic Buyer for your sales objective into a Coach in his or her own organization.

The benefits of using your Economic Buyer as a Coach are obvious:

- The Economic Buyer is likely to understand better than the other Buying Influences how the buying organization actually works—that is, how purchasing decisions are made. So this person can guide you to the other key players.
- If the Economic Buyer is convinced of the concept advantages of your proposal, you'll have less trouble selling its advantages to the other Buying Influences.
- The simple fact that the Economic Buyer is usually a top manager means that this person's counsel will carry weight with the other key players for your sale.
- Turning your Economic Buyer into a Coach significantly reduces the risk of a veto late in the selling cycle.

For different but related reasons, it's always good to get to the Economic Buyer early and to develop a good Coach early. Turning the Economic Buyer into a Coach does both these things simultaneously.

If the Economic Buyer favors your proposal early in the game, one good way of turning this person into a Coach is to ask for Coaching about *another person.* "Dan," you can say, "I'd appreciate some Coaching on the best approach to take with Will Johnson." Such a question reinforces your position with the Economic Buyer *and* improves the Coaching possibilities.

Asking for Coaching

When you've winnowed out the false Coaches and have found someone who you believe fulfills the three Coaching criteria, you should ask that person for Coaching. We mean this advice literally. The term "Coaching," because of its use in sports, has a very positive connotation in our culture. It decodes as "I'm competent and I'll do my own work; just give me some direction." Because of its positive connotation, most people welcome the opportunity to do Coaching. So use the word: "Coaching." *Don't* say, "I need your help," or "Can you refer me to the right people for this sale?" The words "refer" and "help" and "recommendation" decode badly: They're heard as "I'm incompetent; I need you to carry the ball for me."

By asking for Coaching rather than for a referral, you'll discover a happy paradox. The sales representative who asks for a referral or for help may not get either one. The sales representative who asks for Coaching usually gets the information he needs—and the referral besides.

A fundamental point to remember is the one we mentioned above, when we defined the difference between an inside salesman and a Coach. Your Coach's role is to provide information, direction, guidance—and in many cases access to the other Buying Influences. *But the Coach doesn't do your selling for you.* Be wary of giving any potential Coach the idea that that's what you want.

Your Coaching Network

You should try to develop at least one Coach per major sales objective. But often one is not enough. Often too, even a good Coach whom you've effectively developed for one sales objective will prove useless for future sales objectives. So your long-term aim should be to develop a *network* of Coaches whose expertise you can draw on as needed within an account. The larger and more complex the account, the greater the need for a network of Coaches.

There are two basic reasons that you need to develop a Coaching network. One is that every sale is *unique;* you need a different Coach or Coaches for each individual sales objective. The other reason is that, even for a single sales objective, there are still so many ways to be *misinformed* that success is usually the result of relying not on one person's information, but on a variety of data from many sources. The more Coaches you have working with you on a given sale, the better chance you'll have of eliminating the many varied Red Flags that can be involved in any sale.

Coaches for This Sale

A friend of ours in computer sales discovered the importance of having a Coaching network last year, when he nearly blew a major software deal by relying initially on a single Coach, a person he described as "my old buddy Mel." Mel had Coached him very well on a couple of former deals, and naturally our friend went to him for direction when he was about to propose a third.

On this third sale, though, Mel was lukewarm. He gave our friend advice that boiled down to "Hang in there—you're doing fine." Encouraging, sure—but not the kind of information the salesman needed to be sure of his position. For about a month he kept going back to Mel, with negligible results, until he suddenly realized his problem. On the previous sales, Mel had been one of the User Buyers as well as the Coach; he'd seen that it was in his immediate self-interest to have our friend make those deals. On this sales proposal, however, our friend was trying to sell a software package that had nothing to do with Mel's department. Because Mel felt that he had nothing to gain from the transaction, his "assistance" was more cordial than illuminating.

"When I realized that," the salesman told us, "the light really went on. I saw that he was still my friend, but that he had no interest in this sale. I'd have to look for another Coach."

He did so in a way that illustrates the importance of networking. Once he saw that Mel was the wrong man for *this* unique sales objective, our friend went to him and admitted his dilemma. "Look, Mel," he said, "I'm in a bind here. Is there anyone who can give me the kind of information on this sale that you gave me on the last two?" In effect our friend was still using Mel as a Coach, but in a totally different, and much more effective, manner. By getting his "old friend" to guide him toward another sale-specific Coach, he accomplished three valuable things:

1. He reinforced his former Win-Win relationship with Mel by letting Mel know that he valued and appreciated his advice.

2. He acquired the right Coach for this sale—a woman who saw a Win in the sale for herself.

3. He widened the network of possible Coaches on which he could draw in the future.

Networking as a Checking Mechanism
The second reason you need to develop a variety of Coaches is that, even within each individual sale, there are still plenty of chances to be misinformed. The more people you have giving you information on a given sales goal, the more opportunity you'll have to check each individual person's assessment against other views. In addition, the more Red Flags you'll be likely to turn into opportunities.

An area sales director in food sales, a man we'll call Rod, uses a "total coverage" technique in setting up and nurturing his Coaching network. "I always try to use everybody I can as a Coach," he explains. "I deal mostly with the vice-presidential level, and almost everybody at that level has some information you can use. I get Jack Smith to give me a handle on Mary Jones's Wins, and then I get Mary to tell me about Jack's. That way I can double-check what each person is telling me, so I never end up out in the cold."

Rod's technique has several times helped him become salesman of the year. It works because it incorporates several of the Strategic Selling principles we've described:

- In a sophisticated way, it covers—and re-covers— the bases to be sure that as many Red Flags as possible are turned into opportunities.
- It effectively focuses attention on the individual Buyers' probable Wins.
- And it highlights the basic rule that every sales strategy has to be constantly tested and reassessed to remain effective.

The obvious problem you'll encounter in using networking as a testing mechanism, of course, is that you'll uncover not just *verifying* information, but *conflicting* information. Since no two Coaches are ever going to perceive a given selling situation in precisely the same way, you'll inevitably be involved in sales where one Coach tells you one thing about a key Buying Influence, and a second Coach tells you the opposite.

Sorting your way through this difficulty means being able to assess each Coach's information independently against the reality *you* perceive.

We used this strategy recently to resolve the fundamental question of who was really the Economic Buyer for a pending sale. Our initial Coach for the deal, a Technical Buyer, said that a vice-president of sales, a man we'll call Fox, would give final approval for the sale. "He's been here forever," the Technical Buyer said. "And he'll be here when we're all gone."

A User Buyer for the sale, however, gave us conflicting information. According to her, there was a corporate shake-up in the works and Fox was on his way out. The User Buyer had given us good information in the past, but the Technical Buyer was organizationally closer to Fox. Which Coach were we to believe?

To decide the issue, we arranged a meeting with Fox in which we could look unobtrusively for signs of the uncertainty that the User Buyer had warned us about. "The guy is walking on eggs," she'd said. "You see if he looks like somebody who's going to be here in another month." The meeting proved her correct. Fox was uneasy, hesitant to see us, and very reluctant to commit himself. We decided that, even though he'd been the Economic Buyer for other purchases of our programs, he wasn't acting like an Economic Buyer now. We began to look elsewhere for final approval, and a month later Fox was gone. Thanks to our second Coach, and to our reality-testing session, we'd avoided wasting valuable time in presenting our product to a powerless "Economic Buyer."

One final note on your Coaching network. Unless you sell only one product, at a fixed rate, to a single customer, developing more than one Coach per sale is only the beginning in the effective use of a network. Since you very likely work with different products or services, different dollar amounts, and a variety of customers, you need to develop a network that permeates your entire industry and thus touches every possible sales situation. The more reliable Coaches you nurture and develop over time, the more quickly you'll be able to find the right Coach for each aspect of each new sales objective.

The Final Test: Your Feelings

Even after you've verified that each person you're utilizing as a Coach fulfills the three Coaching criteria, even after you've sorted through the "false Coaches" we've described, and even after you have checked your Coaches' conflicting information against your own perceptions of the selling situation, you may still be uncertain about a potential Coach's ability to guide you in a given sale. When this happens, you can fall back on what we've found to be a reliable court of last appeal. When all other means have been exhausted, you should ask yourself how you *feel* about using a given person as a Coach.

This relates back to what we said in our discussion of the Euphoria-Panic Continuum in Chapter 3. We said there that, although you can often be misled by your head, your gut reactions to a given sales situation are usually pretty reliable. If you feel "uneasy" or "a little funny" about a sale, there's a good chance that there's something wrong with your position—even if you don't know what it is.

The point applies to your assessment of Coaches as well, and to your need to test each one against those with conflicting information. Trust those uneasy feelings. If everything a certain Coach is telling you about a given Buyer's Wins or about a given account situation *sounds* right, but something still *feels* wrong, look at that Coach again. If you're uneasy with the guidance you're getting, the chances are you're not talking to a real Coach.

Personal Workshop 7: Testing Your Coach

By this point in your strategic analysis, you should already have identified at least one Coach. The purpose of this Personal Workshop is to have you *test* that individual to see whether or not he or she can in fact provide good Coaching. So pull out your Buying Influences Chart, your Alternate Positions list, the Win-Results Chart, and your Red Flags. Since your Coach is a principal key to your other Buyers, the chances are that much of the information you've written in on these various charts came directly or indirectly from the Coach. You're going to test it now for reliability.

Step 1: Do you have credibility with your Coach?
Begin by measuring your Coach against the first of the three Coaching criteria. If you have two or more Coaches identified—as in our sample Buying Influences Chart—assess them separately, one by one. There's nothing subtle or

esoteric about this step. To test whether or not you have credibility with Andy Kelly, for example, ask yourself these questions:

- How has Andy *Won* with me in the past?
- If he hasn't Won with me personally, has he at least Won with my *company*?
- Am I certain that I have Andy's *trust*?

As always, be specific in your answers. If you can say, "I sold Andy that promo deal when he was with Smith Industries, and it helped him get a vice-presidency"—then you can be fairly certain that you've earned his trust. But if you can't say something like this—if you can't identify a *concrete,* and preferably *recent,* Win that you've brought him—look at him again. Unless he believes that you can be trusted to deliver Wins for him, *you* may not be able to trust *him.*

Step 2: Does he have credibility with the buying company?

Now look for evidence that Andy can provide you with reliable information on *this* sale, to *this* company. To get that information, he must be trusted by the buying organization. If he's not, his efforts on your behalf will at best be useless, and at worst could lead you to undermine your own position.

Past history is your best yardstick here. If Andy told you about a marketing decision at Contour Industries two months before it became public, he looks like a good bet for a Coach: Somebody at Contour obviously trusts him enough to give him an inside track. But if your last experience with him was that he misidentified an Economic Buyer for you, think twice about using him now.

Testing the credibility of your Coach with the buying organization is particularly important if he doesn't come from that organization himself. Coaches you draw from your own firm, or from the golf club and convention network, may or may not be able to guide you effectively. They *may* make excellent Coaches—but you can't assume that to be so until you test them.

Even if the Coach you've tentatively chosen to help you get into Contour is part of Contour himself, you *still* have to test his credibility. As you know, not everyone sitting at a nine-foot desk actually knows what's going on. Don't rely on titles and offices to test your Coach for the second criterion. It doesn't matter what his corporate position is if what he tells you is accurate.

Use your Coaching network too to test one Coach against another. What is Doris Green saying about Andy? What does he say about her? Which one of them, judging objectively, is closer to the Contour reality?

Step 3: Does your Coach want you to make this sale?

Since your Coach's role is to guide you in the sale, it's necessary for this person to be not only able but *eager* to give you proper direction. The only way to guarantee this eagerness is to demonstrate to your Coach that there's something in the sale, personally, for him or her. Your Coach always has to perceive the sale as a Win. So put Andy to the test again by asking yourself this question:

> *How is this person's self-interest served by my making this sale?*

You need a clear, concrete answer to that question—something like this: "The sale will enhance his perception of himself by making him look like a problem solver." If you know how Andy will Win when you Win, then you know he fulfills the third Coaching criterion. If you don't have such an answer, you can't be certain that you have a reliable Coach.

If that's the case—if you can't identify a supposed Coach's reason for wanting you in there—then you need to reconsider your position with him. He can only be the key you want if he perceives that he'll Win with you in this sale.

One way of determining whether or not a possible Coach sees himself as playing Win-Win with you is to examine critically the information he has *already* given you. Do that by asking yourself these questions:

1. Has this Coach helped me to find the real key players for my sales objective—and to understand the exact *role* each of them is playing?
2. Has this Coach helped me to identify areas of uncertainty (Red Flags) in my position—and given me sound, workable advice for eliminating them?
3. Has this Coach given me reliable information regarding the *receptivity* of each of my Buyers to my specific sales proposal?
4. Has this Coach supplied me with *unique* and *useful* data on the Win-Results I need to deliver to each of the Buyers to manage the sale into a Win-Win outcome?

You should get positive answers to most, if not all, of these questions. If you don't, your "Coach" isn't providing the information you need.

Step 4: Assess your current position with your Coach.

If your Coach isn't providing you with appropriate data for this sale, you should investigate why not. If you've discovered through this exercise that Andy Kelly isn't working out to your satisfaction, take this discovery as a Red Flag for opportunity and go on. Find out why he isn't working out.

- If it's because you lack credibility with him, is there something you can do to create or restore it? Can you remind him of a past Win he may have forgotten?
- If it's because he lacks credibility with the buying organization, can he at least guide you to someone in that organization who *does* have credibility? Or would your best option here simply be to get rid of Andy and look elsewhere for a Coach?
- If it's because he sees no Win in this sale for him, what can you do to change that? What information can *you* give *him* that shows his self-interest will be served by the sale? Or, if he sees no Win in the sale for him, is he correct? Would a better option be to acknowledge that he has nothing to gain

from the sale—and go on to choose or develop another Coach?

Remember that there's more than one Coach in the corporate sea; sometimes your most suitable option is the difficult one of "firing" one Coach and getting someone else—someone who can better guide you in the sale.

Step 5: Revise your Alternate Positions list.

Now use the information you've uncovered in this workshop to revise your Alternate Positions list. Look at the Red Flags that still remain on your Buying Influences and Win-Results charts. Concentrate first on options that can eliminate or reduce the impact of those Red Flags. Pay special attention to the information your Coach can still provide you to help you do this. Frame the questions you need to ask your Coach, and write them down as new items on the Alternate Positions list.

For example, if you still don't know exactly what's in your sale for your Economic Buyer, Dan Farley, one Alternate Position could be "Get Doris Green to explain how Farley can Win." If Technical Buyer Steinberg's inventory problem is still unclear to you, you might put down, "Ask Andy Kelly why Steinberg is so worried about his department."

After you've listed options in which your Coach can be of assistance, list options that improve your position with the Coach. Consider the questions that you asked about your Coach in Step 4 of this workshop. Do the answers to those questions suggest further Alternate Positions?

Continue to assess each possible Alternate Position against the two-part rule of thumb that has been the hallmark of all your revisions. Make sure that every strategy option you consider eliminates or reduces the impact or a Red Flag, leverages from a Strength, or does both.

A Final Word: Reassessment

As we come to the end of the second part of this book, we want to emphasize one point that's particularly suggested by the Personal Workshop you've just completed, but is implicit in all aspects of Strategic Selling. The point is that, to be effective as a sales strategist over time, you must continually *reassess* your position with regard to your individual sales goals, and with regard to all the Key Elements that will help you to realize those goals.

One reason that your Coach is indispensable to your strategy is that he or she can help you, on a regular basis, to perform this necessary reassessment. The way you use your Coach reflects to a great degree the way you manage your sale. If you take this unique Buying Influence as merely an inside salesman or a "buddy," you'll almost certainly develop poor Coaches and use the potentially good ones in inefficient ways. But if you *test* your Coaches' information and then use this information to apply the Key Elements of strategy to your sale, you'll find your position in that sale continually, and predictably, improving.

You must do this over and over. A sound strategic analysis is only as good as its last reassessment. In using your Coaches wisely to guide you through each reassessment, you'll find that this critical Buying Influence can be the key not only to the other Buyers, but to a predictable Win-Win record over time.

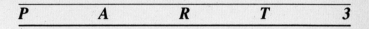

MULTIACCOUNT STRATEGY: MANAGING YOUR SELLING TIME

▲

► 13 ◄

OF TIME AND MONEY

Up to now you've been applying our Strategic Selling principles to a single, specific sales objective—the one you defined for yourself in the Personal Workshop on position in Chapter 3. Experience has shown us that, when you handle several accounts or prospects, it's easy to become strategically confused unless you break your objectives in each account into distinct, separate sales goals. So we've insisted that you keep your chosen sales objective clearly in mind.

You're not always going to be as single-minded in your analysis as we've asked you to be up to now, because this initial, "test case" objective isn't your only objective. You have several accounts and prospects and in each account there are a number of distinct sales goals that you're working toward at the same time. Once you finish this book, you'll be able to apply the principles of Strategic Selling to all those individual goals, all the time—and thereby achieve repeatable and predictable sales results.

In order to do this effectively, you have to be able to do two additional things:

- So that you understand how each individual objective fits into your larger, multiaccount picture, you have to take a *broader view* of your selling needs than the one we've been suggesting up to now.
- So that each individual objective contributes to a predictable, consistent income over time, you have to be able to *divide your time* efficiently among them all.

Our fifth Key Element of strategy is designed to help you do both these things. We call this Key Element the Sales Funnel. It's an integral part of our Strategic Selling approach because, as we've demonstrated to sales representatives and managers in many businesses, it enables you to manage your single *most precious resource* effectively, so that you get maximum benefits over time from every sale and every account.

Your Most Precious Resource: Selling Time

Everyone we know in sales has at one time or another complained, "What I need is a forty-eight-hour day."

This is a complaint of people in many walks of life, but it's especially aggravating to sales professionals because, in addition to the actual *selling* time we have to put in (which most of us enjoy), we also have to put in time on many nonselling tasks. And these tasks take up the *bulk* of every sales representative's time.

Think of how many hours a week you spend on the following tasks:

- Selling internally to your own company
- Making out expense reports
- Doing other paperwork
- Attending meetings
- Handling customer complaints

- Expediting orders
- Training customers to use your product or service
- Traveling

Don't misunderstand us. We don't mean that these nonselling tasks are unimportant. We know as well as you do that they're essential to your long-term success. But they aren't what we call selling.

When we talk about selling time, we mean something very specific. We mean the time you actually spend face to face (or phone to phone) with your customers. In our Strategic Selling programs, we use the following definition:

> *Selling time: any time spent talking to a Buying Influence about Growth or Trouble, or asking questions of a Buying Influence to uncover a Growth or Trouble discrepancy*

When our participants understand our definition of selling time, they usually tell us that they're lucky to get five or ten hours a week to devote to this fundamental professional activity. Most top salespeople, in fact, spend somewhere between 5 and 15 percent of their total working time actively engaged in face-to-face selling. Among the thousands of sales representatives and managers we've counseled, we have yet to meet one person who spends more than a quarter of the work week actually talking to Buying Influences about Growth or Trouble.

Nobody likes this state of affairs, but it's a fact of every salesperson's life. As much as we would like to spend more time with our customers and less behind a desk or a steering wheel, selling time is still the single resource of which we never have enough. If it isn't managed well, the representative typically falls victim to a deadly pattern of fluctuating and unpredictable income—the pattern we call the Roller Coaster Effect.

The Roller Coaster Effect

If you've been in sales for more than a few months, you're probably already familiar with the Roller Coaster Effect.

This way of describing uneven income over time is represented by the chart below.

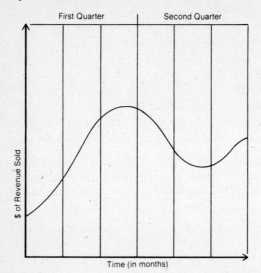

As you can see, the chart plots the relationship between each monthly accounting period and dollars of revenue sold—or, more bluntly, between time and money. Obviously, according to this chart, time does not always equal money; to be more precise, the amount of time that you put in on a month-to-month basis isn't necessarily going to be reflected in a steady (or steadily rising) income.

If you recognize this chart as being an approximation of your own "time and money" pattern, you've got a lot of company. Unevenness of income over time is so common among people in sales that many lifetime managers and sales representatives consider it a kind of natural law. As a regional manager once confessed to us, shrugging his shoulders in resignation, "That's the way the selling road runs. You've just got to hang on and wait it through."

Not true, we told him. The Roller Coaster Effect is *not* an inevitable feature of the sales representative's long-term income profile. And you *do* have an alternative to "hanging on" until better times come through.

We know, as you do, that *some* cyclical fluctuations in

income are inevitable; they're built into your business. There are seasonal variations, annual budgets, and microeconomic trends that impinge on every sales representative's work. However, our experience shows that the worst fluctuations of the Roller Coaster Effect are caused *not* by these economic forces, but by the salesperson's own poor management of selling time. That's something we can help you control.

What the Sales Funnel Does

The fundamental purpose of the Sales Funnel is to help you manage your selling time more effectively, so that you avoid the deepest valleys of your personal selling cycles and thus ensure that you translate that time into real money, not just for today's sales goals, but all the way down the line. In the following two chapters you'll learn how to use this time-management tool to accomplish the following essential selling tasks:

- *Sorting* your many sales objectives into three basic categories, or levels of the Sales Funnel
- *Tracking* each sales objective's progress as it moves from one level into the next
- *Setting priorities* for working on the objectives in each level of the Funnel to ensure that you don't neglect any one of the three
- *Allocating time* to the objectives in each level of the Funnel in a way that's appropriate to your specific situation.
- *Forecasting* future income based on how your objectives are moving through the three levels of the Funnel

When you use the Sales Funnel to accomplish these related tasks, you not only utilize time more efficiently, you also achieve the broader perspective needed for success in all your sales objectives over time.

So let's see how the Sales Funnel works.

► 14 ◄

KEY ELEMENT 5:
THE SALES FUNNEL

The funnel metaphor that we use as the basis of our fifth Key Element of strategy may not be entirely unfamiliar to you. Many sales representatives talk about "throwing prospects into the pipeline," "into the hopper," or "into the top of the funnel" and then waiting for completed orders to come out at the other end.

We've already mentioned that we don't wait for orders, but actively *work* the funnel, so that orders (and thus income) are predictable. Our Sales Funnel is also more sophisticated in that we divide the Funnel conceptually into three distinct parts, or levels, corresponding to three different types of selling work.

The first thing you need to know to use the Sales Funnel concept effectively is how to *sort* your sales objectives into these three levels.

Sorting: The Three Parts of the Funnel

The Sales Funnel concept is represented by the chart below.

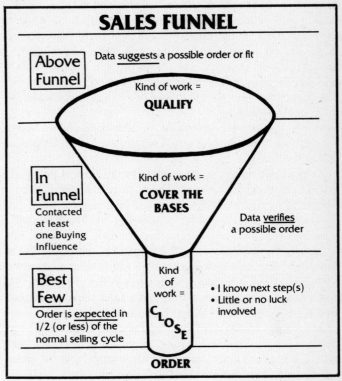

SALES FUNNEL

Above Funnel
Data suggests a possible order or fit
Kind of work =
QUALIFY

In Funnel
Contacted at least one Buying Influence
Kind of work =
COVER THE BASES
Data <u>verifies</u> a possible order

Best Few
Order is expected in 1/2 (or less) of the normal selling cycle
Kind of work = CLOSE
• I know next step(s)
• Little or no luck involved

ORDER

You'll notice that in this chart there are three distinct parts to the Sales Funnel. We call these parts *Above the Funnel, In the Funnel,* and *Best Few.* You'll also notice that each of these three parts is associated with a particular kind of selling work. This is a central feature of the Funnel: Each part of the Funnel is by definition associated with one, and *only* one, kind of work.

As a sales professional, you must be able to do all three kinds of work. You have to be able to:

- Prospect and qualify
- Cover the bases
- Close the order

But, since you have many possible orders working at the same time, and since they're all at different stages of completion, you're not going to be doing the same kind of work on all of them at the same time. You'll be prospecting or qualifying on some pieces of business while you're closing in others and covering the bases in yet others. You'll achieve the predictable and sound income you want only if you consistently *do the right kind of work* on each possible order *at the right time.*

That's the reason you need to sort your work tasks. The Sales Funnel is, first and foremost, a tool to help you do that.

Before describing the three parts of the Funnel in detail, we want to make three key observations about the tool as a whole:

First, the Sales Funnel helps you sort and track the progress of individual possible orders or sales objectives, *not* accounts. You can't say that the "Apex account" belongs in Best Few. You can only say that "getting Apex to approve a pilot installation by May 15" belongs in Best Few.

Second, two things are reduced as a sales objective moves down the Funnel: the expected *time* to the order and the level of *uncertainty* involved. Each sales objective begins at the top of the Funnel, often with a long time span to the order and many uncertainties, and ends up at the bottom, with the order closed and uncertainties hopefully under control.

Finally, each level of the Funnel is related to certain *prerequisites,* and to one and only one *kind of selling work.* We'll explain these points now, with regard to each of the Funnel's three levels.

Above the Funnel

The *prerequisite* for identifying a possible order as being Above the Funnel is that you have data which *suggests* a fit between your product or service and the prospective buying company's needs. Examples of this suggestive data:

- You read a news report about a firm's expansion that could be facilitated by your product or service.
- Your company receives a "bingo card," or a simple request for information, from a potential customer.
- A colleague who has sold a different product or service to the firm tells you there's a chance for a sale.
- The customer's existing contract with a competitor is about to expire.
- The customer's equipment is aging, indicating a need for new capital investment.

These are only a few samples, but you get the idea. You don't need to be too exclusionary at this point. As long as there's even an outside chance of a fit, throw the prospect's name Above the Funnel.

The *kind of work* that needs to be done on a prospect that's Above the Funnel is to *qualify,* or *verify* your suggestive data. You do that by contacting the Buying Influences, including your Coach or Coaches.

Verification of your data may take many forms. It may mean simply that a given Buying Influence shows interest in an initial phone call or presentation. It may mean that this person starts Coaching you on the other Buying Influences. Or it may mean that you get a direct request for a demonstration.

But one element of the verification process is essential. You must contact at least one Buying Influence and identify a Growth or Trouble discrepancy that your product or service can address. This is your *minimum* selling task on a piece of business Above the Funnel.

In the Funnel

The *prerequisite* for placing a sales objective In the Funnel is that you've verified the possibility of an order: You've contacted at least one Buying Influence and spoken about Growth or Trouble.

The *kind of work* that you need to perform in this part of

the Funnel is to *cover the bases*. This entails using all the Key Elements of strategy that we've already discussed. In covering the bases, you perform the following tasks:

- Identify all the Buying Influences for your sales objective, and ensure that each one is contacted by the person best qualified to do so.
- Understand the Response Mode of every Buyer, and concentrate on eliminating the perceived discrepancies of all Buyers in Growth or Trouble Mode.
- Identify the Results each Buyer needs to Win, and make sure that each one understands that your proposal will serve his or her self-interest.
- Continually reassess the sales picture so that you eliminate Red Flags and use the principle of capitalizing on your Strengths.

We said that *time and uncertainty decrease* as you move a sales objective down the Funnel. Your overall purpose in covering the bases here is to ensure that this continues to happen.

Best Few

The *prerequisite* for placing a sales objective into the Best Few category is that you've all but eliminated *luck* and *uncertainty* as factors in the final buying decision.

We realize that this is a subjective judgment, and for that reason we acknowledge that the dividing line between In the Funnel and Best Few isn't quite as sharp as the line between Above the Funnel and In the Funnel. But it's *not* simply a matter of guesswork. You can test whether or not a possible order is really ready to go into the Best Few level of the Funnel by remembering the following specifics:

- In Best Few, there are *few discrete tasks* left to be performed and you know exactly what they are. In other words, the *kind of work* to be done involves "end tasks" such as overcoming last-minute objections, dealing with basic issues, getting final confirmation, order signing, and so on.

- On a Best Few objective, you've *covered the bases* so well that you've moved entirely beyond trial and error or guessing. For example, you know all your Buyers, you've addressed their Win-Results, and you've laid out a plan to eliminate any remaining Red Flags.
- Finally, in Best Few, there's at least a *90 percent* probability that you'll close the order in *one half* or less the time of your *normal selling cycle*.

This last point needs clarification, since it introduces an unfamiliar term—"normal selling cycle"—that is crucial to the effective use of the Sales Funnel.

Your Normal Selling Cycle

When we talk about your normal selling cycle, we mean the amount of time that it typically takes you to move an order from the top to the bottom of the Sales Funnel—in other words, the amount of time between initial contact and the agreement to buy.

We're aware that selling cycles vary dramatically from industry to industry, and from product to product within the same industry or same company. Selling cycles are influenced by many factors, including the cost of the product, the identities of the Buying Influences, and the complexity of the buying decisions. We know people in sales who have sold special promotions to retail chains in a matter of one or two weeks, and other people who have spent seven or eight years handling an aircraft sale to a government. There's no such thing as a universally "normal" selling cycle.

What we're concerned with here is *your* normal selling cycle, for your business and your service or product line. Although your orders won't all move at the same rate, most of them will probably follow an average cycle. That average is what we mean by "normal."

Take a few minutes right now to determine your own normal selling cycle. Think over the sales you've made in the last year or two, and consider how long each one took from first sales call to signing on the dotted line. In determining your personal average, throw out the renewals you did in your sleep, and those oddball orders that you moved to the signing two days after meeting the first Buyer. Throw out also the drawn-out orders that reflected extraordinary business conditions or peculiarly difficult situations or Buyers. Concentrate on what's left and take the average of that.

For example, if most of your sales take somewhere between three and nine months to close—from first sales call to an official contractual agreement—then your normal selling cycle is about six months. If it generally takes you somewhere between ten and twenty weeks to move from first sales call to the close, your normal selling cycle is fifteen weeks.

We emphasize the importance of understanding your normal selling cycle because it's one of the keys to knowing when a sales objective should move from In the Funnel into Best Few. We've already given you other keys to knowing when to place an order Above the Funnel, and when to move it from Above the Funnel to In the Funnel.

Moving a piece of business from one level of the Funnel down into the next level is what we call *tracking* it. You have to do this at the appropriate time for each individual piece of business. If you mentally move a sales objective down too early or too late, you can easily end up doing the *wrong kind of work* on that sales objective—and therefore put your order in jeopardy. An example will illustrate what we mean.

Barry, a friend of ours who sells word-processing equipment to small businesses, tried to sell a system two years ago to a company that couldn't afford it at the time. The company's officers obviously wanted the system and Barry had done an admirable job of covering the bases with all the Buying Influences involved. The only hitch was the budget. "We'll put it in for the next fiscal year," they told him. "But we've definitely got a deal."

They told him that in January, and at that time they did have a deal. That is, they really did intend to buy from

Barry, as soon as money became available. The trouble was that the new budget wasn't due to be approved until July. As Barry found out too late, a lot can happen in six months.

Normally, he would have closed a deal like this one in about five or six months. But since things had gone so well up to January, he considered the order in hand. In other words, he mentally moved the order *out* of the In-the-Funnel position into Best Few. And he figured that the only work he had to do between January and July was to wait for the new budget to go through.

That was a big mistake. When he went back to the buying firm in July, he found that he'd lost the sale to a competitor—one who had stayed on top of the situation right up to the last minute.

If Barry had kept the "one half of normal selling cycle" rule in mind, he wouldn't have made this classic error. Realizing that six months was more than half his normal selling cycle, he would have kept the order In the Funnel, and kept covering the bases with his Buyers, right on into the summer. If he'd done that, he might not have been blindsided by the competition.

The lesson is this: In tracking your sales objectives down the Funnel, you have to remember the prerequisites and the kinds of work that are relevant to each level of the Funnel. The Sales Funnel becomes operationally effective only when you satisfy the prerequisites before moving an objective down the Funnel, and when you do the right kind of work at the right time for every objective in the Funnel.

You'll practice these principles now, in a Personal Workshop.

Personal Workshop 8: The Sales Funnel

In this Personal Workshop you're going to sort your own current sales objectives, to see how near each of them is to being completed, and to determine what specific tasks you still have to perform to move them further down the Funnel. You'll need your notebook, pencils, and your Alternate Positions list. The exercise should take about thirty minutes.

Step 1: List your sales objectives.

Open your notebook so that you have two clean pages facing you. Remembering that the Sales Funnel sorts and tracks sales objectives or possible orders, *not* accounts, list the individual sales objectives on which you're currently working. *Be specific.* In Chapter 3 we said that an individual sales objective:

- Is *measurable*. It gives numerical answers to the questions who, what, and when.
- Focuses on a *single outcome* that you're trying to bring about in an account.
- Can be defined in a *simple* rather than compound sentence.

You may have only a few objectives to list, or dozens. Just be sure to list working orders, not accounts. You can't track "Handle the Tintax account" in the Sales Funnel; what you need to list is "Sell Tintax one gross of our #39 package by June 15."

Step 2: Sort your current possible orders or sales.

Now sort the possible sales you've just listed into the three parts of the Sales Funnel. Do this on the right-hand page of the open notebook. At the top of the page write the heading "Sales Funnel." Divide the page into three columns, and at the top of each one place a subheading describing one of the three parts of the Funnel.

We want you to do this in a special sequence. Make the subheading of the left-hand column "Best Few," that of the middle column "Above the Funnel," and that of the right-hand column "In the Funnel." When you're done, the worksheet should look like the example on page 243.

We're aware that this probably isn't the sequence you would have chosen on your own. We'll explain in the next chapter why it's crucial to your success.

Now sort your sales objectives into the three columns, depending on the kind of work still to be done to bring each one to completion. Be sure to include the objective that you've been using as a test case in this book. You should end up with sales objectives in *each* column.

```
                        SALES FUNNEL
                    _____

   BEST  FEW      ABOVE THE FUNNEL     IN THE FUNNEL
```

Step 3: Test your sorting.

To ensure that the Sales Funnel scenario you've just constructed is a realistic rather than wishful one, test each entry in the columns by asking yourself specific questions:

- For each entry in the "Best Few" column, ask: "Have I covered all the bases here? Am I ninety percent certain that I can close this piece of business in less than half my normal selling cycle? Do I know what specific tasks I need to perform to ensure I can close the deal?"
- For each entry in the "Above the Funnel" column, ask: "Do I have any data suggesting that there's a possible fit between this prospect's needs and my product or service?"
- For each entry in the "In the Funnel" column, ask: "Have I confirmed the data that suggests a possible fit? Have I contacted at least one Buying Influence and verified the firm's interest?"

If you get a resounding yes to all of these questions, go on to the next step. If not, make the necessary sorting revisions and then go on.

Step 4: Analyze your information.

Now look at your entire sales picture as you've sorted it. What you have is a "snapshot in time" of your *current* over- all sales situation. Use that snapshot, and use everything else you know about your accounts, to look for patterns of movement and position within the three parts of the Fun- nel. You want to look especially for indications that your Funnel is either drying up or getting jammed up—that is, indications that you don't have *enough* business moving down, or that you have too *many* sales objectives stuck at one level of the Funnel.

Ideally, each of the three parts of the Funnel should have *some* objectives in it at all times. They ought to be moving toward the close at a predictable, steady rate. If you find that's not the case—and especially if you find that a given objective has been stuck in the Funnel for more than your normal selling cycle—then you have to consider modifying your strategy by taking Alternate Positions.

Step 5: Revise your Alternate Positions list.

The final Step in any Sales Funnel analysis is to search for ways in which you can move your various sales objectives steadily and predictably toward the close. Assess how your objectives are moving down the Funnel now. Start with the sales objective you've been working on all along, and ask yourself this question:

> *What specific tasks can I perform right now to move this particular sales objective further down the Sales Funnel?*

The answers to this question should always relate to the specific *kind of work* that's required at the level of the Fun- nel where your sales objective is located. For example, if that objective is now Above the Funnel, appropriate Alter- nate Positions will involve prospecting and qualifying work that seeks to verify a suggested fit. If the objective is In the Funnel, reliable Alternate Positions will involve covering the bases. And if it's in Best Few, good Alternate Positions will involve performing the end tasks that nail down the order.

Write down the answers to the question on your Alternate Positions list. Remember that, in addition to relating to the appropriate kind of work, every Alternate Position you list must also eliminate a Red Flag, capitalize on a Strength, or do both.

Since the Sales Funnel is designed to help you plan strategies for all your sales objectives, eventually you'll submit all of them to the same kind of analysis you're doing here. You can't do that yet, because you don't have enough information about those other objectives. Once you finish the book, you can begin to gather that information and perform further Funnel analyses. The analysis that you've performed here on your chosen sales objective will serve as the *model* for those future analyses. As you use the Sales Funnel concept again and again over time, it will become an invaluable tool in helping you set strategies for *all* your slow-moving or seemingly stuck objectives.

Whatever your current account situation is, we're now going to introduce two concepts that, when used interactively over time, are guaranteed to improve it.

► 15 ◄

USING THE SALES FUNNEL TO SET WORK PRIORITIES AND ALLOCATE TIME

Your ultimate goal in using the Sales Funnel concept is to be able to move your various sales objectives down the Funnel at a steady and predictable rate, so that your future income is also steady and predictable. You can do that by working on two interrelated tasks:

- Setting appropriate *priorities* for the three kinds of selling work that need to get done
- *Allocating* your limited *selling time* so that these three kinds of work always *do* get done, on a consistent basis.

Setting work priorities and allocating time are *not* synonymous. Although they're frequently lumped together, the people who use the Sales Funnel concept most effectively understand that they're distinct operations.

You need to determine what your priorities are before you can allocate time to them. So we'll take priorities first.

Setting Your Work Priorities

By "setting your work priorities" we mean determining which of the three kinds of work you should do first, which you should do second, and which you should do last.

Obviously we're speaking here not about the work sequence in which an individual sales objective is processed; all prospective orders start with prospecting, go on to covering the bases, and finish by closing. We're speaking about the sequence you should follow in addressing your *total* sales picture. Determining work priorities means deciding which *types* of sales objectives—Best Few, In the Funnel, or Above the Funnel—you should work on first, which you should address second, and which you should leave until last on any given day, or in any given week, assuming you have work to do in all these areas.

If you're like most of the people we work with, your natural inclination is to work the Funnel from the bottom up. That is, you perform the three kinds of work in this sequence:

1. Close orders in Best Few.
2. Cover the bases In the Funnel.
3. Prospect and qualify Above the Funnel.

Psychologically, it seems sensible to work on your objectives in this sequence. Since uncertainty gets smaller as you move down the Funnel, working the Funnel "in reverse" is a comfortable schedule. There's less immediate anxiety involved in starting with the objectives with high certainty (Best Few), then dealing with those with medium certainty (In the Funnel), and putting off until the last minute those with low certainty (Above the Funnel).

Virtually *all* people in sales do this. We've only met two kinds of sales representatives in all our years in the business: those who say they hate to prospect, and those who don't admit the truth and say they like it. The payoff for Above-the-Funnel objectives is so far down the road that almost everybody puts it off until last.

And everybody lives to regret it. This traditional, time-worn approach to the sales representative's work schedule is a fundamental cause of the Roller Coaster Effect.

Roller Coaster Effect: The Cause

In order to flatten out the peaks and valleys of your long-term income profile, you have to have sales objectives moving steadily and predictably from Above the Funnel to In the Funnel to Best Few. The priority structure we've just described as typical ensures that this will *not* happen.

When you put off your prospecting and qualifying work, it becomes, consistently, the kind of work that somehow never gets done. So by the time you finish closing all your Best Few and In-the-Funnel sales objectives, the top of the Funnel runs dry.

The "dry Funnel syndrome" and the Roller Coaster Effect are really only two metaphors for describing the same unwelcome reality. There are two ways of dealing with this reality: the right way and the wrong way.

The wrong way is to wait until the last minute and then panic. We're not being facetious here: This is the "method" for dealing with uneven income that's adopted by nine out of ten people. They ignore their Above the Funnel objectives week after week until everything else has closed. Then, seeing the trouble on the way, they rush around prospecting madly, throwing anything and everything into the Funnel in the hope that they can forestall the inevitable.

This method fails for two reasons. First, if you wait until the last minute to prospect, you simply don't leave enough lead time for a new prospect to generate quick income. Most of the time you can't rush your normal selling cycle: If you've put a new prospect Above the Funnel three months later than you should have, that's how long you're going to have to wait to see it bring results.

Second, prospecting for new orders when you're in a panic state is psychologically ineffective. Remember what we said about being on the panic end of the Euphoria-Panic Continuum. When you're worried about your position, you tend to do everything at once—and nothing produces results. You can't prospect intelligently when you're desperate for new leads. You certainly can't project confidence to one of those leads when you're feeling, "I need this business *now*!"

Roller Coaster Effect: The Solution

The *right* way of dealing with the Roller Coaster Effect is to arrange your work priorities in such a way that you never experience a dry quarter or dry Funnel in the first place.

There's one sequence for approaching the three parts of your Sales Funnel that will ensure the steady movement that you need for predictable commissions. That sequence is:

1. Close your Best Few sales objectives.
2. Prospect and qualify Above the Funnel.
3. Work the objectives In the Funnel.

This is the *only* sequence that can ensure predictable commissions over time.

You'll notice that we follow tradition here in advising you to work on your Best Few sales objectives first. That's common sense. Not only do these objectives provide the best chance of a quick return on investment of your time, you also have more time invested in them, they pay the bills, and they're most vulnerable to capture by the competition, precisely because they're so near completion. Neglecting a Best Few order means risking the worst of all possible worlds: having somebody else pocket the commission for your work.

We differ from tradition in insisting that the next priority should go to objectives Above the Funnel. The only way of being certain that your Funnel won't eventually dry up is to devote some time consistently to Above the Funnel work. And because putting this kind of work off is so easy, we advise you to do it second in the sequence, not last.

This doesn't mean you should let your In the Funnel objectives take care of themselves. They won't. You've got to keep covering the bases on working sales objectives. But we have found that sales representatives waste a great deal of time doing this kind of work, simply because it's *comfortable*. It's a lot more pleasant to take your old pal Harry Barnes to lunch one more time than to strike out for new territory and risk rejection. But you've got to discipline yourself to do that—or you'll risk much more than rejection.

We give our people a simple rule of thumb to help them remember the sequence that we've found effective:

> *Every time you close something, prospect or qualify something else.*

A colleague of ours with an editorial consulting service told us recently that, when we first mentioned this rule to him a couple of years ago, he finally understood what he'd been "doing wrong for ten years."

When we asked him to explain, he said this: "Ever since I started in this business, I've assumed that feast or famine was an inevitable part of it. Since you explained about keeping the Funnel filled, I've been following a new system. I take one morning a week, every week, to scout around for new clients—even if I've got more work than I can handle. It's saved my financial life. I'm now in the incredible position of having to turn down business—and I haven't had a dry month in two years."

The lesson is obvious. Since *everything* starts in the top of the Funnel, the one way to avoid a dry Funnel is to make Above the Funnel work a *regular* priority.

Allocating Time

Once you've established the priorities for the three kinds of work your sales objectives need, you can determine how much time each kind of work needs and allocate it accordingly.

This allocation of time among the three parts of the Sales Funnel isn't static. It differs in this sense from the priority system we've just explained to you. That priority system *is* static. To get optimum results, you have to follow the same sequence of work all the time. Time allocation, on the other hand, is *dynamic*. The *amount of time* that you should give to each level of the Funnel must vary periodically, depending on a number of factors.

The principal factor to consider is the *distribution* in your Sales Funnel of tasks to be done at a given moment in time.

Distribution of Tasks

The Sales Funnel is a snapshot of your total account picture at a single moment in time. As sales objectives move down the Funnel, that picture changes—and you have to adjust your allocation of time in response to this change. Knowing how much time to allocate to each part of the Funnel right now, therefore, means attending to the distribution right now of all the discrete selling tasks you must perform.

Time allocation is a very personal matter. The best allocation of your time may or may not have anything to do with the way your colleagues allocate their time.

Look at the examples in the chart below. The chart indicates the appropriate allocations of time for three different representatives, at the same moment in time.

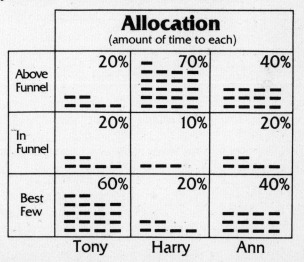

In this chart, the dashes indicate individual tasks and the percentage figures indicate approximately how much time each of the representatives should allocate to working the business in the different parts of the Funnel.

Tony has a majority of tasks in the Best Few category, and he should therefore spend the bulk of his time, in this particular working period, to closing work.

Harry has a great many tasks Above the Funnel, and he should devote the bulk of his time to moving the potential orders there down to In the Funnel.

Ann has a more balanced Funnel picture than the other two sales representatives. She should divide her time approximately equally between Best Few and Above the Funnel, and allocate a relatively small amount of time to tasks In the Funnel.

So, although you always attend to the three parts of the Funnel in a *static,* specified priority sequence, you allocate time in a *dynamic* fashion, as the distribution of your work changes.

Other Time Allocation Factors

Although distribution of work is the primary factor to consider in determining your time allocation, it's not the only one. You'll have to adjust your allocation of time based on other variables. Here are five such variables:

1. Quantity of Work to Be Done. Since every Complex Sale is different, no two sales objectives require exactly the same amount of work. You have to adjust your time allocation to accommodate those sales objectives that demand more (or less) than your customary amount of selling work.

Say you have a total of ten possible orders in your Sales Funnel, and only one of them is in Best Few. By strict mathematics, you should devote not more than 10 percent of your time to closing that one order. But if it's an extremely complicated order—if the closing work involves numerous individual tasks to be performed and you know that failing to perform all of them can imperil the sale—then you're justified in spending more time. Similarly, if 80 percent of your orders are Above the Funnel but all you need to do to move most of them to In the Funnel is make a quick phone call, there's no point in spending 80 percent of your time in qualifying. The Sales Funnel is designed to help you allocate your time most *efficiently*. You make the adjustments that will ensure that, based on the needs of your accounts.

2. *Dollar Payoff Involved*. No matter where an objective is in the Sales Funnel, you'll probably want to give it special attention if it's going to mean a major commission for you down the line. You remember the editorial consultant we mentioned earlier in this chapter. Throughout most of last year, although he had numerous objectives in his Funnel all the time, and although the distribution of his work was constantly changing, he consistently spent well over half his total working time tracking a *single* potential order from Above the Funnel through In the Funnel to Best Few. He did this for an excellent reason: That single piece of business, when it closed, accounted for more than half his income that year.

The bottom line here is . . . the bottom line. It always makes sense to adjust your allocation of time to favor those orders with big payoffs. Assuming, of course, that you don't neglect the rest of the Funnel.

3. *Product Mix Quotas*. On the other side of the coin, you may have to adjust your time allocation to meet specific quota requirements set by your company. You may have to spend more time than you would like to pushing a low-commission product because marketing wants it to sell. Product mix quotas are part of a continual push-pull between the factory and the field, and although few of us in the field really like them, we can't ignore them. Especially not if we're going after the bonuses that meeting these special quotas often generates.

One of our clients, a major instruments manufacturer, produces circuit-board test equipment that can cost several hundred thousand dollars and also oscilloscopes that start at twenty-five hundred. We know several hundred sales representatives in that company, and we have yet to meet one who would prefer to spend selling time pushing the oscilloscopes. But all of them do it anyway. It's part of their sales responsibility.

4. *Investment in the Future*.   About five years ago, we got a feeler from one of the Fortune 500 companies that said it was interested in our programs. We happily put its name Above the Funnel and went about trying to move it down. We've gotten nowhere with it, and maybe we never will. But we still go back to that firm on a *regular* basis, taking time away from more immediately lucrative projects, because we know that, if it ever pans out, it will be more than worth five years of our time.

We don't recommend this as a *standard* course of action. Normally, if a potential order has been Above the Funnel for two or three years and we're not able to budge it, we let it go. We see this order, though, as an investment in the future. We're willing to allot some time to it on a regular basis because the potential payoff is so high.

5. *Buying Cycles*.   You know that individual companies, and individual industries, work on buying cycles that may have nothing at all to do with the way you like to sell, or the scheduling you'd prefer to adopt. But you can't ignore their cycles, since it's virtually impossible to sell outside of them.

This is especially evident in government contracts. One excellent sales representative we know, who deals in sales to state college systems, has learned to adjust her own time allotments to government schedules. Her state government Buyers have their own fiscal cycles; their own systems of bidding, examination, and rebidding; their own scheduling procedures. Our friend is successful partly because she knows the decision process and critically timed events, and is willing to adjust her own preferred schedule to theirs.

Considering what we said in Chapter 7 about your Buyers' *perception of reality,* this is only common sense. No matter how eccentric you may consider your Buyers' purchasing cycles, they're an unavoidable factor in how you arrange your time.

These five factors are only examples. They aren't the only factors influencing your allocation of time, and we're sure you'll find more of your own. But we trust that these five have made our point. The allocation of your time—like everything else in your strategy—must be *constantly reas-*

sessed if it is to remain effective. The goal of this constant reassessment is to keep your potential business moving steadily and predictably down the three parts of your Sales Funnel. The time allocation schedule that does that is the right one for you.

Personal Workshop 9: Priorities/Time Allocation

Now look at the Sales Funnel chart you constructed in the last chapter, and incorporate on it the information we've presented in this chapter.

Step 1: Identify your work priorities.
If you look now at your Sales Funnel chart, you'll understand why we asked you to place the Best Few column to the left, the Above the Funnel column in the middle, and the In the Funnel column to the right. This left-to-right order is the *single optimum sequence* in which you should approach the three kinds of work.

Step 2: Analyze the distribution of your prospective business.
Notice how the various sales objectives you listed in the last Personal Workshop are arranged in the three-part chart. Count the number of distinct, single sales objectives listed in each of the three columns and, at the bottom of each column, write that number down. Compare the number of working sales objectives in each column with your total number of working sales objectives to determine what percentage of your total work load is now in each of the three parts of the Funnel. Write the relevant percentages down at the bottom of the three columns. This will give you an *approximation* of the time you should now be allocating to each part of the Funnel.

Step 3: Weigh other time allocation factors.
Now you should adjust the percentages you have just identified by considering the five "other factors" that frequently

affect the appropriate allocation of time. Ask yourself these questions:

1. Do I need to give more time to sales objectives that are particularly complicated or difficult?
2. Should I shift some of the indicated time allotments to give more time to working business with a high potential dollar value?
3. Do I need to revise this basic allocation to account for current product-mix quotas?
4. Do I need to divert time to a potential order that's stuck in the Funnel right now, but that might pay big dividends in the future?
5. Do I have to accommodate my own time allocation to my various customers' buying cycles?

The answers to these questions may help you reassess the time allocation that's suggested by the distribution of your objectives.

Step 4: Compare real and ideal time allocations.

You now have quite a reliable picture of how you *should* be allocating time to your various sales objectives: a picture, in other words, of the ideal. But it's not always possible to be as systematic in working the Funnel as we would like to be, and we know that some of the things you're actually doing with your accounts right now won't fit into this ideal picture. So we urge you to compare your current reality—including the work priorities you presently follow and how you allocate time—to the ideal you've just constructed.

Do this on an individual basis, for every sales objective now in your Funnel. One by one, ask yourself the following questions:

- Have I been doing the appropriate *kind of work* on this objective, based on its position in the Funnel?
- Have I been working on it in the proper *sequence*—that is, first if it's Best Few, second if it's Above the Funnel, last if it's In the Funnel?

- Have I been allocating the appropriate *amount of time* to it, considering the quantity and quality of the work needed to get the business?

Step 5: Revise your Alternate Positions list.
Finally, you can use the answers to the above questions to revise your Alternate Positions list. Eventually you'll be using the lessons of the Sales Funnel to set appropriate strategies for all your account objectives. You can begin that process now by looking at where your test case objective is in your current Sales Funnel, and what you can do to move it further toward the close.

- If it's Above the Funnel, ask yourself how you can verify the data you have suggesting a possible fit between your product or service and the buying organization's needs.
- If it's In the Funnel, ask yourself whether or not you've adequately covered all the bases required for the successful completion of your deal.
- If it's in Best Few, ask yourself what individual end tasks are yet to be done before you have a signed agreement.

Remembering that every sound Alternate Position eliminates a Red Flag, capitalizes on a Strength, or does both, use the information you uncover here to make the necessary adjustments on your Alternate Positions list.

Save this list, and save the Sales Funnel chart you've been developing. The initial Sales Funnel analysis you've just completed will only become fully operational when you return to it in the future, and use it to create a new picture.

Using the Sales Funnel over Time

This is an essential feature of the Sales Funnel concept— one that you'll begin to appreciate only after you've done several Funnel analyses. A key point of the Sales Funnel is that it gives you a broad-spectrum picture of your account situation *over time.* Therefore, the more often you use the device, the more effectively it will help you to clarify your constantly changing account situation. You now have a single snapshot of that situation as it exists right now. The patterns of development in the situation will become clearer down the line, when you're able to compare this snapshot with future ones.

For example, let's say that the Funnel you just put together showed a heavy cluster of possible business Above the Funnel. Suppose you do another Funnel analysis in a month and discover that only one or two of these sales objectives have moved down to In the Funnel. By comparing the two Funnel analyses, you'll be able to highlight a problem: your possible inability to verify initial, suggestive data.

Or say that the Funnel you just did shows an even spacing of prospective business among the three parts of the Funnel, but that one you do a month from now shows a bunching in Best Few, and an Above the Funnel segment that's dry. That will tell you two things: You have to pay more attention to prospecting, and you have to find out what's holding back those Best Few objectives from being closed.

Lack of movement down the Funnel might also indicate that you categorized a certain piece of business incorrectly in a previous Funnel analysis. For example, a sales objective that you categorized last month as Best Few might really have belonged In the Funnel, because it still had uncovered bases. In such a case, comparing a current analysis with the previous one might help you to understand your earlier mistake.

It's because such comparisons are so useful that we urge you to save not only the Sales Funnel chart you've just done, but every one you do in the future. By comparing these various snapshots of your account situation, you'll eventually be able to construct a kind of motion picture describing the development, from one sales period to another and from one year to another, of your total sales situation.

Frequency of Sales Funnel Analysis
How often should you construct these charts? The question

is asked constantly in our programs. It has no single answer. The frequency with which you should do a new Sales Funnel analysis depends on the amount and rate of *change* in your particular sales situation. Some people will profit from doing a new analysis of their accounts every week, and others can profitably hold off for a month.

Generally speaking, the longer your normal selling cycle, the longer you can reasonably wait between doing Sales Funnel analyses. Just don't wait too long. We advise the participants in our programs to do a new Sales Funnel analysis of their accounts a minimum of once a month. Since you're just beginning to use the concept, we recommend that you do such an analysis, for now, once every two weeks.

The people who use the Sales Funnel concept most effectively start out by doing such an analysis so regularly that it soon becomes second nature to them. That's an ideal to aim for. Once you internalize the use of the Sales Funnel concept in this way, you'll know instinctively when it's time to "do a Funnel analysis" again. And you'll be able to do such an analysis very quickly.

The important point to remember is that use of the Sales Funnel concept must be *periodic* rather than sporadic. You can use the concept profitably even if you only do one analysis a month—provided you're rigorous in adhering to that once-a-month design.

A Forecasting Tool

Used periodically, the Sales Funnel concept has been proven in many businesses to provide the salesperson with an accurate picture not only of current reality, but of future prospects as well. You'll remember that we began our discussion of the Sales Funnel by promising that it would give you a means of *predicting* your future income—and thus of avoiding the unpleasant uncertainties of the Roller Coaster Effect. Many of the people who come to our programs tell us that this is the single most attractive feature of the Sales Funnel concept. "I don't use it just to *track* my business," a southern regional manager told us. "I use it to *forecast* the future."

Several companies to which we've taught the use of the Sales Funnel see this ability to read the future as the concept's greatest advantage over other "forecasting" tools. Hewlett-Packard, the computer and electronics instrument firm to which we've delivered hundreds of our programs, incorporates the Sales Funnel model into its own forecasting system. Saga Corporation, a leading food service and restaurant company, uses it not only to forecast new business but also to track important contract renegotiations. And many of our clients successfully transform the individual Sales Funnel concept into one with regional and national implications: They use their sales representatives' individual Funnel analyses to feed into "branch Funnel analyses," and then into regional and national Funnel projections.

When used consistently, the Sales Funnel gives you the ability to look both forward *and* backward, enabling you to use your scarce selling time efficiently to ensure consistent, regular business. It lets you look at what's happened in the past, to see what's coming in the future, and to allocate your time today in the most strategically effective manner.

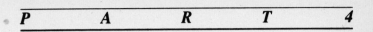
MULTIACCOUNT STRATEGY: FOCUSING ON YOUR WIN-WIN CUSTOMERS

▲

► 16 ◄

KEY ELEMENT 6: IDEAL CUSTOMER

All of us who make our living in sales are under constant pressure to sell: pressure from managers, from colleagues, from family and friends, and from ourselves. Because of this pressure, most of us are constantly tempted to take on marginal or potentially troublesome business that we really ought to stay away from. And few of us can resist that temptation all the time.

As a result, most of us at one time or another have sold business that we later ended up regretting.

We said in Chapter 9, on the Win-Win Matrix, that the real craft of selling isn't in simply getting orders, but in getting what we called Win-Win outcomes. And we said that you get a Win-Win outcome when your selling endeavors lead to the following things:

- The order
- Satisfied customers
- Long-term relationships

- Repeat business
- Strong referrals

The order itself, in other words, is never enough. In Strategic Selling you want to keep away from poor orders—those that don't bring you Win-Win outcomes—and concentrate on getting the good ones.

This means that you have to turn some business down. To many people in sales—especially those who were trained by tradition-conscious managers and trainers—this is simply unthinkable. "Any sale is a good sale," they tell themselves. Or "All dollars are alike."

The people who believe these old saws, though, are rarely if ever the sales leaders in their fields. The top companies understand that no single product is for everybody at any given point in time. They understand too that all dollars are *not* alike, and that if you're going to be successful in the Complex Sale over time, you have to turn some business down. If you don't, you're just going to crowd your Sales Funnel with sales objectives that, even if you bring them to a close, will later prove to be trouble.

In our experience, these poor-quality sales objectives can account for as much as 35 percent of the potential business in most sales representatives' Sales Funnels. You may think that figure is high, but it's based on our conversations with hundreds of regional and national sales managers. These professional overseers of their representatives' accounts tell us that they're forced to throw out, on average, about a third of their people's suggested prospects—because they won't lead to Win-Win outcomes.

In this and the following chapter, we carry the lessons of the Win-Win Matrix to a logical conclusion, by showing you a method for determining which of your potential sales objectives are likely to lead you to Wins and which of them are more likely to be trouble. In using this method, you define, for your own business situation, a hypothetical Ideal Customer. Then you use that Ideal Customer as a standard against which to measure your actual customers.

By focusing on how well the objectives you're selling your actual customers measure up to your Ideal Customer's profile, you'll be able to cut down on that 35 percent of prospects that you don't want in your Sales Funnel in the first place. And you'll be able to concentrate on the customers who are most likely to secure for you, on a regular basis, the five elements of a Win-Win outcome.

Digging for a Match

The reason that up to 35 percent of the prospective business in most people's Sales Funnels at any given time is poor is that these sales representatives lack a dynamic, field-tested process for analyzing their customers' real needs. In all too many companies, the responsibility for doing this is handled by the marketing department, and the bizarre assumption is made that the sales representative actually knows *less* about what the customers want or need than that department does.

The situation is complicated further because many people in marketing have no clear idea of how to meet their customers' needs, and they pass their own confusion on to the sales representative. Even worse, they pass on a traditional ambivalence about the real function of selling that can leave the sales representative uncertain about what his actual job is.

You've probably encountered this ambivalence. Most people in sales have. On the one hand we're told that our mission is to sell as much of our product as we can to anybody who will buy it, at any time. This "cram the product" approach is, of course, the traditional philosophy of the slick-talking huckster—the person who can sell snow to Siberians.

On the other hand, we're told that we should be selling to need—that we should always be "digging for a match" between our product or service and the customer's real requirements. This is the more modern, marketing-based approach to sales.

You cannot have it both ways. Cramming product and digging for a match simply aren't compatible with each other. If you're to be successful in Strategic Selling, you'll have to leave the oldtime huckster philosophy where it belongs—in the past—and learn how to dig for a good fit. Finding a fit between what you need and what your customers need is the heart of our marketing approach to Complex Sales. We're convinced that *no* single product or service is made for everybody, and that you prosper in today's selling environment by finding the matches that serve the self-interest of every one of your customers.

You need to do this on an account-by-account basis, so that you can supplement the data provided to you by your marketing people. What they do might be called macromarketing. It focuses on large economic trends and seeks to uncover the preferences of broad audiences. We're suggesting that you do a kind of "micromarketing" on your accounts. Use your company's marketing data as a base and go on from there. Only by assessing your individual customers' needs, and weighing them against broader market designs, can you adopt effective "matching" strategies for all your accounts.

Meeting Your Own Needs

These strategies must satisfy *your* needs as well as those of your customers. The term "match" implies reciprocity, and indeed the whole point of a Win-Win approach to your sales is to generate outcomes in which *both* you and your customers Win. A significant element in the development of an Ideal Customer profile, therefore, is to concentrate on customers who not only want what you have, but also have what you want.

And we don't mean just money. As we've said, getting the order isn't enough in Strategic Selling. And pocketing a commission, no matter how handsome, isn't enough to make a sale a Win-Win sale.

We can illustrate this point by relating a story told to us recently by the sales vice-president of a large moving-and-storage company.

The company handled a large number of corporate accounts, and advertised "special treatment" for executives whose household goods had to be transferred from one end of the country to the other. About a year ago, the vice-president told us, the company went after a potentially huge new account: a nationwide chain of discount stores whose management people were constantly on the move. In terms of volume, handling this one account would have boosted the moving company's revenues by about 12 percent a year.

But, as good as that sounded, the discount chain turned out to be far from ideal in other ways.

"Because of the seasonal nature of our business," the vice-president explained, "we prefer to handle accounts that will let us move their people off-season rather than in the summer when we're always short of vans. Also, we like long-distance moves rather than short hops, large households rather than apartments, and ideally about a month's lead time."

These "requirements" of an Ideal Customer made sense to us. Obviously, the moving company understood what types of accounts brought it the best profit margins, and preferred to go after them.

"The discount chain didn't fill that bill?" we asked him.

"Couldn't have been worse," he said disgustedly. "They gave us plenty of volume, sure, but it was nothing but grief. Their standard pattern was to give us three days' notice and then expect us to move a management trainee across state—and usually in July. After that first summer, I realized that our people were doing twice as much work for half the revenue. So we let the business go."

The lesson should be clear. It's not enough to sell to a customer who likes your product or service—as the discount chain liked the moving service. You also have to make sure that as many of your customers as possible come as close as possible to meeting *your* needs as a seller. You don't develop Win-Win scenarios on a one-way street.

The Fourth Part of the Sales Funnel

In every salesperson's environment, there are almost limitless possibilities for contacting prospects and making sales, unless you're in a *very* mature territory and industry. If you don't begin to focus on the real Win-Win possibilities as early as possible in your selling cycle, you'll almost certainly find yourself in the common, but unhappy, position of not knowing what to do with that 35 percent of prospects that nobody needs, but most salespeople get anyway.

In our discussion of the Sales Funnel, we identified three parts or levels of the Funnel, into which we advised you to sort your sales objectives. Now we're going to add a fourth level to our Sales Funnel diagram—one that you need to attend to *before* you work on the other three. This "amplified" Sales Funnel is pictured below.

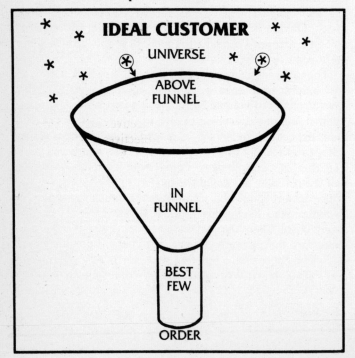

You'll notice that the fourth part of the Sales Funnel is actually outside of the Funnel; it's the Universe of possible business, including all your true, Win-Win prospects and also the many potential poor prospects that you might be tempted to go for. We place the Universe level outside of the Funnel because we want to emphasize the importance of getting rid of the poor prospects first, before they even get into the Funnel. Since it often takes more time and effort to work a poor prospect down the Sales Funnel than it does to work a good one, this is also a way of improving the return on investment of your selling time.

In working this preliminary level of the Sales Funnel, you'll be performing two critical tasks. You will:

- *Sort out* potentially poor prospects so that you can focus your attention on those closest to your Ideal Customer standard—those that will most likely give you a Win-Win outcome
- *Anticipate problems* that might arise with your marginal prospects and customers, so that you'll be prepared to deal with them if and when they arise

In performing these two tasks, you'll do exactly what the Sales Funnel is meant to help you do: understand the real probability of closing each sales objective, and continue to reduce uncertainty about those objectives that are worth working through the Funnel.

► 17 ◄

YOUR IDEAL CUSTOMER PROFILE: DEMOGRAPHICS AND PSYCHOGRAPHICS

When we use the term "Ideal Customer," we're not referring to an actual, real-life customer. You'll never find the mythical perfect customer. The Ideal Customer is a *standard* against which to measure your actual customers. In this chapter you'll develop that standard for yourself by analyzing your current best customers to see what criteria make them best. Then you'll use those criteria to define a composite picture of the hypothetical perfect customer; this picture will be your Ideal Customer Profile.

In drawing up this profile, you need to consider two categories of possible customer characteristics. The first is called *demographics;* the second is called *psychographics.*

Demographics and Psychographics

Demographics are the physical characteristics that define the individual buying environment. Since most marketing departments work exclusively with demographic data in determining what and how to sell, you're probably already familiar with the term.

To the sociologist and statistician, "demographics" refers to the size and composition of selected human populations. Here, the term is borrowed from social science and modified only slightly, so that it refers to the size and composition of individual *buying* populations.

Examples of demographics for our purposes would include the following:

- Size of the market audience and number of end users of your product or service
- Age and condition of the buying firm's present equipment
- Geographical distance of the buying firm from your firm's shipping points
- Proximity to your service and support centers
- Compatibility of your product or service with the buying firm's existing facilities

Notice that all these examples share one feature: They describe objective, measurable characteristics.

"Psychographics," unlike "demographics," is not yet a widely used term outside of some advertising agencies and marketing departments. In fact, your marketing people may not have heard it before. Yet understanding psychographics is critical to success in the Complex Sale, and we therefore make it an integral part of our Strategic Selling programs.

Psychographics are the *values and attitudes* shared by the individual Buyers within a company, and held collectively by the company itself. In today's business world, such shared values are common, since most successful managers participate to some degree in their companies' internal cultures.

Examples of psychographics would include:

- Importance placed on reputation in the marketplace
- Ethical standards

- Attitudes toward people, including customers, suppliers, and employees
- Openness to innovation
- Relative importance placed on quality rather than quantity of sales or performance

Psychographics aren't as accessible to measurement as are demographics, because they're not usually objective. But they're equally important, because they define the culture to which you're selling.

Company Cultures

One of the principal lessons of such recent books as William Ouchi's *Theory Z* and Thomas Peters and Robert Waterman's *In Search of Excellence* is that today's most successful corporations owe their success in part to the fact that their employees—from the CEO on down—are conscious and eager participants in a uniform company culture. Their people, no matter how individual and diverse they may be in their private lives, also share certain assumptions and values that make their communal, working life follow a perceivable internal pattern.

We don't mean that people in today's top companies behave like the hypothetical "organization man" of the 1950s, slavishly adhering to a gray, pinstriped model. On the contrary. The most successful companies usually generate company cultures that emphasize innovation rather than tradition, quality of service rather than the old-fashioned "bottom line only" mentality. A few examples from our clients:

- Saga Corporation prides itself on selling quality food service and emphasizes value, not price, in its persentations. Saga people all accept the general proposition that they aren't for everyone; they best serve accounts desiring a premium-line service. A paradoxical result is that quality pays: Saga is now one of the volume leaders in its field.
- The Coca-Cola culture is marked by a dedication

to making Coke a first-class company in every respect. Whether they're choosing an advertising campaign or buying art for corporate headquarters, supervising quality control or handling customer inquiries, Coke managers try to make "number one" the watchword of every corporate decision.

- Finally, at Hewlett-Packard, there's a company-wide recognized insistence on building products that fill *real needs* in the electronic instruments and computers field. People who work at this firm are committed, across the board, to making the name Hewlett-Packard synonymous with quality, value, and "state of the art." Innovation in research has therefore become a central aspect of the internal corporate culture.

These few examples point to the fact that, in today's corporate environment, most of the people you sell to are likely to share many of the social and business attitudes of others in their respective companies.

Social scientists would say that business people within a firm share a set of "normative values," that is, values that generally define the basic acceptable range of behavior and belief within any given social group. Since corporations are certainly social groups, it makes perfect sense that they will generate such normative values, and that the people who become most successful in a given company will be those who most readily lock on to, or adapt to, its values.

To revert to Strategic Selling terminology, we can say that a company's normative values are one of its most significant *psychographic* characteristics. And these values apply not only to the corporate entity as a whole, but to all of the individual people who make buying decisions for that entity.

This observation has enormous implications for the sales representative, although those implications haven't very often been made clear. Essentially, what the existence of corporate psychographics means to you is that, in positioning yourself with your various accounts, you can gain an immense advantage over your competitors by analyzing not just the "hard facts"—the demographics—of each account, but values and attitudes—the psychographics—as well.

The Importance of Psychographics

Because psychographics define companies as well as individuals, and because both vendors and buyers display psychographic characteristics, you can take a major first step in "segmenting the Universe" of your various potential customers by determining which of them most closely approximates the psychographic profile of *your* firm—that is, by determining which of your customers share most of your values and attitudes about doing business. Built into your product and services are *your* company's values and attitudes, and the customers who come closest to matching your Ideal Customer standards will be those who buy into those values and attitudes—or who can be educated into doing so.

For example, let's say you sell a product whose principal advantage over the competition is its quality and value over time. If you're selling to a firm that sees price alone as the critical factor in choosing among vendors, you'll probably have trouble. But if you're selling to a firm that concentrates on "price performance"—a firm that's willing to pay a little extra to get a more exact match to its needs—then your competitor's low bid probably won't be enough to carry the day.

A friend of ours at Saga understands this principle very well. "We sell quality," he told us recently, "and I refuse to try for accounts where the appreciation of quality is not a fundamental perception. They've got to share that attitude or there just won't be a match with what we offer them." This three-time salesman of the year boasts a success rate of well over 50 percent with his major presentations and, as he admitted to us, "I haven't been low bid in ten years."

What's implicit in this story is something that we've been emphasizing throughout this book. It's that the *real* reason people buy isn't simply that your product or service matches their objective business needs. People buy not only to get Results, but to get personal Wins as well. They buy because they perceive that your sale will satisfy their personal values and attitudes—and thus satisfy their own self-interest.

It all comes back to Winning. In Chapters 9 and 10, where we urged you to set up Win-Win scenarios with all your Buying Influences, we said that the best way to do that was to deliver them Win-Results. The same thing is true on the *account-wide,* or *corporate,* level. The best way to Win with a given account over time is to understand that company's psychographic profile, because that profile is one important key to how each of its individual Buyers Win.

If you're like most people in sales, up to now you've probably been concentrating only on demographics in determining which accounts are your best prospects. Here we present a Personal Workshop that gives you the opportunity to utilize both demographic *and* psychographics in defining your best potential accounts.

Personal Workshop 10: Ideal Customer

In this workshop you can create your own personal Ideal Customer Profile, based on your current and past accounts, and then use that profile to test the real prospects for a Win-Win sale with all your sales objectives.

Step 1: Draw your Ideal Customer chart.

Turn your notebook lengthwise and begin by drawing up a worksheet that will generate your Ideal Customer Profile. At the top of the page write the heading "Ideal Customer." Divide the page into five equal columns and label them with the following subheadings, from left to right: "Best Customers," "Characteristics of Best," "Ideal Customer Profile," "Characteristics of Worst," and "Worst Customers." When it's finished, the chart should look like the example on page 276.

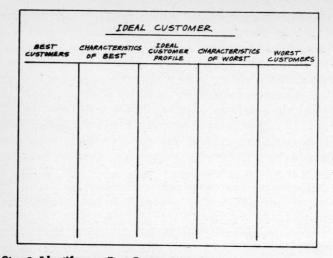

BEST CUSTOMERS	CHARACTERISTICS OF BEST	IDEAL CUSTOMER PROFILE	CHARACTERISTICS OF WORST	WORST CUSTOMERS

IDEAL CUSTOMER

Step 2: Identify your Best Customers.

List, in the left-hand column, your best current and past customers. We mean customers, not prospects; limit yourself to accounts where you've already done some business.

By "best" here we mean whatever *you* mean by "best." You set the criteria. The accounts we want you to concentrate on are those that have given you the maximum Wins and the minimum amount of trouble. You're the best person to decide what criteria you should use in focusing on those accounts. Keep your own gut feelings in mind. Usually, you find that you *feel* great about your "Best Customers"—regardless of the amount of dollar revenue generated by them.

List as many as you want of these Best Customers, but follow this guideline for establishing a cutoff point: First, write down your single Best Customer; then, write down number two; and so on down the line, until you come to a name that's significantly different in your eyes from the last one you wrote down. Stop there. If there's a quantum difference in quality between number three and number four, for example, make number three the last entry on this list. This list identifies your *crème de la crème* accounts.

Step 3: Identify your Worst Customers.

Now you can go to the right-hand column of your Ideal

Customer chart and list your worst past and current customers. Again, *you* set the criteria. Concentrate on those accounts where either you or the customer, or both of you, have lost, even though you've closed the order. Again, trust your own gut feelings. Again, stop when you reach a quantum difference between the last name you wrote down and the next one that comes to mind. And again, identify these "Worst Customers" regardless of the dollars they've spent.

Step 4: List Best Customer characteristics.

In the second column from the left, list those characteristics that are common to, or unique to, the Best Customers you've just identified. You may include both demographic and psychographic characteristics here, but you should pay special attention to the latter.

To give you some examples of the kind of psychographic characteristics we mean, our program participants often list things like this:

- Trusts my company's performance
- Innovative, progressive management
- Is loyal to the vendors selected
- Committed to quality control
- Willing to pay for "value-added" aspects of my product
- Highest business ethics and integrity
- Wants a Win-Win relationship on every sale

Use these examples as a guide, but list the characteristics *you* personally find most attractive among your own Best Customers.

One caution. Don't list things like "Has money to buy," "Needs my product," "Is creditworthy," or "Is going to decide soon." We assume that *all* your customers, not just your best ones, meet these minimum business requirements. Focus on characteristics—either objective or psychographic—that distinguish your Best Customers from the rest.

Step 5: List Worst Customer characteristics.

In the second column from the right, you can now do the

same thing for your Worst Customers. List as many characteristics as you can that distinguish the customers in the right-hand column of your chart from the rest of the accounts you deal with. Examples from our seminar participants:

- Inflexible on price, unwilling to make adjustments
- Slow in making buying decisions
- No loyalty to my company or to me
- No interest in the product, only in price
- Authoritarian management system
- Secretive and unwilling to cooperate
- Want me to Lose so they can Win

Again, your goal is to come up with a useful list of negative characteristics that are common to all, or most, of your Worst Customers. And again, *you* set the criteria.

Step 6: Create your Ideal Customer Profile.
Now, in the central column of your Ideal Customer chart, you can define the standard against which your customers should be measured.

This step of the workshop is a process of distillation. Study the lists you've just made of Best Customer characteristics and Worst Customer characteristics, and distill out of the items there a new list of characteristics that you consider *most significant*. This process may take a little time. Don't rush it.

In assessing the items on your "Characteristics of Best" list, transfer only the most significant ones into the center column. In assessing the items on the "Characteristics of Worst" list, transfer *opposites* of the significant items listed.

For example, if you've identified "appreciation of quality" as a significant Best Customer characteristic, you simply list that characteristic in the central column of the chart. If a characteristic common to your Worst Customers is that they're "unable to make decisions," write in the center column something like this: "Has a process for making buying decisions quickly."

Once you've transferred all the relevant characteristics to

the center column, go through the distillation process one more time. Study the items in the center column carefully, and identify the *five most significant* ones.

Then turn to a clean page of your notebook and write "Ideal Customer Profile" at the top. Write down only the five most significant characteristics under that heading.

This is your *Ideal Customer Profile.*

Step 7: Test your current accounts.

You now have a tool with which to measure two things: the compatibility of each of your sales accounts with the characteristics you personally find most desirable in a customer, and the problems that are most likely to arise in accounts that do *not* meet those characteristics. In other words, you have a tool for *sorting* your prospects and *anticipating* problems. You can do these two things now, beginning by evaluating the account to which you're trying to sell the test case objective that you've been working with since Chapter 3.

To do this, measure that account against each of your five Ideal Customer Profile characteristics in turn. Go on down the list and, for each characteristic, ask yourself this question:

> *How well does this particular customer match
> with this ideal characteristic?*

Then rate the customer on each item, using the same -5 to $+5$ rating scale that we introduced to you in Chapter 8. If there's a very strong or near-perfect match with a given characteristic, give your customer a $+5$ rating for that characteristic. If there's no match at all for another characteristic, give the customer a -5 rating.

When you're done going down the list, you'll have five numbers, positive and negative. Taken together, they are a measurement of this customer against your Ideal Customer standard.

Once you've performed this exercise for your test case account, you can use it to rate your other accounts and prospects as well. For each of these actual customers or potential customers, generate a new set of five numbers based on that customer's matches, or mismatches, to your list of ideal characteristics.

Each set of numbers will, of course, be different. But each set, like the set you generated for your test case account, will give you a reliable picture of how close that customer is to your standard. The higher the positive numbers, and the more of them there are, the greater the likelihood that you can consistently reach Win-Win outcomes; conversely, the more negative numbers you have, the greater the chances that you'll have problems, at least in those areas where the profile match is poor.

These figures, though, are only *rough* guides. Your orders are individual and unique, and we wouldn't presume to advise you either to drop a mathematically "bad" account or to become overly confident about selling a mathematically "good" one. What we do know is that, other things being equal, the above figures give fairly reliable assessments of the *probability* of a given account's leading to consistent Win-Win sales.

Step 8: Revise your Alternate Positions list.

Once you know how close a given account is to your Ideal Customer Profile, you're in a position to make a decision about how to improve your strategy for that account. Assuming there's a less than perfect match between a given account and your Ideal Customer Profile (this will almost always be the case), you can now do *one* of the following:

- Decide to *sort* a working order from that account out of your Sales Funnel because you realize it has a low probability of becoming a good order
- *Anticipate* the problems that will arise with the order, based on its imperfect match, and devise strategies to deal with them

You can make this choice now by considering each of your current customers in turn, starting with the customer or prospect to which you're trying to sell the chosen sales objective you're analyzing in this book. Assess the ratings that you just gave each customer, and then decide what Alternate Positions you might adopt to increase the likelihood of a Win-Win outcome. As we said in the previous workshop, you'll be able to do a fuller analysis on the customer for your chosen sales objective than on your other customers, because you have more information there. Your analysis of that customer will serve as a *model* for all future Ideal Customer analyses.

Obviously subjective judgment is involved here, and in using that judgment, you should take into consideration everything you've learned about your accounts, and your sales objectives, thus far. The ratings you've just developed are only a rough guide. *We don't advise anyone to use the Ideal Customer Profile as a cop-out for avoiding difficult sales*—only as a method for establishing the basic criteria that you need for Win-Win outcomes.

You should use those criteria as a base-line judgment, not a final one. For example, if your Ideal Customer Profile indicates that the Goliath account has several −4 or −5 matches, it would seem reasonable to think about dropping it. But if the potential commissions from that account are enormous, if the marketing people at your company are pushing you toward products that Goliath particularly needs, or if the "future investment" possibilities there are huge, then it might still be worth your time.

On the other side of the ledger, if you have a very strong profile for a given company, but that company has dealt exclusively with your major competitor for ten years and shows no signs of shifting loyalties, you may just be wasting your time in trying to make its people see the "perfect match" between what you have and what they need.

Remember that the Ideal Customer Profile is to be used to anticipate and deal with problems as well as to sort out potential bad business. This means that you should look at the *individual* characteristics on the list, not just the profile as a whole.

For example, if you've decided to keep Goliath orders in your Sales Funnel because of a huge potential commission value, you can improve your position with that account by analyzing each profile characteristic in turn, to see where the problems with that account lie. If Goliath scored low on your Ideal Customer rating largely because it's slow in responding to proposals, you may want to add "Adjust my selling schedule to accommodate Goliath cycle" to your Alternate Positions list. If Goliath has no apparent interest in quality and always takes low bid, you may want to add "Try to show them that our product will be the least expensive solution for them in the long run."

The key point here is that the closer an individual account comes to your Ideal Customer Profile, the easier the sale; the further away from the profile, the more troubles you'll encounter. The main virtue of the profile, as both a sorting and an anticipation device, is in enabling you to identify specific problems and weigh them against potential gains.

A Balanced "Admissions Policy"

What you're aiming for here is a balance. It almost never makes good strategic sense to throw into your Sales Funnel accounts whose Ideal Customer Profiles indicate they share *none* of your company's values and attitudes. On the other hand, no sales representative has the luxury of selling *only* those accounts that perfectly match the Ideal Customer Profile. Your goal is to reduce uncertainties in your sales and ensure Win-Win outcomes; usually, the best way to accomplish these goals is to walk the fine line somewhere between a policy of taking anybody who knocks on your door and one of focusing only on the "best."

Remembering that the Ideal Customer concept is designed to help you segment your Universe of potential customers *before* you start them in the Funnel, you can think of the testing we've been describing as a kind of screening process, similar to that which is employed by college admissions committees.

Those committees, although they often have very exact and exacting requirements for their potential students to meet, also employ a great deal of give-and-take in making final decisions. Most admissions boards today tend to look not only for a "balanced" student body, but also for reasonably balanced personalities in the individual students they select. That means that a certain student who didn't score high on the Scholastic Aptitude Test may still get in if there's evidence from other data that he or she has much to offer the college community in terms of sports ability, industriousness, or social adaptability. On the other hand, a student with great scores on this standardized test may not be admitted if he or she seems to have a narrow, "tunnel vision" attitude—thåt is, if it's likely that the school will Lose by having this person as a member of the community.

Your goal, as always, is to Win. And to see to it that all your Buyers, in all your accounts, Win as well. The best way to do that, we've found, is to use your Ideal Customer Profile as a base-line test and then weigh the information it gives you against everything else you know about the account.

A Final Assessment of Position

The concept of Ideal Customer is the last of the Six Key Elements of strategy that comprise our approach to the Complex Sale. We've presented it to you last for two reasons:

1. Ideal Customer is the logical outgrowth of the Win-Win approach to your customers that we've recommended in this book. Win-Win is the heart of Strategic Selling; we've chosen to close the discussion of the Six Key Elements with Ideal Customer because it reinforces the central importance of the Win-Win approach.

2. Ideal Customer also enables you to rethink your sales objectives and accounts in a broader perspective and a new light. Now that you understand how to use an Ideal Customer Profile, you're in a position to reassess everything else you've learned so far; Ideal Customer ties it all together.

You'll understand better how Ideal Customer ties everything together if you take a few minutes now to review the other five Key Elements of strategy in the light of Ideal Customer. We suggest you take out all the material you've developed in this book. With this material laid out before you, ask yourself the following questions:

- *Buying Influences.* Looking at your Buying Influences Chart, ask if the difficulties you've had in getting to your Buying Influences are related to their company's imperfect match to your Ideal Customer Profile. What specific demographic and psychographic mismatches have made selling them uncertain?

- *Red Flags/Leverage from Strength.* Look at the Red Flags on your Buyers Chart and on your Win-Results chart. Is there a correlation between them and the Ideal Customer Profile items that show a poor match to the customer for your sales objective? Can you use the items that show a good match as areas of Strength to leverage against these Red Flags?

- *Response Modes.* Which of the items on your Ideal Customer Profile explain a willingness on the part of your Buyers to accept change? Which items explain a reluctance?

- *Win-Results.* Compare the Win-Results chart with the Ideal Customer Profile. Do the demographic items on the profile translate into objective business Results? Do the psychographic items translate into Wins for the individual Buyers in the account? Do those Buyers *know* that you value their account and are trying to play Win-Win with them?

- *Sales Funnel.* If your chosen sales objective has been moving steadily and predictably down the Funnel, does your Ideal Customer Profile suggest why? If it's stuck at one level of the Funnel, does the profile suggest specific mismatches that you still have to address?

As we've stressed repeatedly, the Six Key Elements of strategy only become fully effective when they're used *interactively,* as a system. Asking yourself the above questions is a way of helping you see how the six of them all fit together.

By now you have a great deal of data. You've analyzed your chosen sales objective with regard to all six Key Elements. You've revised your Alternate Positions list several times, to incorporate the results of that ongoing analysis. And you've just checked your data one last time. There's only one thing left to do.

That's to use the information you have in drafting a precise Action Plan to move you closer to your stated sales objective.

FROM ANALYSIS
TO ACTION

▲

► 18 ◄

YOUR ACTION PLAN

You now have all the principles you'll ever need to set viable strategies not only for the sales objective you've been working with in this book, but for every future sales objective as well. Those principles in themselves constitute a body of knowledge about selling that will put you strategically ahead of 90 percent of your competition. To use them most effectively in practice, however, we suggest that you employ a dynamic vehicle called an *Action Plan*.

Stated simply, an Action Plan is a list of concrete, practical actions that grow out of the basic elements of Strategic Selling, and that you can perform before sales calls to move you closer to a given sales objective. It provides a bridge that leads from the analysis that you do *before* a sales call to the selling that you do *in* the call. As the final step in your strategy, it has the purpose of assuring you that each call will count, because you know before you make it that you're meeting the right person in the right place at the right time.

Don't be misled, however, by our use of the phrase "final step." An Action Plan is final only in the sense that it's the first step in preparing for each individual sales call. The Action Plan is also a dynamic vehicle that must change from call to call. It's part of an ongoing *process* of assessment, feedback, and reassessment that makes you continually responsive to change.

In this chapter, you'll make the bridge between theory and practice for your own chosen sales objective, in terms of (a) your current position with your Buyers, and (b) what you expect to accomplish the next time you're face to face with them. At the same time, the Action Plan you create here will be a model for future plans (with the proviso that each Action Plan, like each sales call, will be *unique*). You'll be able to use it, therefore, both specifically with regard to your test case objective and generically, as an example of an essential step in every ongoing assessment.

An Essential Ground Rule

In drafting a list of practical actions to improve your current strategic position, the emphasis is on *practical*. You want to be sure that your action can *in fact* move you closer to attaining your objective. In our Strategic Selling programs, we find that one simple Ground Rule helps our participants keep practicality in mind:

> *Each action that you list as part of your Action Plan should capitalize on a Strength, eliminate or reduce the impact of a Red Flag, or do both.*

We've been stressing the importance of Red Flags and Strengths throughout the book. We emphasize the Red Flags/Strengths principle here, and even phrase it in the form of a rule, as a base-line check on wishful thinking—a means of testing the *real* potential of actions for moving you closer to attaining your sales objective.

It's worthwhile mentioning again that, even though Red

Flags are danger signals, they should never be seen as negative. Identifying potential dangers is the most positive thing you can do in any selling situation. It's the best assurance you have that your Action Plans are working against real weaknesses and building upon real Strengths in your specific strategic position, as that position changes over time.

Putting the Theory into Action

In creating your list of practical actions—your own model Action Plan—you might find it useful, at least at the outset, to begin with the Alternate Positions list that you've been developing throughout the book. With that list in front of you, look at your current position with regard to each of our Strategic Selling concepts. As you go, make a list in your notebook of any actions you might take, in the next sales call, to improve that position. Focus on these four areas:

- Your sales objective
- The Buying Influences involved in that sales objective
- The Response Mode of each Buyer
- The Win-Results of each Buyer

Test each area briefly, asking yourself questions to uncover remaining Red Flags, and then considering which actions can turn them into opportunities.

Your Sales Objective
To succeed in any sales endeavor, you have to understand clearly what you're trying to accomplish in the account that isn't happening right now. A sound sales objective is always *specific, measurable,* and *realistic;* in addition, it always has a clearly defined *time frame*—that is, you know when you expect to accomplish it. If you don't define your goal precisely, and have a good reason for believing you can accomplish it by a certain date, you put yourself in the position of the computer programmer who doesn't understand the pur-

pose of his program; the messy outcome of that situation is often described by programmers as "Garbage in, garbage out."

Look at the sales objective you defined for yourself in Chapter 3. Does it meet the conditions we're setting out here? If not, you must consider redefining it.

An example: Suppose you've identified your current sales objective as "Sell Goliath Industries pilot program by May 1." It's now late March, and negotiations have stalled. Everybody at Goliath seems interested in your proposal but, according to Joe Garcia, the manufacturing manager, "It's just a bad time of year for us to commit." You may have to redefine and/or reschedule your objective, and to take actions now that will help you do that realistically. Example: "Arrange meeting at Goliath next week to have Garcia explain buying cycle."

Notice that the phrasing of this hypothetical action is *precise,* is geared to improving your current position *now,* and answers very *specific* questions. It tells you:

- *Who* will be involved in the sales call or other meeting. In the case described here, only you and one Buyer are involved. Remember, though, that a single call may involve more than one Buying Influence—and that it may or may not involve you, personally, as the person best qualified to perform every action.

- *Where* and *when* the meeting will take place. Remember that actions may be implemented in your own organization or on neutral ground as well as at the buying firm's place of business. And remember that the ideal time to implement an action is as soon as it's convenient for you and your Buyers.

- *What* specific information you expect the call to give you. Until you're actually positioned to make the close—and often even in a closing call—each action should help you to either confirm or invalidate suspected information, or secure information you don't have.

Of course, in addition to specifying the who, when, where, and what of the sales call, each action you include in your Action Plan must also follow the Ground Rule. In this example that basic condition is met because the suggested action is designed to reduce the impact of one of the automatic Red Flags that we described in Chapter 6: *lack of information*. It thus turns that weakness into an *opportunity* for improvement.

Buying Influences

We've emphasized that understanding the identities of all the key players for your sales objective is the foundation of every good strategy, and we've given you a method for locating those players by defining the *four* Buying Influence *roles* that are always present in every Complex Sale. It's essential, before any given sales call, that you assess your position with each of these key figures.

Using the Buying Influences Chart that you made up in Chapter 5 and your Alternate Positions list as starting points, you should now list actions that will address Red Flags in this critical area. The goal of these actions should be to ensure that all of the people playing each of the four Buying Influence roles for your sale are covered adequately—by the person *best qualified* to do so.

You have to begin, of course, by making sure that you know the identity of each of those people. You should have at least one name in each of the four boxes of your Buying Influences Chart. If you don't, you should address actions to that automatic Red Flag. *What* Coaching data do you need to fill in the empty space? *Who* can get you that data? *When* and *where* can you meet that person? The answers to these questions should suggest specific actions designed to capitalize on Strengths and remove Red Flags.

Suppose the boxes are all filled in but the key players are not all *covered*. Maybe you can't get in to see Farley, your Economic Buyer, because according to his secretary "he never sees salesmen." Here you might want to arrange for an executive of like rank to see him. One action resulting from that plan would be to make an appointment with someone in your own organization—ideally, someone who has already given you good Coaching—to determine who's best qualified to get past the secretarial screen. Notice that, although this action is still preparing you for upcoming sales calls on your Buyers, it's implemented not on their territory but on your own; the *where* in this case might be your own boss's office.

Another scenario: Farley is strongly in favor of your proposal, but you can't overcome the resistance of Steinberg, a Technical Buyer who has an unidentified "problem" with your proposal. Here you might consider using Coaching downward, from the Economic Buyer to middle management. One possible action: "Meet Thursday with Farley to determine why Steinberg feels he's Losing." Notice the Ground Rule again: this action capitalizes on the Strength of Farley's support to leverage against the Red Flag of Steinberg's resistance.

Remember, however, that whenever you meet an Economic Buyer, you need a Valid Business Reason for doing so. Farley will be more disposed to give you the information you need if you first bring him information *he* finds useful. Suggested actions: Remind Farley of an upcoming conference on national productivity decline, set up an executive briefing on your past Win-Win sales, or bring him a journal article on problem solving. As always, you should know where and when each of these possible actions is to be implemented.

Response Modes

The key point to remember with regard to Response Modes is that there are only *two* modes in which a given Buyer is likely to buy: Growth and Trouble. In these two modes—and only in these two—Buyers perceive a *discrepancy* between their current business reality and the Results that they need to Win. By definition, having a Buyer in one of these two modes is a Strength (if there's a positive rating), and having one in Even Keel or Overconfident Mode is a Red Flag (no matter what the rating).

With your Buying Influences Chart and Alternate Positions list still before you, list actions that would highlight your Buyers' perceived discrepancy between reality and Results—and that would also demonstrate to the Buyers in Growth or Trouble Mode that your proposal can eliminate that discrepancy.

In the sample Buying Influences Chart that we presented in Chapter 8, for example, we identified Dan Farley (Economic Buyer) and Doris Green (User, Coach) as in Growth Mode, and Gary Steinberg (Technical) and Andy Kelly (Coach) as in Trouble Mode. The best immediate actions here would probably focus on these four people, rather than on Will Johnson (Technical), who's in Overconfident Mode, or on Harry Barnes (User, Technical) who's in Even Keel.

Suggested actions: First, "Lunch with Green and Farley Friday to reinforce Growth potential of proposal"—an action that observes the Ground Rule by capitalizing on a Strength. Then, to overcome Steinberg's negativity, "Tour of Steinberg's department next Tuesday with Kelly so Kelly can show how proposal will solve Steinberg's problem"— an action that reduces the impact of a Red Flag. Remember again, you don't have to sell everybody yourself; Kelly may be better qualified to sell Steinberg, because they share a perception of Trouble.

One caution. The four Response Modes must be viewed as *situation* perceptions, not personality types; that means they can change at any time. Only if you first understand each Buyer's perception of the situation can you be sure that you're addressing that person's real concerns in the actual sales call.

Win-Results

The fundamental goal of every good sales strategy should be to ensure Win-Results for all your Buying Influences, as well as Wins for yourself. The key point here is that Winning, the most important reason anyone buys, isn't measurable or quantifiable: *Wins* reinforce *emotional* values and attitudes. Objective business *Results* are the *means* by which Buyers obtain Wins, but they're only a beginning. A major pitfall in selling is to deliver Results alone. Unless you understand *how* your Buyers Win as well as the Results they need, you won't be able to manage your sales into repeatable Win-Win outcomes.

Are you sure that your sales proposal can provide each of your Buyers a corporate Result that will provide a personal Win?

Look at your Win-Results chart. You should have identified at least one business Result that each Buyer wants from this sale, *and* how that person will Win when you deliver the Result.

On the sample Win-Results chart we set up in Chapter 10, for example, we failed to identify a Win for either Farley or Steinberg. We placed Red Flags there to make our lack of data visible. If you were managing this sale, your Action Plan would include specifics for setting up meetings to eliminate those Red Flags. Coaching from people who knew Farley and Steinberg better than you would help you determine the who, when, and where of those meetings. A sample action: "Appointment Friday with Andy Kelly; have him explain Farley's Wins."

Two warnings: First, although it may seem unnecessary for you to know everybody's Wins on every sale—and although you can in fact close deals without knowing this— delivering Results alone is still a hazardous strategy. Since you're in the account for the long run, the sooner you know how each of your Buyers Wins, the more effectively you'll be able to meet that person's needs in future sales. Ignoring a Buyer's Wins will eventually undermine your position with the entire account.

Getting everybody to Win to the same extent may not be possible on every Complex Sale. But your goal should remain to provide the highest degree of Winning and the lowest degree of Losing for everyone concerned. Sometimes the best you can do is to minimize the Losses. In our judgment, this is still playing Win-Win.

Second, don't forget your *own* Wins. You wouldn't think sales professionals would have to be reminded of this, but they do: We've already mentioned how frequently sales representatives give away the store in the vain hope that their Buyers will one day pay them back. We urge you to drop from your list any action that might put you in this type of Lose-Win scenario—and to drop it just as quickly as you would drop an action that tends toward Win-Lose.

The "Final" List

We're often asked how many actions should be included in an Action Plan.

We recommend a short list of actions because an Action Plan is a *dynamic* instrument designed to help you improve your *current* position. Once you've implemented the actions in a sales call, that position by definition will have changed. You'll then have to reassess your strategy and devise the next Action Plan. The point is that strategy has to change as the sales situation changes. In a future-shock world, there's no point in loading yourself down with an action agenda that stretches six months into the future and that may be irrelevant by the time you get around to implementing it.

If you can draft a plan including just *four* or *five* actions that move you visibly and demonstrably closer to your sales goal, you'll have accomplished everything you need to accomplish to continue improving your position for the current sales objective, and for all your future objectives. And on future objectives, with practice, you'll be able to select the best actions much more quickly—often without actually writing them down. Although the actions you choose in the future will be unique to their own situations, the selection *process* you're performing here is the *model* for all those future efforts.

Often, you can get your "final" list down to this optimum number of four or five by measuring each possible inclusion against three criteria. The best four or five actions will be:

- *Logical:* They'll build naturally on the work you've already done toward your sales objective.
- *Urgent:* They'll have a high priority.
- *Viable:* They'll be actions that, given your current position, you can realistically accomplish in the next one or two sales calls.

These criteria for choosing the best actions, of course, are meant to amplify rather than replace the Red Flags/ Strengths Ground Rule. Every one of the best four or five actions will still observe that rule.

A Wider Perspective

You'll notice that we haven't yet mentioned the Sales Funnel or the Ideal Customer Profile. That's not because they're unimportant, but because they relate more to long-term, multiaccount planning than to preparing for individual tactical sales calls. However, if you're having trouble defining valid actions, you may want to use these two Key Elements of strategy to help you.

For example, the Goliath Industries scenario described earlier in this chapter is really a case of a stuck order. If, after redefining your sales objective, you're still uncertain about what subsequent actions to take, you might want to look at the Sales Funnel, to determine whether or not you're doing the right *kind of work* on this sales objective, based on its current placement in the Funnel.

Or you might want to test the overall viability of a sales objective against your Ideal Customer Profile. If none of the actions you're considering seems likely to improve your position significantly, maybe you're working on a dead-end account. Check the account's alignment with your profile. In a small but significant number of situations, the best action may be to let a piece of business go.

The Sales Funnel and the Ideal Customer Profile may not always be as relevant to setting up individual sales calls as the four concepts we've just discussed. But these two Key Elements do provide a wider perspective on your total account picture that can act as an extra check on the potential reliability of your actions.

The Acid Test

One final test to measure the validity of your chosen actions. In Chapter 3, when we presented the Euphoria-Panic

Continuum, we mentioned that your own gut reactions often provide confirmation of your real position faster and more reliably than cerebral analysis does. Judging how you *feel* about your position can also be an acid test for the four or five "best" actions you've selected. So refer to the Euphoria-Panic Continuum one more time—you'll find it on page 49—and use it as a final check of your plan.

For each action that you're now considering implementing in your Action Plan, ask yourself whether or not it makes you feel more *comfortable* about the overall sales situation. If all the actions on your list help to reduce your uneasiness and to eliminate uncertainties, they probably really are your best actions. If they don't do that, you should retest that plan to zero in on what's making you uncomfortable, and why. And do so before the next sales call.

From Strategy to Tactics—and Back Again

The Action Plan you've just devised, in addition to providing you a model for future use, has prepared you to make a given call on a given Buyer or Buyers. Since the selling process is dynamic, once you make that call the plan will be rendered obsolete precisely because it has done its job. And it will be time to consider new actions.

The point, as we mentioned early in the book, is that strategy and tactics, although they're different, aren't disconnected. They work together, like one hand washing the other. Every Action Plan you create will enable you to enter an individual sales call so well prepared that, once you're face to face with your Buyer, you can use your tactical skills to your best advantage. At the same time, each call will give you information about what's required to accomplish your sales objective that you didn't have before you went in. You won't let that information lie there. You'll *use* it to reassess your position, reconsider your Strengths and Red Flags, and plan your next set of actions.

The tactical implementation of an Action Plan, in short,

is never the end of strategy. As part of an ongoing process, it's a bridge to the *next* analysis, the *next* Action Plan, the *next* sales call, the *next* improvement of position. To repeat a central axiom: Every sales strategy is only as good as its last reassessment.

► 19 ◄

STRATEGY WHEN YOU HAVE NO TIME

An Action Plan for determining the best actions you can take to reach or move you closer to your sales objective typically takes about forty-five minutes to devise properly. If you had the time, you could perform this kind of in-depth planning on all your accounts, for all your sales objectives, before every sales call. Your sales figures would undoubtedly justify the expenditure of effort.

In the real world, though, you won't always have this much time to devote to every upcoming call. Even though creating an Action Plan becomes easier and quicker the more you do it, time pressures are still likely to make that forty-five minute ideal unrealistic for many sales objectives.

This doesn't mean that you should decide by chance which sales objectives deserve the full treatment. And it certainly doesn't mean that you should enter *any* sales call without the benefit of *some* strategic planning. In determining how to give the appropriate amount of planning to each objective, we urge you to consider a two-part solution.

First: Determine which accounts and which objectives really deserve a "long form" Action Plan such as the one you devised in the preceding chapter—and give them the forty-five minutes they need. Second: Adopt a "short form" model of analysis for those sales objectives and those upcoming sales calls where conditions just don't allow time for the full treatment.

When You Need the Long-Form Analysis

At one time or another, you'll probably find yourself in one of the following situations:

1. You've just "inherited" an important account from another sales representative.
2. You're handling a big dollar account, or one in which there will be severe negative impact if you fail to get the order.
3. You're in a tough battle with the competition.
4. You don't know who the competition is.
5. You're handling an account that represents an important new market, industry, or customer.
6. Your sales objective is stuck in the Sales Funnel, the expected closing date has passed, and you don't know what to do next.
7. You're about to review the status of a difficult account with your sales manager.
8. You lack a piece of information that's essential to the sale and you don't know how to get it.

In cases such as these, we never advise anyone to opt for a short-form analysis. Whenever the sales objective you're considering involves big money, can significantly alter your long-term sales picture, or is filled with uncertainties, a complete analysis is called for. Spending time working on strategy before the next sales call, we've found, always pays off in these situations. To put it negatively but more cogently, if you try to approach difficult sales situations like these *without* strategy, you'll only be fooling yourself—and offering your throat to the competition.

When to Use Short-Form Analysis

When the objective you're aiming for doesn't involve a huge dollar amount, when the risks involved aren't particularly high, when you're not working against a high degree of uncertainty, or when there are few Buying Influences involved, a short-form approach can often be of sufficient benefit to see you through the next sales call.

When a complete Action Plan isn't essential, or when you simply don't have time to construct one, we suggest that you employ one of two modifications of the forty-five-minute model. Which one to use depends on the individual situation.

Modified Analysis 1: The Ten-Minute "Quick and Dirty" Analysis

Suppose you recently inherited an account with a modest but reliable sales volume. Your current sales objective is to get that account to approve a pilot program for a new product line within the next six months. You've met the Economic Buyer and a couple of User Buyers, and are scheduled to meet the Economic Buyer again this afternoon at four. You wanted to draft an Action Plan for this meeting, but your other accounts took up all your time. It's now twenty to four. What kind of strategic planning can you do?

A brief analysis, like all the analyses you've been doing in this book, involves asking yourself questions designed to uncover areas of uncertainty and suggest ways to improve your position with the Buying Influences. When you only have ten or fifteen minutes, you obviously have to narrow the questions down to the most essential ones. We suggest the following four:

- Do I know who all my *Buyers* are? That is, do I know the identities and buying roles of all the key players for this sales objective? If not, do I *at least* know the Economic Buyer for this sale?

- Do I know these Buyers' *Win-Results*? Do I know how each of them will Win personally by getting a business Result that my proposal can deliver?
- Am I capitalizing on *Strengths* and working to eliminate or reduce the impact of *Red Flags*?
- Do I have at least one reliable *Coach* for this sale?

If you can answer all of these questions positively, you're in a fairly sound strategic position. In the sales call, you can build on what you already know to continue addressing Win-Results, leveraging from Strength, and eliminating Red Flags.

If you can't answer these questions affirmatively, you know that you have to use that sales call to begin providing the answers. The benefit of asking these four questions *before* you go in to see your Buyer is that, even if you draw a blank, you'll know *where* you're missing information, and what kind of data you need to get from that Buyer. Often the most valuable thing you can accomplish in a sales call is not to give a sterling presentation, but to get this needed information.

How you get a Buyer to give you this information—that is, how you ask questions designed to better your understanding of the sale—is a matter of tactics, not strategy. Tactics are essential to good selling, of course, but they're beyond the scope of this book. Strategic Selling is designed to give you the fullest possible understanding of the sales situation *before* you see the Buyer. A "quick and dirty" method for increasing that understanding is to find out how well you can answer the four suggested questions.

Modified Analysis 2: The "Crisis in the Elevator" Analysis

Sometimes, of course, you don't even have the ten minutes you need to investigate these questions properly. So here's an even briefer model.

Maybe it's a small account, where you didn't really think that strategic analysis was "necessary." Maybe it's a "routine" renewal, in an account where "nothing ever changes." Maybe it's a new account for you, and your man-

•

ager has just dropped a note on your desk that reads, "Just found out Lacey, at CPI, is leaving for Australia in the morning. Can you give him a call this afternoon?"

For whatever reason (and the above reasons, as you know, are only the tip of the iceberg), you find yourself in an elevator bound for the seventeenth floor, with fifty-two seconds to zero hour.

Even if you've never done any conscious strategic planning for this account and this sales objective, you still know *something* about it—even if it's only office scuttlebutt about the customer or the names of a couple of key players. What you need to do in that fifty-two seconds is to identify just what you *do* know so that, when you meet the Buyer, you'll at least have made your current position—shaky as it might be—visible.

As in any analysis, making your position visible means asking yourself appropriate questions. The less time available for analysis, the more fundamental the questions. This question is the most fundamental of all:

- *Do I know who my Buying Influences are?* If not, do I *at least* know the Economic Buyer for the sale?

Answering this question, especially in fifty-two seconds, isn't going to give you a detailed picture of any account. But identifying the account's key players, and reminding yourself of the roles they're playing for your specific sales objective, concentrates on what we've repeatedly said is the foundation of good strategy. If you don't know who the key players are, and how they fit into your sale, you really know nothing at all.

Admittedly, not knowing who your User Buyers are, for example, isn't a very good position. But it's a much better position than *not knowing* that you don't know. If you *realize* that you know nothing, you should also realize that you must use the upcoming sales call to begin filling in the blanks.

The bottom line here is that any strategic analysis performed in advance of a sales call is going to be to your advantage—even if all it gives you is a knowledge of your own missing data. The only absolutely untenable position is to go into a sales call cold, with no information and no strategic principles to guide you.

In the words of a branch sales manager we know who attributes a recent record quarter to our system, "Going into a call without asking who your Buyers are is like walking into a room with a blindfold on. Before taking your program, I used to do that all the time—and ended up bumping my shins. Asking that one basic question is like taking the blindfold off. I don't always know exactly where I am in every sale, but I know where the furniture is."

Strategy First—Again

We don't advise anyone to use the "elevator" or the "quick and dirty" analysis as a *substitute* for a more detailed analysis. The ten-minute model functions best as a quick review of an account situation with which you're already familiar. The crisis model is just that—an expedient for emergencies. Sometimes neither of these models will be appropriate, and you'll have to make the time for a full-fledged Action Plan analysis. The model you should adopt in each case depends on how much preparation is necessary to make you feel comfortable before the next call.

It all comes back to strategy, and to our observation in Chapter 2: Strategy and tactics are both essential to long-term sales success, but strategy must always come *first*. No matter which model you decide is appropriate for a given sales objective and a given account, you'll still profit from Strategic Selling only if you do your strategic analysis *before* the selling event. The moment when you sit down in Farley's office is no time to be wondering whether or not he really *is* the Economic Buyer. Address your strategic questions first, and you'll be free in the selling event to do what you do best—sell.

If you always put strategy first, you'll be assured that no matter how small a *quantity* of time you have available, it will always be *quality* time.

► 20 ◄

STRATEGIC SELLING: A LIFETIME APPROACH

Many sales-training programs end with a snappy little speech about "positive mental attitude" and "hard work," at the end of which the trainer wishes the assembled sales representatives "good luck" out in the trenches.

We don't end our programs that way, and we won't end this book that way, because in our system "luck" plays a negligible role. Strategic Selling is successful precisely because it reduces the uncertainties associated with luck, trial and error, and blind chance; it works because it's founded on logic and on a sound understanding of all the Key Elements of the Complex Sale. In our system, you make your *own* luck.

The reason that Strategic Selling professionals are able to make their own luck, even in the constantly changing world of future shock that all of us inhabit, is that they're constantly alert to the importance of two keys to sales success.

The first of these keys is *method*. Strategic Selling professionals approach their sales with a planned system of selling steps that are logical, visible, and repeatable. These sales-people understand that, in selling as in any other human activity, it's *the way the professional does things* that sets him or her apart from the competition.

The second key is something that we've stressed again and again in our Personal Workshops. It's the importance of *constant reassessment.* Since change is the only constant in your Complex Sales, and since you can only be undermined by change if you fail to adapt to it, you'll get the most out of our Strategic Selling system if you see it as a *dynamic* system—one that's always in the process of refinement.

There's a logical conclusion to be drawn from this observation: The more you *use* Strategic Selling, the better it works for you. Not only that, but the *easier* the system becomes to use.

When we described the use of the Sales Funnel, we observed that repetition makes Funnel analysis a progressively simpler task, so that eventually it becomes almost second nature. Once you've worked through a Sales Funnel analysis several times, the techniques and concepts involved become *internalized,* and you're able to perform further analyses in a quicker and more efficient manner.

The same thing can be said about Strategic Selling as a whole. Not only do the Six Key Elements individually become easier to use with practice, but the system itself becomes *self-reinforcing* over time. We've observed this consistently in follow-up surveys we do of our program participants: The most successful ones owe their success to the constant use of our strategic principles, in all their accounts, all the time. In the words of a Midwest branch manager who attributes his latest salesmanager-of-the-year award to our programs, "The more I practice, the luckier I get."

That says it all. We hope you'll take this observation as so many of our participants take it, as a watchword for future success. Strategic Selling is a *lifetime* approach to the Complex Sale. The analysis that you performed on your test-case sales objective in this book is a model. As you continue to apply and refine this model in future sales efforts, increasingly you'll be able to say, "It's the way I go about it that makes me number one."

"Luck," a savvy slogan writer once observed, is "where preparation meets opportunity." Strategic Selling, it has been frequently proven, can prepare any dedicated professional to meet sales opportunities more effectively. If, by using the principles and techniques presented in this book, you and your Buying Influences continue to Win in all your sales goals—then we will have Won as well.

INDEX